Unproductive School Choice Debates

Unproductive School Choice Debates

All Sides Assert Much That Is Wrong, Misleading, or Irrelevant

John Merrifield
Nathan Gray

Foreword by Terry Moe

ROWMAN & LITTLEFIELD
Lanham • Boulder • New York • London

Published by Rowman & Littlefield
An imprint of The Rowman & Littlefield Publishing Group, Inc.
4501 Forbes Boulevard, Suite 200, Lanham, Maryland 20706
www.rowman.com

86-90 Paul Street, London EC2A 4NE, United Kingdom

Copyright © 2023 by John Merrifield and Nathan Gray

All rights reserved. No part of this book may be reproduced in any form or by any electronic or mechanical means, including information storage and retrieval systems, without written permission from the publisher, except by a reviewer who may quote passages in a review.

British Library Cataloguing in Publication Information Available

Library of Congress Cataloging-in-Publication Data

Names: Merrifield, John, 1955– author. | Gray, Nathan, 1972– author.
Title: The unproductive school choice debate : all sides assert much that is wrong, misleading, or irrelevant / John Merrifield, Nathan Gray.
Description: Lanham, Maryland : Rowman & Littlefield, [2023] | Includes bibliographical references and index. | Summary: "This book asserts a controversial proposition: that a system dominated by attendance-zoned, political process managed, uniformly comprehensive mega-schools (TPS) cannot adequately address unique educational needs and interests"—Provided by publisher.
Identifiers: LCCN 2023000026 (print) | LCCN 2023000027 (ebook) | ISBN 9781475870916 (cloth) | ISBN 9781475870923 (paperback) | ISBN 9781475870930 (epub)
Subjects: LCSH: Educational vouchers—United States--Evaluation. | Privatization in education—United States—Evaluation. | Education—Parent participation—United States. | School choice—United States.
Classification: LCC LB2828.8 .M47 2023 (print) | LCC LB2828.8 (ebook) | DDC 379.1/11—dc23/eng/20230203
LC record available at https://lccn.loc.gov/2023000026
LC ebook record available at https://lccn.loc.gov/2023000027

Contents

Memorial to Seymour Sarason	vii
Foreword	ix
Preface: Still a "Nation at Risk"	xiii
Introduction	xvii
Chapter 1: Elements of an Open Education Industry	1
Chapter 2: Hyped "Experiments" in Near Irrelevance: Escape Hatches ≠ Reform Catalysts	19
Chapter 3: Chartered Public Schools: Mostly Chance, Not Choice	39
Chapter 4: Fallacies About School Choice	57
Chapter 5: Government Regulation Issues	77
Chapter 6: The Neglect of Costs	85
Chapter 7: Fund Children or Institutions?	103
Chapter 8: Federal, State, and Local Roles and Perspectives	117
Chapter 9: Equity and Equality	129
Chapter 10: Diversity Issues	141
Chapter 11: Important Policy Choices	153
Chapter 12: Strategic and Tactical Mistakes	163
Chapter 13: Teachers	177

Chapter 14: Outlook and Political Strategy	193
References	211
Index	225

Memorial to Seymour Sarason

We lost Dr. Sarason in 2010. In his 90 years, he wrote 40 books and 60 articles[1] on education practice and policy, and a brilliant foreword for *The School Choice Wars* (2001).

We note his passing and accomplishments here because he may have been the original disappointed education reform debate referee. It was certainly a major theme of his work.

As he did in the *Wars* foreword, he would note that key narratives seemed unlikely to be productive, in part because widely used "labels, in practice, were predictably a source of confusion and failure" (p. vii).

Like him, we believe historians will be bewildered "that the reform movement continues to have too little to show that is a source of encouragement or optimism." And that's after his warnings, and 22 years after coauthor JM's *The School Choice Wars* sounded many alarms, which according to Dr. Sarason "made a seminal contribution to explaining why the current school choice wars cannot change our educational system." Hopefully we have sounded the alarms again.

Dr. Sarason made a herculean effort, and we, too, will keep trying to chart a course toward much higher performing K–12 school systems. The fate of our civilization hangs in the balance.

NOTE

1. https://en.wikipedia.org/wiki/Seymour_Sarason

Foreword

Milton Friedman was a libertarian economist and Nobel laureate. He was also the father of the school choice movement, introducing Americans (and the world) to the concept of vouchers in a pioneering article published in 1955.

His argument was devastatingly simple. There was no need, he claimed, for government-run schools. The government could simply provide parents with vouchers, which they could then use to pay their children's tuition at the private schools of their choice. They would thus have far more educational options than the existing public school system provides them, and far more control over their kids' educations. The private schools, meantime, because they must compete for enrollments and money, would have incentives to be responsive to the needs of parents and students and provide high-quality educations—incentives woefully lacking in the government monopoly.

For more than two decades, the voucher concept was regarded as little more than a provocative intellectual curiosity. The public saw no serious need for education reform, and vouchers gained no political traction. But that changed in the early 1980s, when one of the most influential reports ever issued by the federal government, *A Nation at Risk*, hit like a bombshell. It warned Americans that the "educational foundations of our society are presently being eroded by a rising tide of mediocrity that threatens our very future as a nation and a people."

The response was immediate. Policy makers and reformers in all 50 states scrambled to improve their public schools. They began with incremental reforms that tinkered about the edges, such as higher spending and stronger teacher certification requirements. By the late 1980s, however, that tinkering seemed to not bring significant change, and they became more open to reforms that promised to deal with the fundamentals of the system itself. Two distinct movements emerged promising to do just that: the movement for school accountability and the movement for school choice—both of which went on to dominate American education reform in the decades ahead.

Thanks to *A Nation at Risk* and its powerful wake, Friedman's ideas about school choice made the leap from obscurity to center stage.

The choice and accountability movements are very different. For its part, accountability is in no sense revolutionary. It takes the existing education system as given, part of the nation's institutional woodwork, and seeks to improve its performance through better top-down management—involving, for example, stricter academic standards, the testing of students, and evaluations of schools and teachers. Some states adopted accountability reforms in the 1990s, but the biggest victories for reformers came at the national level with No Child Left Behind (NCLB) in 2001 and President Obama's Race to the Top contest to encourage state-level innovation, which ran from 2009 through 2013. The energy behind the accountability movement has flagged in recent years, however, and NCLB no longer exists. Although evidence suggests that accountability has been modestly successful in lifting student achievement, this is hardly the kind of outcome *A Nation at Risk* hoped to produce.

School choice, in stark contrast to accountability, actually *is* revolutionary. At least potentially. It allows students, money, and jobs to leave the regular, government-run public schools and flow to schools of choice that are *not* run by the government. Depending on the specific reforms, these choice schools may be independently governed charter schools that are costless to students and remain within the public sector. Or they may be private schools whose tuitions are fully or partially paid by the government through vouchers—as Friedman intended—or through more recent voucher-like programs such as tax credit scholarships and education savings accounts.

If pursued seriously and expansively, all of these choice programs have the capacity to provide families with attractive options to the existing public school system. But they also have the capacity to *replace* the existing system with a new, far more dynamic system of autonomous choice schools—schools with much stronger incentives to be responsive to parents, to see that kids are well educated, and to meet the diversity of the American population.

Yet, in the nearly 40 years since *A Nation at Risk*, there has been no choice-based revolution. Not even close. As of today, charter schools enroll about 7% of America's public school kids. And the private school component of the choice movement—the component tracing its lineage most directly to Friedman's original ideas—has fared much worse, with roughly 1% of the nation's school kids attending private schools with help from vouchers, tax credit scholarships, or education savings accounts. This, despite the fact that the great majority of America's parents say they'd like to be able to choose where their kids go to school.

So why, after four decades of reformist struggle, has school choice made so little progress? As I have argued extensively in my own work, the answer has a lot to do with politics and, more specifically, with the formidable power of key vested interests—mainly the teacher unions, but also the school districts—that have deep stakes in the existing public system, see choice (correctly) as an existential threat, and have used their massive clout to resist it. Very successfully.

There's much more to be learned, however, if we are to fully understand the choice movement's lack of progress. And in the book you are about to read, John Merrifield and Nathan Gray shed important new light on the subject. They argue, among other things, that the choice systems that have actually been adopted over the years in states and districts around the country are distorted, anemic versions of what a well-designed true choice system ought to look like; and that, because different real-world choice systems are burdened in very different ways by excessive rules, small size, underfunding, and the like, they are not somehow the same and cannot meaningfully be lumped together as though they are homogeneous "choice systems." The upshot, the authors contend, is that almost all research that claims to tell us about "school choice" is misleading or irrelevant. It cannot be taken as direct evidence of the impacts of choice, nor can it be taken as direct evidence of what choice has to offer in improving schools, learning, and the lives of students and families.

As you can see, Merrifield and Gray are not mainstream researchers intent on making incremental contributions. They are thinking big, offering a searing critique of the mainstream, and demanding new ways of understanding what choice is and how it needs to be studied. Where others see a coherent, informative body of research, they see massive, debilitating confusion—and seek to bring clarity.

They are speaking, moreover, not just about the failures of research, but also about the failures of choice advocates—the proponents out there in the political trenches pushing for the adoption of choice systems—to understand the very thing they are supporting and trying to get done. These advocates have been responsible for the adoption of choice systems that are only pale reflections of what a true choice system should be, and they don't even realize it. Merrifield and Gray are attempting to set them straight, to clarify their goals and strategies, and to show how choice can be advanced more productively in future political struggles.

Finally, I should point out that the authors' vision of the best possible choice system is one that is constructed along libertarian lines, relying on virtually unfettered markets to see that America's children get the schooling they need. Milton Friedman would heartily agree. I must say, to be honest, that I see things somewhat differently. I am not a libertarian. I support choice, including private school choice, but with rules to ensure that the system promotes equal opportunity, student achievement, financial transparency, and other important values.

But this kind of disagreement is par for the course among academics. I don't expect to agree with everything Merrifield and Gray have to say here. What I admire is that they are thinking outside the box, making provocative arguments that anyone interested in school choice will find challenging, tantalizingly subversive, and well worth contemplating. That's what contributions are made of.

Terry M. Moe
Stanford University

Preface

Still a "Nation at Risk"

Coauthor JM was planning to write a second edition of his critically acclaimed *The School Choice Wars* (2001) when he realized that 2023 would be the 40th anniversary of the original, famous, strongly worded *Nation at Risk* (1983) report[1] of Reagan education secretary Terrel Bell's National Commission. It said that "the educational foundations of our society are presently being eroded by a rising tide of mediocrity that threatens our very future as a Nation and a people. If an unfriendly foreign power had attempted to impose on America the mediocre educational performance that exists today, we might well have viewed it as an act of war."

"Mediocre" is an overly kind characterization of 12th-grade math proficiency levels at just 24%, reading at just 37%.[2] According to the Obama administration's secretary of education, Arne Duncan, 82% of U.S. public schools "are not passing the test in educating our children."[3] At the eighth-grade level—the last for which state data are available—math proficiency levels are as low as 21%, with no state topping 47%—all of that after a tripling of inflation-adjusted per-pupil spending since 1965 when federal involvement grew exponentially.[4]

Alongside this huge overall spending growth and dramatically increased federal involvement, many states addressed *savage inequalities*[5] (Kozol, 1992), often by court order,[6] but noteworthy improvements did not arise. The New Jersey "Abbott districts"[7] and Kansas City, Missouri, are the poster children for failure to turn major funding increases into improved outcomes.[8]

Because the frenzy of post–*Nation at Risk* activity left the root causes intact, five less well-known, equally alarming warnings followed.[9] It is becoming increasingly apparent, especially from the craziness of the COVID-19 years, that the strong language of the *Nation at Risk* report was prescient and is still true. *An undereducated and miseducated population is at risk of self-destruction through bad policy making.* Indeed, enough examples, such as those cited by Hubbard and Kane (2013), were known in Thomas Jefferson's time for him to assert that, "if a nation expects to be ignorant and free, in a state of civilization, it expects what never was and never will be."[10]

And in sharp contrast to the promises of the founders of the current 51 systems that they would bring a diverse population closer together, the current systems create enormous social tensions that damage the collective decision-making process at all levels of government.[11] All 51 current systems do that by (1) concentrating poverty around the worst schools, which makes them even worse, and (2) forcing society to resolve contentious, divisive issues through politics that individuals could resolve for themselves by making different selections from a dynamic menu of specialized schooling options.

This year is also the 30th anniversary of Myron Lieberman's *Public Education: An Autopsy* (1993). It launched coauthor JM's interest in school system reform, including his conviction that we need school choice expansion[12] to better address the always large, and often growing, diversity of schoolchildren *and educators*.[13]

It is also the 10th anniversary of Mike's passing (Myron's friends called him Mike). Coauthor JM also gives Mike credit for his focus on objectivity maximization, which yielded JM's nascent Institute for Objective Policy Assessment (IOPA), an embodiment of a strategy to overcome the human tendency toward subjectivity and unrecognized bias by creating objective assessment "packages" from informed diverse perspectives. IOPA will host discussion forums for each chapter of this book (https://myiopa.org).

Because Mike was instrumental in motivating the writing of *The School Choice Wars* (2001) and deciding what it needed to address, and because of the 1983, 1993, and 2013 anniversaries, we decided to repurpose the *Choice Wars* updates and connect the central message of *The School Choice Wars* and this book to Mike's 1994 article, "The School Choice Fiasco," which was Mike's way of calling out an unproductive school choice debate.[14]

Spanning over 30 years, the central message is still that "much that is said and written about school choice expansion is dangerously false, misleading, and irrelevant." We indeed have a persistent school choice fiasco, which has the same theme as Mike's 2007 *The Educational Morass*. Part of that theme is that alongside inertia, long-standing, well-funded efforts to bolster pro-choice-expansion candidates and messages have failed to significantly expand parents' ability to find or afford a better-fit alternative to their assigned public school. We have been on the wrong track policy-wise, and to a great extent on the wrong track in terms of policy reform advocacy, despite a twice-declared "Year of School Choice"[15]—most recently because of the COVID-fostered awakening,[16] through critical race theory advocacy in schools and lengthy, extensive school closures. This book will argue that well-intended efforts still often hinder school choice expansion.

To end the dangerous current stalemates in the pursuit of school systems that no longer leave large numbers behind—in which nearly everyone succeeds (finds a good fit)—we need a big-picture reassessment of where we are, where we need to be, and how to get there by adjusting our (1) research agenda, (2) allocation of political resources, and (3) narratives and messaging. Assisting that reassessment and adjustment process is the primary aim of this book. It is a global imperative.

Both "Build Back Better" from the left and "Make America Great Again" from the right seem to assert that our nation, definitely "at risk," *was* the longtime leader of the free world. The reassessment and adjustment process must adequately address student diversity to change *was* to is. To do that, we have to identify a functionally and politically optimal school choice expansion.

NOTES

1. https://en.wikipedia.org/wiki/A_Nation_at_Risk
2. https://www.nationsreportcard.gov/
3. https://www.publicschoolreview.com/blog/why-82-of-public-schools-are-failing
4. Eighth-grade math, https://www.nationsreportcard.gov/mathematics/states/achievement/?grade=8
5. Excellent examples: (1) Jonathan Kozol, *Savage Inequalities* (New York: Harper Perennial, 1992); (2) Robert Lowe's and Barbara Miner's, eds., "Selling Out Our Schools," a special report of *Rethinking Schools*, an urban educational journal; (3) Carol Ascher and Richard Gray, "Substituting the Privilege of Choice for the Right to Equality," *Education Week* (June 2, 1999): 33, 44.
6. http://hanushek.stanford.edu/publications/courting-failure-how-school-finance-lawsuits-exploit-judges-good-intentions-and-harm
7. https://www.politifact.com/factchecks/2011/dec/01/chris-christie/Chris-Christie-claims-31-former-Abbott-districts-r/
8. https://www.cato.org/publications/commentary/americas-most-costly-educational-failure
9. https://www.schoolsystemreformstudies.net/nation-at-risk-vi/
10. https://www.goodreads.com/quotes/11289-if-a-nation-expects-to-be-ignorant-and-free-in
11. https://www.umass.edu/umpress/title/short-route-chaos, https://www.cato.org/publications/policy-analysis/why-we-fight-how-public-schools-cause-social-conflict
12. Nearly every family in the United States chooses an assigned public school by deciding where to live. Assigned school relative quality is the number-one concern of many homebuyers. School choice expansion means reducing the public funding discrimination against families for whom an assigned school is a poor fit for at least

one child *and* providing for system openness to potential alternatives to the assigned school.

13. We have greatly increased the diversity of educators by adding technology developers and software designers to the list of people who can participate in the creation of viable schooling options.

14. https://nationalaffairs.com/public_interest/detail/the-school-choice-fiasco

15. https://www.wsj.com/articles/school-choice-momentum-in-the-states-11612568327

16. https://www.wsj.com/articles/betsy-devos-is-on-a-mission-to-rescue-teachers-unions-hostages-school-reform-education-k-12-family-policy-change-11655845136

Introduction

> When you're fighting from the trenches . . . your point of view is distorted by the fog of war.
>
> —Ken Elias[1]

Even among longtime participants in the school system reform conversation, there is still persistent confusion and controversy about the key reasons to genuinely expand parental choice among existing and potential K–12 schooling options. The most important reason—and still the least noted—is to end "Nation at Risk" low school system performance.

Already in 2000, when coauthor JM wrote *The School Choice Wars*, the children that began school when *A Nation at Risk* (National Commission on Excellence in Education, 1983) arrived, left systems that even top Democrats—typically stubborn defenders of current governance and funding processes—say are "a disaster."[2] Now we see that 40 years of frenzied, failed attempts to achieve improvement without transformational change of the governance and funding systems yielded five more "Nation at Risk" declarations.[3]

School choice expansion can add entrepreneurial initiative to educator initiative. Together, they will relentlessly revise the menu of schooling options to better match the always large and often growing diversity of children and educators. Then every motivated student succeeds (engaged by a good fit), and no child is left behind (NCLB).

Indeed, the titles of this century's two major pieces of federal education legislation—NCLB and ESSA (Every Student Succeeds Act)—are a boldface, front-center formal reaffirmation that the undereducation and miseducation produced by America's 51 school systems is an existential threat. We expect "school choice expansion" to deliver a rise in (1) system-wide fit, and (2) the number and accessibility of schooling options far beyond the choices that exist for families able to relocate to school attendance zones with better traditional public schools (TPSs). Our definition of "school system" is all of the schooling options, government provided and privately provided.

The COVID-19 pandemic highlighted another reason to wisely orchestrate an expansion of our menu of schooling options. The knowledge deficits and financial costs of an expensive system that leaves a lot of children behind are becoming increasingly unaffordable, as are the repeated costly, predictable failures to progress through central plan optimization.

Since the publication of *The School Choice Wars* (2001), policy error has become increasingly common, likely, and costly. Lately, that has included failure to dodge disasters such as online instruction from teachers unaccustomed to doing so, and failure to fully harness the political awakening produced by the COVID-19 pandemic. School system reform proposals have been mostly[4] rare and weak. Objectively catastrophic policy proposals, *in general*, are increasingly common, and they get the most support from the most recent graduates of our schools. And the debt added by the federal fiscal response to COVID will create increasingly overextended state and local governments that will desperately need to achieve more with less.

With regard to the so-far inadequate capturing of the pandemic opportunity,[5] momentum may outlast the pandemic.[6] Parents' closer look at public school politics and bureaucracy, especially slowness to reopen, may have "shifted opinions over the crest." But huge barriers remain. For example, many rural and suburban areas still oppose choice expansion proposals, which "explains why many solidly red states, such as Idaho, North Dakota, and Wyoming [also Texas and Utah] have few or no voucher [choice] programs."[7]

Moreover, it may not just be the pandemic that has parents reeling about their children's schooling prospects. In the midst of COVID (summer of 2020), cultural issues reached a fever pitch as many people took to the streets highlighting race tensions once again. The arguments quickly turned to the source of these issues, and the debate regarding critical race theory raged.

Evidence regarding how parents feel about education policy is best seen in the 2021 Virginia governor race, which pivoted on parents taking a greater interest in TPS curricula. Glenn Youngkin's victory was attributed mostly to that issue. The pandemic and cultural issues yielded many state political settings ripe for transformational choice expansion, a time when widespread confusion about key issues can be quite costly. It may have already reduced the political feasibility of key provisions of productive policies such as (1) universal eligibility where expanded choice is available; (2) inclusion of private schools; (3) the payment process (Chapter 11 compares direct payments, "scholarships," vouchers, tuition tax credits, and education savings accounts); and (4) allowing of shared financing of tuition.[8]

The long list of policy details can obscure key central themes such as the literal *need* to match the engagement-in-learning factors of diverse students with educators' diverse skills. True equity means "equal fit,"[9] a goal that is not widely recognized, much less even roughly realized through the current pursuit of equal access to instructional content.

The status quo is hope defying experience that having diverse educators teach the same material with the same methods to diverse students will yield equal, good outcomes. That fails because of weak and perverse incentives and because individual talents and strengths are much too diverse. *No amount of funding, or teacher training, can make one size come close to fitting all.* The *Nation at Risk*[10] credible threat exists because widespread academic disengagement created a lot of miseducated and undereducated citizens.

This book asserts a controversial proposition: that a system dominated by attendance-zoned, political process managed, uniformly comprehensive (Brown, 1992) mega-schools (TPSs) cannot adequately address unique educational needs and interests. Since this book argues for transformational choice expansions, it ignores or dismisses some of the existing alleged evidence (Merrifield, 2008b) and common arguments responsible for the confusing school choice policy wars.

The nearly universal propensity to make sweeping generalizations about policies that barely expand access to current schooling options[11] is a huge problem. Those generalizations created unnecessary controversy and confusion, even among school choice activists and researchers. The generalizations are typically drawn from research findings relevant only to some kinds of school choice expansion strategies (Merrifield, 2008a). For example:

1. Chartered public schools (CPSs) are the most common and most intensively researched alternatives to assigned traditional public schools (TPSs), but CPSs arguably mostly represent school chance, not choice (see Chapter 4). Outcomes of particular charter school laws may not even reasonably predict outcomes of chartering in other states. Many common differences in the 45 charter laws are very important. Also quite important are provisions, such as price control, that all charter laws have in common.
2. Generalizations drawn from studies of chartering may be assigned to "school choice" generally, often including proposed versions with key provisions not included in any other charter law or private school choice program; for example, provisions such as price formation, which are norms of market settings.
3. The vast majority of school choice expansions severely limit eligibility and/or family empowerment to select a TPS alternative, which

prevented the much-needed major change in schooling options and measured school system performance.

We see dueling generalizations when policy advocates emphasize the outcomes that support their policy preferences and downplay—or completely exclude—the results that do not.[12] As will be argued throughout this book, a key aspect of the persistent policy failure is that often all of the dueling generalizations are wrong, misleading, or irrelevant.

Of central concern are the common inferences that the effects of zero rivalry and barely rivalrous situations—often mistakenly alleged to be genuinely competitive—are good indicators of the effects of truly competitive situations. Failure to discredit such inferences reduces the political feasibility of parental choice plans that would establish a truly competitive or, more critically, an open education industry (OEI)—a terrible outcome since likely transformational parental choice is a promising but only minimally explored governance strategy. This book focuses on OEI versions of parental choice strategies because it:

- is the transformative versions of choice expansion policies that are the needed focus of the people who believe that mere adjustment/tinkering is insufficient for a "Nation at Risk" (the United States has 51 low-performing school systems);[13]
- aims to force policy debate participants to clearly define what they mean when they support or criticize "school choice," "parental choice," or "education choice";
- makes it possible to analyze policies from a consistently held concept of choice; and
- allows assessment of one of the most critical arguments for transformative parental choice, that OEI benefits would top the transition costs.

OEIs, though small and scattered in history, have a great track record. Samuel Blumenfeld (1981), Andrew Coulson (1999), and E. G., West (1994) studied the United States' pre-TPS, OEI era (before 1840).

CONFUSION ABOUT PARENTAL CHOICE

Expanding parental choice means some mix of greater access to new, diverse schooling options (genuine choices) and improved access to existing choices. A policy that triggers entrepreneurial initiative yields specialization aimed at matching the schooling preferences of diverse schoolchildren. A critical, positive result of school specialization is that which schools are best will vary by child, which can blissfully erode the devastating, poverty-concentrating neighborhood stratification by income that results when TPS policy uniformity causes the highest-income families to win the bidding war for the homes near the best versions (which often still aren't very good) of what all TPSs offer.

There are many types of parental choice policies in part because choice advocates have diverse beliefs about education goals and how choice policies can help achieve those goals. Each reason puts different demands on choice policy specifics. The strategy of doing whatever is possible in the short run also underlies choice policy variety and confusion about what parental choice might achieve immediately versus what different forms might eventually achieve.

In 1955 and 1962, Milton Friedman proposed universal choice through tuition vouchers[14] so that entrepreneurial initiative and competition would invigorate the delivery of K–12 schooling services. Unfortunately, the actual programs that expanded school choice were mostly not universal (Forster & Woodward, 2012; Viteritti, 1999, p. 55); plus they were laden with restrictions that further curbed competitive dynamics. Typically, those early proposals only slightly reduced the public funding bias against private school users. For instance, students receiving vouchers to attend private schools in Washington, DC, receive about a third of the funding[15] per child of DC public schools; so, typically, only a small fraction of families can participate.[16]

Even the funding of choice within the public sector—for example, choice between TPSs and chartered public schools (CPSs; detailed discussion in Chapter 3), and between the assigned TPS and other TPSs—nearly always significantly favors the assigned TPS. For example, the School Choice Demonstration Project found that public charter schools received about $5,828 less (or 27% less) funding per student than TPSs across 14 cities in the United States in the 2015–2016 school year.[17]

Choice expansion advocates' practice of not publicly protesting major restrictions helped choice opponents argue that those expansion efforts divert public funds to benefit a few children supposedly at the expense of the vast majority that must stay in TPSs. Despite the weak basis for such claims (see Chapter 8), and even the fact that it's often the reverse of the truth, those claims helped "status quo + money" proponents make "voucher" the "V-word"[18]—a scarlet letter of the reform wars.

Many choice advocates reacted to the stigma by replacing "voucher" with "school choice," "parental choice," and "scholarship" (Coons & Sugarman, 1999) to refer to the subsidy payment. Because of the scarlet letter effect, and the public being less familiar with tuition tax credits and education savings accounts, choice opponents reintroduce the term "voucher" as much as possible.

Misuse of "public education" and the V-word are clearly seen in the following: "The expansion [of choice programs] has alarmed many public school teachers and advocates who argue that voucher-like programs chip away at the funding and ideals of public education."[19] It implies that the ideal of public education is something other than maximizing each student's abilities—whatever those abilities may be or however diverse they may be. Again, the V-word is associated with depleting public school system resources rather than redirecting them to the most efficient uses—actually educating every student.

The many electoral defeats of voucher proposals lowered proponents' aspirations. The stalling of Milwaukee's 30-year-old program far short of low-restriction universality may have ended (properly) open discussion of incrementalism as a reliable path toward the OEI, transformational version of parental choice.

There is still much agreement with John Miller's 1993 remark that "scholarship sounds so much more appealing than voucher."[20] Indeed, the "Hope Scholarship"[21] label was a key part of the strategy that yielded West Virginia's K–12 funding reform, which is unfortunate.

The transformative, OEI version of parental choice requires universal eligibility, and a universal scholarship program is a confusing contradiction to many people. A scholarship label implies that only a relatively few students will qualify. And scholarship programs available to, even targeted at, low achievers are likewise contradictions. Use of "scholarship" in place of "voucher" or "education savings account" may deter parents who expect the eligibility criteria to include a strong academic background.

Fortunately, it is often possible to easily ditch the name game. Tuition vouchers are no longer the best way to achieve noteworthy school choice expansion. Education savings accounts (ESAs) and education tax credits are better (more in Chapter 11). They are less vulnerable to debilitating regulation. And because ESAs and tax credits can apply to more than one education provider, they facilitate more customization[22] of learning content.

Given the current menu of schooling options, which is a result of current funding and governance policies, it is not surprising that concern for religious freedom is the top motivating factor of some parental choice advocates.[23] Parents who cannot afford private school tuition must send their children to TPSs that cannot give religious instruction and that promote concepts like evolution that some parents regard as anti-religious. Forcing low-income families to send their children to schools that contradict their family values creates social tensions and political hostilities (Arons, 1997; McCluskey, 2007). In fact, some legal and education policy scholars have argued that the U.S. Constitution requires private school choice for equality under the law.[24]

Equity concerns are another widely cited justification for parental choice expansion.²⁵ Economically disadvantaged families cannot afford to live near the best TPS, and most cannot afford to send their children to private schools. From that perspective, efforts to level the financial playing field between TPS, CPS, and privately provided schooling reduce the advantages of affluence. Equity benefits may prove to be the biggest political asset of OEI versions of parental choice expansion efforts. But some analysts cite failed equity rationales to argue for means testing public per-pupil funding and to argue against shared financing of private school tuition (positions opposed in Chapter 9).

CONFUSING TERMINOLOGY

The confusion doesn't end with politically driven substitutions such as "scholarship" for "voucher." It begins with the basics. Public education and public school system are widely seen as synonyms even though the first is a goal and the latter is a delivery process.²⁶ Even Myron Lieberman (1993) equated "public education" and the public school system, and the Wirt and Kirst (1997) politics of education text equates a reduced role for TPSs with "an end of American commitment to public education" (Wirt & Kirst, 1997, p. 51).

But a commitment to effective schooling for all doesn't compel the government to operate schools or deny public funds to families that prefer the schooling services of private entities. Jack Kemp, a 1996 Republican vice-presidential nominee, and Democrat Erskine Bowles, former Clinton administration chief of staff, put it very nicely: "The current model—a non-competitive monopoly—is not the only way to deliver public education."²⁷ Far too few people make the distinction between the goal and a delivery mechanism.

Except when quoting people who use "public education" to refer to the public school delivery system—a misleading practice—this book uses the term "public education" only in Chapter 7's more detailed discussion of that source of confusion. This book's opposition to the public school monopoly on public funding is perfectly consistent with our support for the public education goal of universal education opportunity and shared core values.

This book argues that an OEI is the best way to meet the goal of educating a diverse public. The OEI policy strategy deserves extensive study because of the track record of contestable industries, generally, and the mostly poor track record where the key elements of competitive settings (dynamic, *scarcity-driven price signals*; *easy market entry/exit*; and *profit-loss*—details in Chapter 1) are absent, including primary and secondary education. Such absence forces central planning with its well-known horrific track record.

The terms "public school" and "private school" are also somewhat misleading. The former adequately conveys the public ownership of education facilities, but the exclusive attendance zones of TPSs make them among the least public of government-owned and staffed facilities,[28] especially since there is a housing and property tax premium to gain admission to the better TPSs. TPSs are less public than many privately provided services. Private schools lack attendance zones, but they have major access barriers, especially tuition for students who don't qualify for scholarships, and perhaps entrance requirements.

"One of the truly remarkable features of the education literature is that schools are rarely treated as the government agencies they are" (Hess, 1999). The familiarity of the term "public school" trumps the more accurate, though often offensive, "government school." A key risk created by the term "public school" is the widespread mistaken belief that schooling is a public good, even though schooling lacks both public good conditions: (1) nonpayers cannot be excluded, and (2) use (enrollment) does not affect cost.[29] Frequent mistaken use of the term "public good" is a clear symptom of the current system's massive economic education failures, leading to failure to discern the difference between public good conditions and the potential for schooling to yield positive spillovers from the better educated to the rest of society.

The growing diversity in what constitutes a public school has added to the confusion. Alongside TPSs, the public sector contains magnet schools and chartered public schools (see Chapter 3). Like TPSs, CPSs cannot charge tuition, but unlike TPSs, children are not assigned to CPSs, and CPSs have a degree of independence from the TPS rules that varies widely according to regulatory practice and the state laws that authorize CPSs.

DISSATISFACTION WITH K–12 EDUCATION

Continued widespread dissatisfaction with K–12 academic gains[30] and with miseducation is a major reason this book was written. Wrong, misleading, and irrelevant claims about school choice expansion would matter much less if any of the 51 U.S. school systems were high performing or moving swiftly in that direction.

Despite a Great Recession spending dip by most states, nationwide average per-pupil spending rose 21.2% from 2000 to 2015,[31] with little or no uptick in measured performance.[32] The causes of dissatisfaction still include low test scores, comparisons with other countries' students, differences between school districts, the skill deficits of entry-level job applicants. And even the current very limited private schools menu provides a better fit for many children.

The deficiencies get your attention, but none of the causes establish an appropriate goal. Many of the countries that top the United States in the international comparisons are deeply dissatisfied with their schools, which is not surprising. Though many countries are ahead of the United States, many problematic similarities keep them from being far ahead. In 2012, the top-ranked countries in the widely cited PISA reports (2012, 2015, and 2018), Finland and South Korea, were only ahead of the U.S. results by 8% (Manna & McGuinn, 2013). The 2015 top-ranked countries, Japan and Canada, topped the "Nation at Risk" U.S. results by just over 10%. The 2018 top-ranked countries, Japan and Estonia, topped the U.S. results by barely over 10% in math and just 3.3% in reading.[33] That clustering of outcomes should provide no solace. We know the room to improve the U.S. results—the *need* to improve them—is much larger than 10%.

Suburban TPSs and private schools generally have higher test scores than urban TPSs, but none of the major components of the current system perform acceptably. And none of the states perform at a high level. Former assistant secretary of education Chester Finn's 1991 statement that the states with the best test scores "are at the top of the cellar stairs"[34] is still true. For every state Lance Izumi examined,[35] he documented that the better schools are mostly "Not as Good as You Think." A significant amount of the difference may be the result of greater use of after-school instruction by more affluent families. In every state, a large share of students' scores are below the basic skills level, and a majority are not proficient.

The current public finance monopoly of the public school system undermines public provision *and* private provision of schooling. TPSs suffer low and declining productivity because of perverse and weak incentives and stifling rules from the system level down to the classroom, and private schools suffer from financial inebriation and insufficient competition.

THE CASE FOR AN OPEN EDUCATION INDUSTRY

Promises to spread best practices, match the performance of schools in other places, or regain past achievements are not the reasons to seriously consider implementing an OEI. A business that says its ultimate goal is to match the competition, or match past achievements, would probably vanish quickly, and deservedly so. Part of the persistent policy failure is the noteworthy ability to achieve existing outcomes more cheaply, but that should only signal inefficiency, not a goal. Nation at Risk results for less money are still an existential threat.

Shocking academic deficiencies raise interest in reform, but the intellectual case for an OEI should not hinge on attention-getting evidence of student shortcomings. That case must rest on the dynamic transformative power of having to stay the first choice of a large number of families and the need to pursue some customized learning to genuinely engage diverse schoolchildren in the knowledge-skill acquisition process.

In truly open settings, markets drive specialization and relentless pursuit of improvement. Overwhelming evidence exists showing that a price-change-driven orchestration of what is produced, how, where, and for whom—though often imperfect—is typically superior to "price-less," politically driven delivery systems (Merrifield, 2019).

K–12 education is an unlikely exception to typical central-planning failure. Myron Lieberman's (1993) assessment of the "schooling is different" claim, theory (Walberg & Bast, 2003), and evidence from other industries strongly suggests that an OEI would generate better services at a lower cost than any alternative. That includes all of the foreign systems that rank above the current U.S. school system in the widely publicized international comparisons (Hanushek & Woessman, 2008).

It is true that hardly anyone cares about openness and competition per se,[36] but the politically marketable goals such as equity, academic improvement, and social harmony are likely unattainable without genuine openness to new privately run schooling options.

The reasons for some markets' failure to maximize efficiency—poorly informed buyers (mistakes and fraud), neighborhood effects (often called "externalities" or "spillovers"—positive [Hall, 2006] and negative [DeAngelis, 2018]), not enough competition—are unlikely to cause perverse market accountability effects for schooling (see Chapter 2). However, weak parental choice policy strategies can create or reinforce such effects.[37]

We can capture the spillover benefits of the potential merit of good primary and secondary education without political control of classroom practices and educator credentials.[38] Indeed, such control often yields negative spillovers (DeAngelis, 2018). Lieberman argued that the recurrent, costly nature of schooling purchases promotes consumer informedness, and it raises the value of a good reputation (Lieberman, 1993). Since deceptive practices would stifle the development of valuable long-term relationships with well-informed parents, school operators must offer substantive choices to all parents, even though not all parents choose carefully.

The low value of many education resources in non-school uses (physical assets and the skills of educators) also strengthens competing educators' incentives to pursue continuous improvement and develop long-term customer relationships. Those factors minimize the fast-buck potential that underlies the fraudulent behavior and shoddy service seen in some industries, and widely among CPSs (see Chapter 3) because shortages (wait lists) virtually eliminate accountability to customers. Wait lists create monopoly power for CPSs because CPSs can replace unhappy customers with others desperately waiting in line.[39]

A key point of this book is that an unproductive debate is curbing serious consideration of the likely best policy, an OEI. The approximately level playing field of an OEI creates a substantial niche for some decentralized planning of what is taught, how, where, and to whom. Price change to balance supply and demand orchestrates profit-motivated, decentralized planning. Central planning—nearly universally applied to K–12 schooling, globally—has never produced a thriving economy or industry. To achieve consideration for an expanded role for decentralized planning, we need to greatly improve recognition of key OEI requirements and rigorously assess the policy strategies that would establish those key requirements.

At the same time, a key aim of this book is to raise awareness of choice expansion programs that lack those key elements. Studies of policies that lack those key elements will yield findings that are mostly not germane (misleading and irrelevant) to the assessment of an OEI approach to school system improvement.

It is an unfortunate fact that for many more years it may be hard to credibly, empirically measure effects of true openness in K–12 education. Unless we find well-documented historical OEI examples, we'll have to create some, or rely on credible simulation models. If we create some, it will take a while for new school systems to reach an equilibrium state that is the proper basis for vetting.

Without actual OEIs to study, we must rely on evidence from credibly similar contestable (open) industries, arguments grounded in sound economic and business theory, and wise use of evidence developed from K–12 settings with some competitive dynamics present (e.g., Tooley et al., 2011). That, or quickly seen economic development gains,[40] will have to persuade some policy entrepreneurs to create an OEI to study before empirical support for an OEI as a useful transformation catalyst can confirm or reject the hypothesis implied by indirect evidence and theory. There is already widespread agreement that genuine openness would be a transformation catalyst, but no agreement that the outcomes would be mostly positive.

HOW THE DISCUSSION PROCEEDS

Chapter 1 describes the key elements of an open education industry. The OEI description follows a brief discussion of "monopoly" and the applicability of that term to our current school systems. Chapter 2 argues that much of the widely cited evidence and research—favorable as well as unfavorable—is essentially irrelevant to the merits of a genuine OEI. Chapter 3 focuses on the discussion of the United States' most widely accepted, alleged approach to parental choice expansion, chartered public schools.

Chapter 4 describes the fallacies that pervade the unproductive school choice debate, especially arguments that don't apply to an OEI. Chapters 5–10 discuss regulation and cost issues, confusion between education goals and procedures, equity and equality issues, and diversity and unity issues. The discussion of those issues is in the context of an OEI, and there are frequent comparisons of that perspective and its hypothesized properties and perspectives and the properties of typical published parental choice analyses.

The last section of the book deals with strategic and tactical issues such as working with particular groups; differences between specific choice expansion vehicles (Chapter 11) such as tuition vouchers, education tax credits, and education savings accounts; and different ways of targeting choice expansion. Chapter 12 discusses strategic/tactical mistakes. Many of them parallel the substantive fallacies discussed in Chapter 4.

Chapter 13 compares the current school system, very limited versions of parental choice, and an OEI from teachers' perspectives. Even though market forces contain a large dose of unpredictability, there are still numerous sound reasons to believe that many teachers will prefer an OEI to the current system, and especially prefer an OEI to the narrowly targeted, restriction-laden choice expansions adamantly opposed by teacher unions. Identifying gainers and losers is much more complicated than defining good and bad teachers. Chapter 14 summarizes the outlook for an OEI, including ways to overcome significant political roadblocks and the key policy issues that will arise.

NOTES

1. Letter to the editor, *Wall Street Journal*, October 11, 1994. The 1994 Ken Elias quote may or may not be responsible for the "In the Trenches" title of a section of the Center for Education Reform regular newsletter.

2. (1) California governor Gray Davis quoted in David Broder, "Reforming Education a Tough Assignment," *San Antonio Express-News*, March 2, 1999, 7B; (2) U.S. senator, Democrat Joseph Lieberman (Shokraii, 1998); (3) the U.S. Congress (Kirkpatrick, 1997) has harsh words for the status quo; also see Goals 2000 Education

Act of 1994; and (4) there are repeated "Nation at Risk" warnings (https://www.schoolsystemreformstudies.net/nation-at-risk-vi/), most recently in 2015.

3. http://www.schoolsystemreformstudies.net/wp-content/uploads/2016/10/Nation-at-Risk-Declarations.pdf

4. Key exceptions: Arizona's universal education savings accounts and the West Virginia Hope Scholarship discussed later.

5. https://www.educationnext.org/how-big-was-the-year-of-educational-choice/

6. "School Choice Movement Celebrates Its 'Best Year Ever' Amid Pandemic," The Pew Charitable Trusts, https://www.pewtrusts.org/en/research-and-analysis/blogs/stateline/2021/06/25/school-choice-movement-celebrates-its-best-year-ever-amid-pandemic

7. "School Choice Movement Celebrates Its 'Best Year Ever' Amid Pandemic," The Pew Charitable Trusts, https://www.pewtrusts.org/en/research-and-analysis/blogs/stateline/2021/06/25/school-choice-movement-celebrates-its-best-year-ever-amid-pandemic

8. There are many popular synonyms for "shared financing of tuition," including the term "copayment" used in the 2002 U.S. Supreme Court *Zelman* decision; also "topping off" and "adding on." I will use the term "copayment" or "shared financing" to describe applying the public funding to pay tuition that is larger than the public funding amount. So, for example, if copayment is legal, families can combine a $5,000 tuition voucher with $1,000 of their own funds to pay a $6,000 tuition. If shared financing is illegal, schools must accept the voucher amount as full payment or not admit voucher users. Later chapters will explain why banning copayment amounts to virtual "price control," government virtually deciding what private schooling should cost.

9. See throughout Chapter 9 of Rose (2016).

10. https://edreform.com/wp-content/uploads/2013/02/A_Nation_At_Risk_1983.pdf

11. See especially, and most recently, Ravitch (2010), Chapter 7.

12. For example: https://www.americanprogress.org/issues/education-K–12/reports/2018/03/20/446699/highly-negative-impacts-vouchers/

13. https://www.schoolsystemreformstudies.net/nation-at-risk-vi/

14. Even though tuition vouchers are now widely seen as an inferior means for expanding school choice, the term "voucher" is still the most familiar label, and this book's many references to the term "voucher" should be widely seen (except in Chapter 14 that compares voucher, tax credit, and education savings account approaches to school choice expansion) as denoting any means for yielding decreased discrimination against families that believe a traditional public school is not the best fit for at least one of their children.

15. https://www.washingtonexaminer.com/opinion/school-choice-works-for-a-third-of-the-cost and https://www.edchoice.org/school-choice/school-choice-in-america/

16. https://www.edchoice.org/school-choice/faqs/

17. http://www.uaedreform.org/downloads/2018/11/charter-school-funding-more-inequity-in-the-city.pdf

18. Michael Fox, "Remarks of Ohio State Representative Michael Fox," *State Legislator Guide to Teacher Empowerment* (February 1997), American Legislative Exchange Council, p. 17; *Wall Street Journal* editors, "School Reform Blooms," *Wall Street Journal*, May 5, 1999.

19. https://www.pewtrusts.org/en/research-and-analysis/blogs/stateline/2021/06/25/school-choice-movement-celebrates-its-best-year-ever-amid-pandemic

20. John Miller, "Why School Choice Lost," *Wall Street Journal*, November 4, 1993.

21. West Virginia Legislature 2021 Regular Session—Committee Substitute for House Bill 2013.

22. See Chapter 14 for a detailed discussion of the choice expansion vehicles, and for discussion of course choice and blended learning.

23. https://www.edchoice.org/wp-content/uploads/2018/10/2018-10-Surveying-Florida-Scholarship-Families-byJason-Bedrick-and-Lindsey-Burke.pdf

24. Education policy scholars: https://www.detroitnews.com/story/opinion/2018/06/27/constitution-requires-equality-between-secular-and-religious-education/735193002/; legal scholars: https://scholarship.law.ufl.edu/flr/vol65/iss4/1/

25. Classics: Coons and Sugarman (1999), Viteritti (1999). More recently, see the cover story of the Spring 2012 issue of the widely read *Education Next*.

26. Andrew Coulson, "Are Public Schools Hazardous to Public Education?," *Education Week*, April 7, 1999, 36; also U.S. senator, Democrat Joseph Lieberman (Shokraii, 1998)—concerns about protecting a broken process.

27. Erskine Bowles and Jack Kemp, "An Offer Bush and Gore Can't Refuse," *Wall Street Journal*, June 15, 2000.

28. Defense facilities and jails are exceptions; see also DeRoche's (2020) *A Fine Line*.

29. https://eric.ed.gov/?id=ED586209

30. Additional Nation at Risk Declarations, https://www.schoolsystemreformstudies.net/nation-at-risk-vi/, and Stephanie Banchero, "Scores Stagnate at High Schools," *Wall Street Journal*, August 18, 2010.

31. https://nces.ed.gov/programs/digest/d18/tables/dt18_236.10.asp

32. +3.3% in eighth-grade math, for example, from 2000 to 2019; https://www.nationsreportcard.gov/ndecore/xplore/NDE

33. https://www.oecd.org/pisa/PISA-results_ENGLISH.png

34. Barbara Kantrowitz and Pat Wingert, "A Dismal Report Card," *Newsweek*, June 17, 1991, 65.

35. (1) New Jersey, https://www.pacificresearch.org/wp-content/uploads/2017/06/NAGAYT_NewJersey_F_NewWeb.pdf; (2) Colorado, https://www.pacificresearch.org/wp-content/uploads/2017/06/NAGAYT_Colorado_Web.pdf; (3) Michigan, https://www.pacificresearch.org/wp-content/uploads/2017/06/NAGAYT_Michigan_Fweb.pdf; (4) Texas, https://www.pacificresearch.org/wp-content/uploads/2017/06/NAGAYT_Texas_Final_Web.pdf; (5) Illinois, https://www.pacificresearch.org/wp-content/uploads/2017/06/NAGAYT_Illinois_Final.pdf; (6) California, 2007, especially, but URL no longer available.

36. Frank Luntz and Bob Castro, "Dollars to Classrooms and Parental Choice in Education," Memorandum, April 14, 1998.

37. Merrifield (2008a) and https://www.the74million.org/article/deangelis-when-it-comes-to-school-choice-government-regulated-managed-competition-is-bad-in-theory-and-in-practice/

38. Instruction is *not* a "public good," a very specific term that means that it is impossible to limit access to the good, and that use does not change the quality or quantity available to others. Scenic vistas, lighthouse light, and national defense are "public goods." Schooling is not. Possible spillover benefits to society can make schooling a merit good: a source of positive spillovers.

39. https://www.cato.org/publications/commentary/all-school-choice-great-private-better-public

40. See Chapter 12.

Chapter 1

Elements of an Open Education Industry

This chapter's main objective is clarification of the open education industry (OEI) concept. You may wonder how the OEI concept differs from a competitive education industry (CEI), especially if you read the CEI discussion in *The School Choice Wars* (Merrifield, 2001).

The CEI and OEI concepts are nearly synonymous. For competition, openness to new providers or growth of existing providers are much more important than who the existing providers are or how many of them there are. The term "open" directly conveys that essential feature. With a large share of the schooling options (TPSs) defined by the political process, and perhaps only competition among political jurisdictions, perhaps forever, the essential school system feature—openness—may leave a high-performing formal schooling industry far short of the conditions that would obviously deserve a "CEI" label.

To highlight the key elements of an OEI, we begin with a discussion of monopoly power, which exists because[1] the existing 51 U.S. school systems' governance and funding policies make it difficult to sustain non-public schools. Non-public schools are rare because public schools' nearly total monopoly on public funding forces non-public schools to charge for services already widely available for no additional charge beyond taxes that must be paid. That's a high barrier to non-public school formation. Suppose the government gave away expensive cars. It would be nearly impossible for a private car dealer to operate. Ability to contest market share is the top determinant of openness and industry competitiveness.

Factors other than the public finance monopoly of TPSs can preclude openness in K–12 education. Such factors, which are common outside the United States, include rules that preclude significant differences between the schooling content and quality of public and independent schools. They preclude meaningful choice and genuine rivalry by regulating schooling content, including through central credentialing of educators, by requiring that independent schools accept public funding as full payment (price control), and by prohibiting for-profit schooling options.

MONOPOLY

Market area is a key competitiveness/openness issue. The market for some things is local, while it is regional, national, or international for others. Automakers' market area is global. Below the number needed for intense rivalry to exist, the number of automakers worldwide is quite important, though entry barriers are even more important. The number of automakers in specific places is nearly irrelevant.

In contrast, a one-plumber town is a monopoly, even with many plumbers elsewhere. By itself, however, a one-plumber situation is not a big problem. If a city's lone plumber performs poorly, charges extraordinary rates, or just can't keep up with the demand, the monopoly problem can vanish through in-migration of new plumbers, or training programs can deliver new plumbers. Except for natural monopolies (defined below), monopolies exist only temporarily unless rules block new competitors.

Some analysts claim that publicly funded schools are not monopolies because there are about 100,000 schools in nearly 14,000 diverse school districts.[2] But because it is nearly always extremely costly to opt out of the assigned neighborhood public school (TPS), the large number of TPSs and public school districts nationwide is as irrelevant to the competitiveness of K–12 service areas as the number of plumbers nationwide in the above example. There are four kinds of market entry barriers (the basis for reduced access or outright market closure):

- government policy
- economies of scale—unit production costs are sometimes much lower for larger firms
- patents—supposedly temporary rights to an exclusive franchise
- control over resources required to make a product

Government policy is the main cause of the public school system's monopoly status. Economies of scale are relevant for "brick-and-mortar" schooling options in rural areas.[3] As noted above, the most critical barrier is that government-provided (TPS, mostly) and sometimes government-authorized (CPS) K–12 schooling is available to families at no extra *direct*[4] charge beyond the taxes they must pay. In most attendance zones, the TPS is the only school supported by public funding.

So, though there are private schools, the TPS public finance monopoly gives TPSs, and other public schools such as CPSs and magnet schools, an enormous advantage. Private schools must ask families to pay tuition when there is "free" (no charge beyond taxes they must pay) schooling available. Just imagine if you still had to help fund Walmart after deciding to buy groceries at HEB (big in Texas). The additional charge to families to use private schools is a huge private school entry barrier made even worse by the arrival of CPSs, but that is not all. When a family wants to send its child to another TPS, it typically incurs higher housing costs to access a better TPS.[5]

No U.S. law prevents entrepreneurs from offering instruction to schoolchildren, but the very difficult task of beating a zero-tuition competitor keeps private school market shares very low and largely limited to instructional niches, such as religion, that public schools cannot contest. Though monopoly literally means single seller, practically speaking, monopoly is a matter of degree.

The public school system (TPS + CPS) typically has a 100% share of public funding. Nationwide, pre-COVID, government-funded schools had an 88% market share of K–12 schoolchildren, which held fairly steady until homeschooling expanded in response to COVID-rationalized school closures.[6]

Public schools' nearly 90% market share is much closer to the single-seller case than virtually every formally alleged monopoly. Even the 69% that attends the assigned TPS (2016; 74% in 1999) is a market share that far exceeds the level that usually triggers a U.S. Justice Department antitrust lawsuit. "Under the Sherman Act, monopoly power is considered the ability of a business to control a price within its relevant product market or its geographic market or to exclude a competitor from doing business within its relevant product market or geographic market. In order to meet this definition, it is only necessary to prove that the business had the power to fix prices or exclude competitors."[7]

Face-to-face K–12 schooling is a natural monopoly in sparsely populated areas[8] because it is too expensive to run competing brick-and-mortar schools in place of one TPS. Some areas are so sparsely settled that there are no schools. Children go to schools in larger nearby places.

Monopolies' lack of direct, intense competition leads to higher prices and inefficiencies (Walberg & Bast, 2003). Indeed, the public school system charges taxpayers a high and ever-rising sum. Inefficiency—low and sinking productivity (Hoxby, 2004)—is seen in the tripling of inflation-adjusted per-pupil funding nationwide since 1970, with little or no change in aggregate measures of student performance.[9]

Rapid growth in staff[10] and administrative overhead is a noteworthy inefficiency symptom. A worldwide OECD[11] comparison reveals that, in 1995, the United States was already notably top-heavy. The United States was the only country with fewer teachers than non-teaching staff (a 3:4 ratio vs. a 5:2

average ratio for the other OECD countries), a ratio that has likely persisted or worsened with the U.S. staffing surge.[12] Those are technical inefficiency examples—wasteful production—though likely necessitated by (1) the current funding policies, and (2) typical central-planning processes. Monopoly power has taken its toll on K–12 schooling worldwide.[13]

There are two other kinds of inefficiencies, both of which are also evident in U.S. K–12 education: allocative inefficiency and dynamic inefficiency. Allocative inefficiency is the failure to allocate resources to their most valuable uses. That is evident in the failure to recognize that increasing the accessibility of schooling delivered privately, or perhaps through specialized settings,[14] public or private, including electronically instead of face-to-face, would likely produce larger achievement gains for *some* children in *some* subjects. Allocative inefficiency arguably also arises from political control of textbook content (Ravitch, 2003),[15] curriculum content, and teacher training requirements. Instructional content could include more important information, and teaching could improve through increased specialization, which yields reduced need for challenging differentiated instruction.

Dynamic inefficiency—insufficient improvement—is evident in the school system's failure to systematically pursue research and development and implement innovations.[16] In addition, while change in public schools is undeniable, technological backwardness is the norm, and there is complacency about success and failure. There is no discernible propensity to identify and spread effective practices or to root out unproductive practices and practitioners.[17] According to Dale Ballou and Michael Podgursky (Ballou & Podgursky, 1997), public schools give little weight to the quality of teachers' credentials. Unproductive teachers are only rarely terminated.[18]

GENERAL REQUIREMENTS OF OPEN INDUSTRIES

The absence of a commonly accepted definition of school choice expansion causes much confusion about its desirability and its potential role as a transformation catalyst (see Merrifield, 2008b; Ravitch, 2010). A clear definition won't end controversies, but it might curb those that would result from failure to clarify what is meant by school choice expansion. Likewise, an open industry exists only when four key general elements are present.

1. Freedom of market entry and exit, and profit potential as a possible motive:

Changes in the number of sellers usually reflect changes in industry profitability or other desirability aspects, such as pleasurable nature of the work, risk, and perceived importance. In an open industry, increased desirability attracts additional sellers, thus making the market more competitive, and decreased profitability/desirability does the opposite. With freedom to easily enter or exit a market, changes in the number of sellers keeps the profitability of different open industries comparable. Population is the key determinant of the number of buyers; for K–12, the school-age population. For some industries, the number of buyers varies if the price trend differs (with quality constant) significantly from the overall rate of inflation.

Since universally tiny market shares—so small that no one can influence the market price—maximize the benefits of competition (e.g., see Collinge & Ayers, 1997, p. 241; Ekelund & Tollison, 1997, p. 206), economics texts consistently list "many buyers and sellers" as a key feature of a competitive industry. When consumers have many options, sellers typically won't survive complacency, inefficiency, or inattention to changing consumer wishes. Unpopular sellers face loss of resources if they fail to improve.

A large number of sellers is not an indispensable factor. Contestability (openness)—meaning new firms can contest market share easily—is the critical element of a competitive market. Economists have shown that contestability with only a few sellers at any one time, though not as good as many buyers and sellers, still fosters reasonably competitive behavior (Baumol, Panzar, & Willig, 1982; Borenstein, 1992; Morrison & Winston, 1987). Contestability has to be real. In K–12 education, it is hard to easily contest the government's school supply dominance. Of important note here: many TPSs does not mean many suppliers. The government supplies 70%–90% (depending upon CPS policy) of schooling.

2. Enough well-informed and mobile buyers and sellers:

Competitive pressures are adequate—that is, they establish producer accountability to buyers, including prices near minimum cost—when there are enough mobile, well-informed buyers to affect the financial viability of the sellers.[19] Competitive industries can have many poorly informed, low-mobility participants (Buckley & Schneider, 2003). Indeed, high-fixed-cost industries require very few mobile, well-informed buyers for adequate accountability through competitive pressures.

For example, consider the airline industry, a high-fixed-cost industry because of the money tied up in airplanes, and because depreciation and administrative costs vary little with ticket sales. Because of that, American Airlines once earned a large quarterly profit equal to just one passenger per flight. Ticket prices must reflect airlines' large fixed costs, so the number of passengers per flight has little impact on costs. But a small change in the number of passengers has a large effect on airlines' net revenues. TPS districts often have high fixed costs. Even when those high fixed costs are the result of inefficiency, that overhead can make the districts' status quo viability quite sensitive to small enrollment changes.

3. Producer survival depends on ability to be sufficiently choice worthy.

The suppliers of a service must depend on the consumers they serve. Suppliers can survive only if they provide superior service in at least a local niche.

4. Price changes reflect market pressures, so prices reflect the relative scarcity of a service and thus signal the profitability of increased production (Walberg & Bast, 2003).

In other words, where prices rise relative to production cost, the readily heeded price signal prompts increased production (and vice-versa), a process that orchestrates resource allocation within and between industries. Orchestration through price signals and price change amounts to decentralized planning, the scarcity-driven alternative to product differentiation through regulation ("central planning") that overwhelmingly dominates K–12 schooling worldwide.

Nobel laureate Friedrich Hayek said that the key feature is that "parties should be free to sell and buy at any price at which they can find a partner to the transaction, and that anybody should be free to produce, sell, and buy anything that may be produced at all" (Hayek, 1994, p. 42). It was a key point of Hayek's influential *The Road to Serfdom*, aptly describing the effect of lacking the industry features described above or failing to establish them. The ill-informed policy making that results from low-performing school systems is a key driving force on the road to serfdom.

The lower productivity that results from low-performing school systems is a reinforcing factor. All four factors are essential ingredients. Thomas Sowell (2018) demonstrated that absence of a single factor can yield totally different outcomes, which is why much sloppy analysis of school choice expansion yields wrong, misleading, and irrelevant findings.

APPLICATION TO FORMAL EDUCATION

For a school system, those general factors translate into specific, controversial policy requirements.[20] A parental choice policy produces an OEI if the policy follows two basic principles (I–II) and thus contains five (1–5) key elements.[21]

I. Little regulation of private schools beyond what applies to all entities that serve the general public. Formally define "school" sufficiently to disburse subsidies and curb fraud, but:
   1. Avoid creating formal entry barriers—hindrances to school formation.
   2. Don't curb opportunities to specialize, opportunities for school missions and pedagogies to differ. Specialization[22] is a well-established prerequisite for productivity maximization and is likely nearly as critical to student engagement. Requiring schools to accept all students at random and mandating schools to administer state tests are two examples of regulations that raise costs and reduce the likelihood of specialization.
II. Low informal entry barriers:
   3. Nondiscrimination: each policy jurisdiction's public funding per child can vary by education-relevant characteristics like age and special needs status, but it should not depend on school ownership.
   4. Minimal uncertainty about the future scope of the market.
   5. Avoid price control; allow private tuition copayments (private spending can supplement subsidy funding). That means families *and third parties*, such as scholarship funds, can share the financing of a private school tuition payment.

Overview

Beyond condemnation of onerous permitting requirements, the first general principle (I) means, except to prevent subsidized teaching of unlawful behavior, don't specify the content of schooling, who can offer instruction to children, or how to teach the content. Certainly, publicly funded efforts to facilitate choice expansion are quite proper, and information services such as rigorous, widespread data collection may have to be publicly provided.

Because of spillovers from schooling to the rest of society, the public interest in some minimum competencies is a tempting basis for a public role in specifying some curriculum content, but doing so may be counterproductive. The likely low propensity to privately underdevelop those competencies may not justify the regulatory closure of some instructional niches and the costly, sometimes ugly process of politically specifying, defining, and periodically updating required curriculum content and enforcing compliance.[23] For example, school board politics often led to teaching critical race theory.

Well-conceived *guidelines* can likely achieve higher rates of desirable minimum competencies while avoiding most of the cost of specifying and enforcing curriculum content requirements. Furthermore, since schools need to differ to efficiently address student diversity, the authorities will struggle to justify one-dimensional assessments of school quality.[24] That, plus the huge challenges inherent in the central planning of schooling, makes parental satisfaction the best measure of school performance.[25]

The second general principle (II) means that public policy should not significantly advantage some providers of instruction over others or exclude some providers through limits on what they can *try* to charge for the services offered. Such indirect but often still formidable entry barriers are absent only when tuition subsidy amounts do not depend on the provider of instructional services. For example, the Washington, DC, voucher amount is only about a third of the per-pupil funding amount of DC's TPSs. The TPSs do not have a 100% monopoly on public funding, but their huge financial advantage gives them substantial monopoly clout.[26]

Efficiency considerations don't prevent subsidy payments from varying from one student to the next according to objective factors included in a formal weighted student formula (WSF), but it is inefficient (and unfair to children and educators) for per-pupil subsidy levels to vary by schooling provider.

Nondiscrimination in public funding and the absence of formal barriers will also act as a primary agent of OEI geographic expansion. Consider the situation of an area with an OEI surrounded by places without an open education system.[27] Families suffer no penalty for moving to the area with the OEI besides the actual moving costs. TPSs are still available.

If the families prefer private schools for any of their children, they realize large benefits for going to the area with the OEI, or large losses if they leave the area. Those rewards and penalties exist even without convincing evidence that openness to entrepreneurial initiative and competitive pressures improve TPS schooling outcomes. Development of such evidence will also attract parents that prefer TPSs.[28] Local governments compete for tax base and residents (Tiebout, 1956), so the authorities in adjacent areas might react to the competitive pressures.

Basis and Importance of Low Market Entry Barriers

The large financial penalty for choosing a private school within the current education systems is what keeps private schools' market share extremely low. That any non-elite, nonsectarian private schools survive is quite remarkable. So, the easy entry/exit OEI requirement means nearly equal public funding of mainstream students.[29] A level playing field exists when there are only small differences in the student subsidy level for TPSs, CPSs, and private schools.

Low barriers are important to foster unrelenting attention to better resource use, and because even through our systems' uniformly comprehensive mega-schools, we have not adequately addressed differences in how children learn and differences in what fully engages them in the learning process. We need entrepreneurial initiative to adequately drive innovation and diversity in what is taught, how, where, and to whom.

As already noted previously, specialization is a key element of markets and the entry-exit process (Merrifield, 2005). In an OEI, schools and educators would likely specialize in different subject matters,[30] aptitude levels, and teaching styles.

The U.S. system stifles specialization by assigning the diverse children of each attendance area to a one-size-fits-all neighborhood TPS (Merrifield, 2008a).[31] We are expecting a standard process to be effective for every member of a very diverse student population. That forces educators to struggle to be "all things to all people."[32] That leads to heavy reliance on very challenging degrees of differentiated instruction,[33] one-size-fits-all for required classes, and many elective courses and extracurricular programs.

Yet, even within the severe constraints of the current 51 U.S. school systems, specialization is already a frequent common denominator of success. For example, principals in high-performing high-poverty schools "design their curriculum around the unique strengths and expertise of their staff" (Carter, 2000, p. 27).

The increased demand for private school slots that would result from nondiscriminatory subsidies could raise tuition levels initially. However, because price hikes attract competitors, openness will keep tuition levels low in the long run. And to the extent that barriers to market entry persist or price controls preclude maximum efficiency, rivalry will at least partially funnel above-normal profits into service upgrades. The airline industry before deregulation was a good example of that second-best profit dissipation process. The mostly attractive regulated fares set by the Civil Aeronautics Board (CAB) caused airlines to compete for passengers through valued practices such as higher-quality flight attendants, better meals, and more frequent flights.

The Number of Schooling Options and How to Count the Number of Providers Matters

Even when we satisfy the critical openness requirement, a large number of independent schooling providers—with none of them big enough to affect the market price on their own—is a desirable feature. The effective number of schooling providers is a labor market's number of independent school owners—such as districts, business firms, and religious organizations—not the number of schools. Imagine a labor market with 200 TPSs within a school district, 20 Catholic schools under one archdiocese, and 10 nonreligious private schools owned by one firm. The area has 230 schools, but it doesn't have 230 schooling providers. In fact, it only has three.

A school board decision to privatize management of some schools by contracting it out[34] to a private firm does not change the number of providers. The region may have another school manager, but the attendance area boundaries keep children from gaining any additional options.

Differences between private management of a TPS and private ownership of a school create other problems. Managers face uncertainty about contract renewal. That creates the temptation to maximize short-run profits by cutting corners, and underinvestment because the management contract might not survive long enough to recover investment outlays.

While the profit motive enhances competitive forces considerably,[35] it can become counterproductive in the absence of OEI conditions. A privately managed TPS is still a local monopoly. Wait lists, which are widespread for CPSs, also substantially reduce competitive pressures by giving them monopoly power over their customers (more in Chapter 3).

Demand Certainty and School Continuity Issues

The usefulness of entry ease and nondiscrimination also depends on a high degree of certainty about underlying authority and demand for schooling. Entrepreneurs are much less likely to enter a market if the political support for the key elements of the market is shaky, or if key policies face a credible legal challenge.

Pilot choice expansion programs, narrowly targeted programs, and some privately funded programs will not stimulate major new investments. For example, a 10-year, privately funded full-tuition voucher program located in the Edgewood School District of San Antonio, Texas,[36] filled up existing private schools, expanded some existing schools, but did not lead to much new construction.[37] Uncertain or explicitly temporary programs also diminish parental participation. Families value continuity in the education of their children. They are less likely to choose a new school if its survival could depend on political decisions unrelated to school quality—by any definition—or parent preferences.

Small Market Issues and Homogenization

In places that can support only one school, market contestability still yields useful competitive pressures. Examples of effective education created by rivalry in large markets create pressure to behave competitively in small markets, while also providing innovations to imitate. While contestability usually means some imitation of successful sellers, it does not necessarily mean more homogeneity.

Markets involve individual decisions, so competition reduces the differences between sellers only when buyers become more similar.[38] For example, higher profit margins for Chinese restaurants would increase their size and numbers, but specialization within the restaurant industry would remain the same.

High Stakes and Exit Issues

In an open industry, customer preferences determine the difference between success and financial trouble, with possible extinction through liquidation or bankruptcy. Bankruptcy is an easily monitored, relatively objective indicator of failure, and the possibility of bankruptcy strengthens the incentive to pay attention to customers and make careful decisions. Bankruptcy is rare in the public sector, which is a major reason why there are so many allegedly obsolete government programs. In the private sector, bankruptcy performs the critical task of shifting resources from obsolete and inefficient producers to new and growing businesses.

Bankruptcy would not always force a change in the ownership of school assets. "Under Chapters 11, 12, and 13 [of the Federal Bankruptcy Law], a bankruptcy proceeding involves the rehabilitation of the debtor to allow him to use his future earnings to pay off his creditors."[39] Debtors get time to restructure. Many customers (families as the choosers, schoolchildren as the service consumers) may not notice changes.

In an OEI, bankruptcies would probably not cause many abrupt shutdowns. Children would need a new school on short notice only in the most extreme circumstances. Bankruptcies that require more than restructuring would still usually only shift the physical assets of the school to new managers.

Ownership changes, even sudden midyear changes, will not necessarily disrupt classrooms. New owners have strong incentives to cater to the existing student body's capabilities and desires. That means that new owners are unlikely to quickly abandon the existing faculty and staff or the subject and methodological specialty areas, except where there is an obvious link to the cause of the bankruptcy problem.

The public can establish safeguards against midyear shutdowns. Parents can avoid financially shaky schools if the schools must disclose critical financial data. An analog to bank deposit insurance is another option. The authorities can protect parents and children from midyear shutdowns by requiring schools to post a bond or buy insurance sufficient to run the school until the school year ends. Insurance companies would audit schools and signal which schools are risky through refusal to issue a policy or by demanding high premiums.

Unhappy parents do not yet threaten the survival of TPSs. Most stay because moving a child to another school is costly, and the alternatives are often scarce, unattractive (religion mismatch), or expensive. Furthermore, when children leave a TPS, the school typically only loses the state government allocation. Since the tax money raised locally is usually not lost, departures typically raise a district's per-pupil funding, and they can help growing districts avoid new construction. Districts suffer only if the state's payment tops the cost avoided by having fewer students (see Chapter 6).[40] If there is population growth anywhere in the district, district authorities can avoid budget cuts at any school by reconfiguring the district's attendance areas.

The link between customer satisfaction and funding level is also minimal when funding doesn't come from clients; for example, from endowment funds, legislative appropriations, or management contracts.

Parents can reward good TPS performance, or punish poor service, only through an organized political movement. Educators can ignore calls for change unless parents first convince their representatives—the people who actually fund educators' paychecks—that parent demands are politically significant. And even if many families pressure representatives to change TPSs, the needs of the least advantaged minority groups are still easily ignored.

Parent Informedness and Mobility

In an OEI, the number of families willing and able to transfer their children to another school is large enough to affect the financial viability of schools. Since every producer has immediate costs that do not vary greatly with enrollment levels, it might not take a large number of well-informed and mobile parents to greatly impact school finances.

The parents who are unaware of school differences will benefit from the efforts to please the informed, mobile parents. For example, all car buyers benefit from safety features that appeal to safety-conscious buyers. The benefits of openness do not depend on all parents being motivated and able to choose the best school for their children.

One of the most cited objections—largely irrelevant—to openness is that parents may make poor decisions about schooling for their kids. It is certainly true of some parents, but the likely benefits outweigh those costs. A few informed consumers often enhance products for all buyers. That point is largely absent from the political debate of choice expansion. And even the least advantaged families usually make good educational decisions for their kids.[41]

No Price Controls—Flexible Prices

Price movement is a primary source of information and incentives, and an indispensable element of the market process (Schuettinger & Butler, 1979). Price changes are the main reason for market entry or exit. Increased demand competes prices upward. That raises industry profitability and motivates entry. As more services become available, prices drop, the output of the industry stabilizes, and inefficient producers close. Only the best firms persistently earn above-normal profits.

The price-change-driven entry-exit process performs the crucial function of allocating resources to competing uses, and it helps motivate continuous service improvement. Each resource is put to its most valuable use when prices are flexible and comprehensive and therefore reflect changes in scarcity. Prices are "comprehensive" when they accurately reflect all of the costs of producing and consuming a product, including spillovers.

School systems globally—certainly the 51 U.S. systems—are typically price-less. TPS tuition stays at zero regardless of changes in key underlying demand and supply factors. The political process drives a centrally planned resource allocation process and then self-assesses performance. Even with a carefully constructed weighted student formula (WSF) as a starting point, there are many reasons to allow parental and third-party supplementation of subsidy payments.[42] "Skin in the game" is a good reason to demand some supplementation, and because of unique subjective factors, parents may want to purchase schooling that costs more than the WSF-based subsidy amount.

Unfortunately, most private school choice programs and prominent proposals[43] do not establish a basis for scarcity-determined prices. The actual and proposed programs are either too small, or they bar private schools from charging more than the public funding. Government price control is much less likely when subsidies are available as private tuition tax credits or education savings accounts (more detail in Chapter 11), which is a key reason they are generally the best means for facilitating parental choice expansion.

Requiring private schools to accept the subsidy amount as full payment (prohibiting copayment, banning privately funded "add-ons")[44] shrinks the future menu of schooling options. Except that expensive, elite private schools would survive, a universal program that bans add-ons creates a price ceiling at the subsidy amount.

Consider the following example. Say a voucher is worth $5,000. Then a $5,000 per year private school would cost families only the school taxes they must pay. An "add-on" ban means that families cannot use the voucher to help pay tuition of $5,001 or more. Just $1 in extra cost would cost families $5,001. So, a $5,000 voucher linked to a copayment ban would eliminate school choices costing somewhat more than $5,000 and greatly reduce the demand for school choices costing significantly more than $5,000. For example, there likely wouldn't be any $6,000 instructional approaches on the menu, and very few $7,000 instructional approaches.

Many of the families that would be willing to buy the $7,000 package by supplementing the $5,000 voucher with $2,000 of their own money would not pay the full $7,000 themselves. Instead of paying an extra $7,000 for an additional $2,000 worth of schooling, many parents would use the voucher at a school that would accept it as full payment (if one is available) and then seek additional education informally by paying for tutoring, summer programs, and home education tools such as games and software. That $7,000 educational option would also cost less than $7,000 in the long run *if* market entry occurs. But prohibiting copayment above $5,000 reduces the financial incentive and ability to pursue market entry.

The shortages that result from voucher values below the market-clearing prices eliminate private schools' incentive to be customer friendly or to aggressively pursue innovation. The important connection between persistent shortages and declining product quality is widely agreed to among economists, but not well known. The reason is straightforward—shortages give producers monopoly power, as described in Reisman's (1998) *Capitalism*. In this case, the shortage is in the number of producers of particular schools. Since the shortage is literally other school producers, the public school system enjoys additional monopoly power.

Regulation

Though competitive pressures create accountability, many people who don't trust families to choose adequate schooling content may seek regulation of factors such as tuition, discipline policies, personnel characteristics, state testing, and subject matter content. Such regulation limits the scope of specialization and potential avenues of innovation, and it can become a barrier to entry. Therefore, to achieve an OEI, only the rules that apply nearly uniformly throughout the economy (e.g., health; safety; fraud; discrimination by race, creed, gender, or national origin) should apply to the producers of K–12 schooling.

A low minimum enrollment level might be enough to curb the establishment of extremist schools at taxpayer expense (Lieberman, 1993, pp. 290–292). However, such a restriction would just be possibly costly insurance against a very unlikely event. There is no evidence that private school students are more likely to foster extremist behavior. On the contrary, Shakeel and Wolf (2018) found that U.S. homegrown terrorists were more likely to attend public than private schools. The rule could substantially limit the benefits of allowing children to attend small schools.

Since the critical elements discussed in this chapter are widely neglected, the school choice wars have yet to tell us much about the desirability of an open education industry, which is a key basis for persistent education policy failures. Getting the key participants in the school choice wars and the public to link choice, openness, and the key elements discussed in this chapter must begin with an assessment of the alleged school choice evidence (Egalite, 2013; Merrifield, 2008b), including especially its limitations. The next chapter reviews the scientific evidence on existing private school choice programs and the unintended negative consequences of obsession with analysis of restriction-laden, narrowly targeted programs.

NOTES

1. The "natural monopoly" exception is discussed shortly.
2. Robert Lowe and Barbara Miner interview, in Lowe and Miner (1996).
3. Diseconomies of scale are actually the norm in urban areas, where the strategy to address student diversity is comprehensiveness, which often leads to hard-to-manage, huge schools. For a study of larger vs. smaller, see Cushman (2000), or for an extensive discussion, see Powell et al. (1985).
4. Free schooling is a very costly delusion. Families pay more for housing the better the area's assigned TPS.
5. See note 4.
6. https://nces.ed.gov/pubs2019/2019106.pdf; see page 6.
7. https://www.freeadvice.com/legal/what-is-monopoly-power-under-the-sherman-act/
8. A single dominant "seller." Especially in industries, such as schooling, where product diversity is valued, a natural monopoly does not preclude small-scale alternatives such as online schooling, micro-schools, and homeschooling.
9. https://www.wsj.com/articles/money-for-children-not-schools-students-education-K-12-cost-prices-inflation-system-math-reading-11655924112
10. https://www.edchoice.org/research/back-staffing-surge/; https://reason.org/commentary/how-K-12-support-services-spending-can-divert-education-funding-from-instruction
11. Organization for Economic Co-operation and Development, *Education at a Glance: OECD Indicators* (Paris: OECD, 1995).
12. The 2009 OECD "Education at Glance" appears to be the last to contain the basis for comparing teachers to non-teaching staff, which indicated that U.S. teachers barely outnumbered non-teaching staff.
13. https://www.cato.org/publications/policy-analysis/markets-vs-monopolies-education-global-review-evidence
14. https://object.cato.org/sites/cato.org/files/serials/files/cato-journal/2005/5/cj25n2-9.pdf

15. https://fordhaminstitute.org/national/research/mad-mad-world-textbook-adoption

16. D. W. Miller, "The Black Hole of Education Research," *Chronicle of Higher Education*, August 6, 1999. Also, Lieberman (2007).

17. Lieberman (1993) summarizes the evidence on those issues.

18. https://tntp.org/publications/view/the-widget-effect-failure-to-act-on-differences-in-teacher-effectiveness

19. Note that political accountability is much weaker than competitive market accountability. Low-quality services do not jeopardize government agencies' financial viability. And, as Eric Hanushek aptly states, "Nobody's career is really dependent upon the children doing well" ("Incentives: The Fundamental Problem in Education," *School Reform News*, January 2000, 17).

20. https://object.cato.org/sites/cato.org/files/serials/files/cato-journal/2005/5/cj25n2-9.pdf

21. Quantified into the JSC 2011 EFI.

22. https://object.cato.org/sites/cato.org/files/serials/files/cato-journal/2005/5/cj25n2-9.pdf

23. See Burke and Bedrick, Chapter 9 of *School Choice Myths* (2020), and Arons and McCluskey's "Why We Fight" (2007).

24. One-dimensional perception of school quality (Sahlgren, 2013), teacher quality, and student ability is one of the most confounding aspects of parental choice debates and school system reform conversations.

25. https://www.cato.org/blog/we-shouldnt-need-use-science-grant-educational-freedom

26. https://www.cato.org/publications/commentary/school-choice-works-third-cost

27. The privately funded 1998–2008 tuition voucher program for residents of the Edgewood School District in San Antonio, Texas (Merrifield & Gray, 2009, http://faculty.business.utsa.edu/jmerrifi/evp.pdf).

28. http://object.cato.org/sites/cato.org/files/serials/files/cato-journal/2013/1/cj33n1-7.pdf

29. I define mainstream child more broadly than just lacking any learning disabilities. If a student can find appropriate education services for the dollar value of public per-student support, or close to that amount if some private contribution to tuition payments is expected, the student is mainstream. That will be the vast majority. Public Law 94-142 assures non-mainstream students—children with especially severe disabilities—with sufficient taxpayer support to implement an individual education plan.

30. There is some subject area specialization within the public school system, mostly by public schools of choice, CPSs, and magnet schools.

31. According to 1993 data from the National Center for Education Statistics (NCES), 80% of the grade 3–12 student population attends the assigned TPS. The 2009 figure is 69%. NCES did not say why their data excluded grades K–2, but the percentage will be higher at those grade levels.

32. Frank C. Nelsen, "Parental Choice: Will Vouchers Solve the School Crisis?," *Christianity Today*, August 19, 1991, 29.

33. https://www.schoolsystemreformstudies.net/differentiation-of-instruction-delusion/; https://www.educationnext.org/making-differentiated-instruction-work/

34. Marie Gryphon, "Edison's Mess Is No Referendum on Privatization," *Washington Times*, June 9, 2002. Detractors of privatization are eagerly piling on, publishing story after op-ed about Edison's woes. Edison's failures would prove, they maintain, that private contracting has been a failed fad; that private companies can't do more with less, and that the stability of politically-driven school management is preferable to the uncertainty of private management.

35. David G. Brennan, "Innovation and Profit: What Education Needs Most (Brennan interviewed by George Clowes)," *School Reform News*, July 2004, 14–15.

36. Merrifield and Gray (2009), http://faculty.business.utsa.edu/jmerrifi/evp.pdf

37. There was one major expansion. It converted to CPS status when the privately funded voucher program ran out of money. A large new school was built by the person who was the main source of the voucher funding.

38. In contrast, the political arena is about collective choices. Therefore, competition in the political arena reduces differences between the choices.

39. The Legal Information Institute web page (www.law.cornell.edu/topics/bankruptcy.htm) quote refers to the chapters of the Federal Bankruptcy Statute (Title 11 of the U.S. Code).

40. The Friedman Foundation study on average versus marginal; also old Texas Public Policy Foundation.

41. Jason Bedrick and Corey A. DeAngelis, "Parents Know Better than Standardized Tests," *Wall Street Journal*, August 28, 2019, https://www.wsj.com/articles/parents-know-better-than-standardized-tests-11567033335

42. Many synonyms: "tuition copayment," "shared financing of tuition," "top-off," "add-on."

43. True of most actual and proposed, past and current, programs. There are some exceptions, for example, California's Prop 174 (defeated in 1993), the November 2000 Voucher2000 proposition (also California), and New Mexico governor Gary Johnson's universal voucher proposals.

44. "Topping off," "shared financing," and "copayment" are widely used synonyms for voucher add-ons.

Chapter 2

Hyped "Experiments" in Near Irrelevance

Escape Hatches ≠ Reform Catalysts

> Every time we don't tell the truth, we play a part in destroying kids' lives.
>
> —Howard Fuller[1]

Major changes can seem risky even when the status quo is terrible. Therein lies the desire to "go small" as an experiment.[2] We get the same disappointing results when leaders "go small" to appear proactive with low resistance. Years of intense study of restriction-laden, mostly tiny choice programs are likely a key reason for failure to implement low-restriction choice expansions large enough to foster much-needed school system reform.

Academic scholars cannot publish studies—publish or perish—of low-restriction, larger-scale choice programs until leaders willing to confront major resistance enact such programs. And after larger-scale programs exist, full, true academic effects will surface slowly. Because of the imperative to publish, the focus has been on available data, which is unable to yield much useful insight. Chapter 12 explains how intense scrutiny of low-dose, small-scale, restriction-laden programs can be counterproductive.

Longtime, widespread linkage of "choice," "competition," and "experiment" created the false perception that competition was an effect of the recent choice expansions. However, those expansions didn't qualify as the OEI experiments[3] that may be politically necessary for widespread adoption of a reform catalyst, because (1) time to generate and process the results may be very costly, and (2) creation of such an experiment will require at least one state to adopt a large-scale program[4]—not necessarily statewide—on the basis of guidance from theory and what can be validly gleaned from our experience with restriction-laden programs, mostly on a small scale. Economic theory and abundant evidence from past K–12 education systems (West, 1994) justify the low-restriction, large-scale programs that other places will see as experiments. But it may take an accidental experiment whereby key conditions emerge from the pursuit of another policy objective.

A key basis of the persistent policy failure is that political and intellectual interest in the effects of what are small-scale escape hatches[5] may have (1) greatly delayed access to better-fit schooling for millions of disengaged children ("left behind"); (2) kept school choice expansions small and rare; and (3) yielded an empirical basis ("let's examine the evidence") for misleading generalizations of high-restriction outcomes to the low-restriction reforms big enough to foster school system transformation.[6]

Methodological rigor didn't make highly regulated and narrowly targeted programs into OEI experiments.[7] They compared the effectiveness of the choices, when what we need is rigorous documentation of differences in school systems with large-scale choice expansions, and without. Evidence from other industries indicates that entrepreneurial initiative will yield an entire industry working competitively to define and fill the changing engagement niches.

Milton Friedman differentiated[8] "charity voucher" programs from the reform catalyst "education vouchers" he envisioned. Diane Ravitch's (2010) Chapter 7 is the best example of the frequent, often deliberate, failure to differentiate. Her chapter does not specify the key elements of any of the many choice programs she asserts as compelling evidence that choice has been a failed strategy and will continue to be so.

Likewise, Joshua Cowen's assessment[9] of the experience with narrowly targeted, restriction-laden U.S. choice expansions barely notes the small scale of the U.S. programs, and then paints with a broad brush. Especially egregious is his willingness to assert as a general result the *New York Times* description[10] of the negative achievement effects of an especially restriction-laden Louisiana voucher program. There is no description of the extremely debilitating conditions of that single example of negative effects (Mills & Wolf, 2017), which we review a bit further below. Indeed, the choice expansion opposition narrative is grounded on the typically small effects of choice expansion.

The Ravitch and Cowen broad-brush condemnations are examples of the legacy of reckless inferences that restriction-laden choice expansions are true experiments. That has reduced the political feasibility of genuine OEI policies. Indeed, Andrew Coulson (1999) argued that "the greatest threat to the [political] success of school choice stems from the diversity of the reforms that bear its name.[11] The problem is [perceived] guilt by association" with small-scale programs. Small academic gains from small choice expansions tarnished more than the limited conditions that actually existed.[12]

Perceived success only spread restriction-laden programs (Merrifield, 2020).[13] Widespread reliance on outcomes of non-OEI systems reduces the political feasibility of OEIs. Even though it should not take a social scientist to understand that apples-to-oranges comparisons are potentially egregious methodological errors, social scientists and policy makers are making such errors.

It is not widely recognized that restriction-laden programs cannot tell us what to expect from an OEI. However, unexpectedly noteworthy are the small programs' significant social benefits such as reduced teen pregnancy and crime, plus post-schooling attainment gains (Wolf, Witte, & Kisida, 2019). Poor study design[14] and acts of deliberate deception ("spin") are also significant risks, especially given the propensity for sound-bite-driven political warfare.

LARGELY IRRELEVANT AND DANGEROUSLY MISLEADING

Webster's dictionary defines "experiment" as "test, trial" and "tentative procedure or policy." Stefan Thomke, author of *Experimentation Works* (2020), notes that experimentation is "the ideal driver of small changes," but that "not all innovation decisions can be tested." Since school system change (innovation or a large change), not the academic gains of a few transferees, is the critical issue in a nation already in policy-making error-driven decline, the intensely studied, tiny school system changes and the oldest school choice programs should have been nearly irrelevant to everyone but their few participants.

Parents should know if a schooling strategy change will help their child, but it was still amazing, and given the political hype, lucky, that way-below-noteworthy choice expansions still yielded detectable academic gains. The results of the small program studies returned the results one would expect: mostly very small, positive, statistically significant effects. The treatment was simply too weak to convey whether an OEI would yield truly significant results.

With price controls,[15] for-profit bans,[16] participation deterrents, and eligibility curbs, no one should expect any of the U.S. school choice programs that have existed long enough to credibly study to yield noteworthy school system change. The 1990s studies only told us what happened to test scores, excluding the self-selection effects that are a key benefit of choice expansion, when a few children moved to a private school that is viable in the current school system.

Cash from a few small vouchers cannot greatly enhance private school abilities, or prompt much new school formation, because even the best inexpensive private schools cannot expect large jumps in per-pupil funding. Unless the program is big enough to entice education entrepreneurs to enter the market, there won't even be much new rivalry in the private sector. Without significant education market entry, very few families will have multiple genuine private schooling options.

Rules that forced random admission of voucher holders and state exam use often kept the best private schools on the sidelines (DeAngelis, 2019b; DeAngelis et al., 2019; Stuit & Doan, 2013; Sude, DeAngelis, & Wolf, 2018). By reducing the number of genuinely specialized options (DeAngelis, 2019b; DeAngelis & Burke, 2017; DeAngelis & Dills, 2019), the rules often had the opposite of the desired effect.

Louisiana's statewide, small-scale parental choice program, which was the first to yield negative effects (Mills & Wolf, 2017), seemed designed to fail. Only low-income families from the attendance zones of officially failed TPSs are eligible, and participating private schools must accept students randomly, administer the state test, and accept the low voucher amount as full payment (price control). Onerous rules (Bedrick, 2016; Sude, DeAngelis, & Wolf, 2018), especially the low price cap, disproportionately discouraged the highest-quality private schools, which partially explained the negative effects (Abdulkadiroğlu et al., 2018; Lee et al., 2019). Low price caps also stifle the formation of new private schools.

The extensively studied choice expansions—public school choice, privately funded vouchers, and the Cleveland and Milwaukee publicly funded vouchers[17]—were not OEI experiments. But because many studies used rigorous study methods (Greene, 2000; Greene et al., 1997; Rouse, 1998), they are legitimate charity voucher experiments. Chapter 4 discusses expansion of parental choice through CPSs, so we omit CPSs from the balance of this chapter and focus on parental choice expansion through education tax credits and publicly funded tuition vouchers. Education savings accounts (ESAs) have not been in use long enough to study rigorously.[18]

CONFUSION

The mismatch between the rhetoric about competition and highly restrictive school choice policies created considerable confusion (Cobb, 1992). Caroline Hoxby (2000) asserted a "Novel Way to Assess School Competition," part of a *Wall Street Journal* article[19] in which the author and her editors showed that they didn't understand the big differences between the conditions of rivalry between businesses and "Tiebout competition," which is rivalry between governments such as school districts. The reviewers and editors of the economics flagship journal that published Hoxby's assessment of competition between school districts did not compel her to clearly differentiate Tiebout competition from competition among businesses.

Nearly all analysts and activists ignored Frederick Hess's (2002) point that the rivalry evident in cities with school choice expansions ("the pick axe"—small adjustments, escape hatches) was a far cry from what exists ("bulldozer"—transformational change, extinction of the non–choice worthy), continuously, in a typical marketplace. "The market bulldozer is not in evidence in urban school systems, although there are hints of the pick axe" (p. 17).

TRIVIAL, INAPPROPRIATE SUCCESS CRITERIA

Prominent choice advocate Daniel McGroarty (1996) stated the mistaken, high-stakes focus of the alleged experiments with "choice and competition" (market-based education) very clearly:

> For many observers, the success or failure of school choice hinges on hard statistical data: Are choice students' test scores higher than those of their public school peers?

He did not grasp that policy makers should ignore such comparisons. What is truly being tested—whether parents can discern better schooling options—is intuitively true.

At a time when we need to optimize school systems (all of the schools, public and private), we are rigorously studying, and endlessly debating, the effect of moving students within a nearly static, low-performing system.[20] Although different rules and relationships exist depending on the type of school, *all* can have a significant role in educating the public. The school system reform narrative is a prisoner of the political debate—which is better, public or private—when we should focus on maximizing student outcomes without regard to the public-private school ownership mix.

Ideology is sadly a key factor. Left-leaning people want the state to dominate schooling policies. Conservatives believe it should not. The beauty of an OEI is that it admits our total ignorance of the optimal conditions and unleashes the immense knowledge each of us has about our own situations and shares it with others through a price system and our individual choices and preferences. But what Rene Sanchez of the *Washington Post* noted in 1997 is sadly still mostly true: "Researchers are feuding over a bottom-line question—whether [choice] students do substantially better."[21] It's simply the wrong question. Answers are borderline irrelevant.

The restriction-laden, mostly small program studies typically defined "success" on just test score effects. But two reviews of rigorous school choice studies indicate that test scores are weak proxies for long-term outcomes such as high school graduation, college enrollment, employment, crime, and health (DeAngelis, 2019a; Hitt et al., 2018).

THE MILWAUKEE PARENTAL CHOICE PROGRAM (MPCP)

Severe Restrictions

In the widely cited early studies (e.g., Rouse, 1998; Greene, 2000; Greene et al., 1999), only 1%–1.5% of Milwaukee Public School (MPS) students were eligible, and voucher users couldn't attend religious private schools (Witte et al., 2007). Voucher users could not top 49% of participating private schools' total enrollment. Those rules disqualified all but six of the private schools that existed when the MPCP began in 1990. Over 80% of the voucher users attended three of them (Greene, Peterson, & Du, 1997). The schools' space limitations and the legal cloud that engulfed the MPCP in its first year kept voucher use below the 1% cap.

A change in the voucher enrollment limit from 49% to 65% increased the number of eligible schools to 23 with enough total space for all voucher users, though most attended just a few of them. The schools still must admit voucher users randomly, and mostly accept a voucher equal to the state share of MPS funding—about 67% in 2017–2018—as full payment.[22] Private schools had to allow voucher users to opt out of religious programs, require their administrators and teachers to have bachelor's degrees, and administer state standardized testing to voucher users in 3rd, 4th, 8th, 9th, 10th, and 11th grade.

Weak Incentives and Wishful Thinking

Incentives matter. Financially poor private schools struggling against the zero-tuition public school system may have to participate in restriction-laden "choice" programs to survive, while long-standing, established private schools can survive without participating in the program. So, in addition to the low relevance of private-public comparisons, the comparison will likely suffer from selection bias that exists when weaker private schools participate in choice programs at a higher rate than higher-performing schools.

Once the number of voucher applicants tops voucher availability, the choice program provides no financial incentive for TPSs to pursue improvement. Less than huge improvements would only cut the number of unsuccessful voucher applicants. Since gradual improvement would not reduce voucher use, increased media attention was the only new incentive for MPS leaders to pursue improvement.

With so few eligible private schools in the initial years, most voucher users probably had access to only one of them, and because the number of vouchers initially exceeded the available space, there wasn't even much private school rivalry pressure. The requirement that schools accept the voucher amount as full payment[23] eliminated the key incentive of improved per-pupil funding. New testing and accreditation mandates (2005) further reduced private schools' incentive to participate in the program (Witte et al., 2007).

As the continued unsatisfactory performance of the MPS attests (already, in June 2000, the governor threatened a state takeover), the MPS gains were small (Ford & Andersson, 2019). Nine studies found that competitive pressures helped cause small TPS improvements (e.g., Carnoy et al., 2007; Chakrabarti, 2008; EdChoice, 2019; Egalite, 2013; Greene & Forster, 2002; Greene & Marsh, 2009; Jabbar et al., 2019; Mader, 2010).[24]

One of the specific MPS responses—a promise to fund personalized summer reading instruction—also illustrates a key difference between settings that promote limited rivalry and truly competitive market settings. Reading instruction may not be a cost-effective expenditure, or there may be better uses for the money. The MPS can fund inefficient programs because people must pay taxes. Without competing choices, inefficient programs are harder to identify and eliminate. Genuine rivalry purges inefficient programs by offering customers better buys.

We need a careful study of the MPCP's impact on the whole Milwaukee school system, including the private schools. Researchers must determine if the MPCP program's small size and many restrictions were the reasons the school system didn't improve much. Two studies found that voucher program regulations can have unintended negative effects on program quality (DeAngelis et al., 2019a,[25] 2019b[26]), and some correlational studies found similar results (e.g., DeAngelis, 2019b;[27] DeAngelis & Burke, 2017; Stuit & Doan, 2013; Sude, DeAngelis, & Wolf, 2018). Otherwise, there might be more assertions such as President Obama's that school choice doesn't make "much difference,"[28] and the very early Carnegie Foundation's *1992* report's claim that parental choice is a pointless reform because "Milwaukee's plan has failed to demonstrate [in one year?!] that vouchers can . . . spark school [TPS] improvement."[29]

Inappropriate, Misleading Evaluation Criteria

The performance of the voucher recipients—a maximum of 1.5% of the MPSs in the early published studies—received a lot of publicity. The debate included detail-intensive discussions of the nuances of the voucher student data, the meaning of statistics, and which factors to include in the study.[30] The possible effect on the remaining MPS children received little early attention. And the net effect of adding money along with low-performing TPS transferees to private schools is a key issue that still deserves careful study.

Use of the scores of the unsuccessful voucher applicants as the benchmark for voucher user gains is inconsistent with initial claims (and eventual evidence of small gains) that the voucher program would cause MPS improvements. Such a benchmark is an implicit assertion that the voucher program cannot affect MPS students. Strangely, while asserting that the MPCP was still worthy of study, education reformers acknowledged that the conditions "depart only marginally from past practice" and that it is "a highly compromised choice plan . . . designed to fail" (Peterson, Greene, & Noyes, 1996). The random assignment methodology yielded valid experiments in the slight departures from past practice, but definitely no insight into the effects of OEI conditions.

Peterson et al. found that voucher users ($7,708 voucher in 2017–2018) outperformed comparable, unsuccessful voucher applicants (over $11,500 per student in MPSs)[31] by their third year in the program (Greene, Peterson, & Du, 1997). That parents found better learning environments probably surprised only the scholars aware of the daunting data and statistical issues that can obscure underlying facts. Test scores improved even though most families said they pursued nonacademic goals such as school safety.[32] That's fortunate, because they probably would not have waited three years to realize school safety benefits. Given the political focus on the voucher users' test scores, it is fortunate for the parental choice cause that test scores eventually rose (e.g., Hitt et al., 2018).

It is amazing how many low-income families preferred those weak initial alternatives to their much better-funded assigned TPS. The physical conditions and staffing constraints of the three struggling schools that initially enrolled over 80% of the voucher users (Greene, Peterson, & Du, 1997) reflected the disadvantages our 51 U.S. school systems indirectly impose on private schools. While those three schools avoided bankruptcy, a fourth school did collapse despite the infusion of voucher funds.

The Milwaukee policy changes are an "exciting *reform*"[33] (emphasis added) only if they significantly improve whole systems, including all of the schools, public and private. You measure such effects by comparing school systems with significant policy differences, including, but not limited to, differences in access to diverse TPS alternatives. The appropriate choice expansion "randomized experiment" is for all of the children in some regions to have private school choice without financial penalty and permission to copay tuition, while the status quo survives as the "control" in other, similar regions. Given the political calculus, that seems most likely to occur through an economic development effort directed at persistent, deep pockets of urban poverty through poor-place-targeted universal private school choice (more in Chapter 12).[34]

The comparison of transferees and their MPS peers made parental choice look less effective as a reform than it actually was. The gains by MPS students noted above shrunk the difference between voucher users' and unsuccessful voucher applicants' test scores. In fact, what we allege to be typical but inappropriate (irrelevant and misleading) and bizarre test score comparisons will cause school choice programs to appear less effective[35] the more effective choice expansion is at improving TPS performance.

We're comparing 90-pound weaklings (typical low-budget private schools) and relatively wealthy 500-pound gorilla TPS cartel (school district) members? What can such a bizarre contest actually show us? TPSs are in a political straitjacket and undermotivated. They don't have to be choice worthy. Private schools' resources, constraints, and incentives will be very different in an OEI. Still, analysts on both sides see inconclusive student achievement comparisons as evidence that choice expansion will be an ineffective reform catalyst. The bizarre comparisons at least indicate that the current system's private schools achieve similar results for less money.

Although many of the studies are methodologically advanced—numbers are processed in a myriad of advanced ways—their original design had serious flaws that no manipulation of data can overcome. Choice expansion advocates argue that choice expansion will improve TPS. So, if we compare voucher users to TPS students in the same district, then we are comparing one treatment group (voucher users) to another (students in TPSs that responded to the voucher). Researchers are violating rule number 1 in research design: secure a quality control group.

Small academic gains after three years (Peterson et al., 1996) and parental satisfaction raised participation in the restriction-laden MPCP, and that raised interest in copying it. New York's Mayor Giuliani proposed a Milwaukee-style low-income voucher program.[36] Howard Fuller said the Milwaukee and Cleveland results indicate that such programs "should be expanded to other cities."[37] Clint Bolick said the MPCP "plan should be exported."[38] Nina Rees (2000) said that "conservative lawmakers and minority activists in Colorado plan to promote a MPCP-style pilot program for Denver," though they ultimately did not. More critically, the positive Milwaukee outcomes did not yield movement toward an OEI. As EdChoice CEO Robert Enlow noted in a

2007 letter to the *Wall Street Journal*, "It is simply not a foregone conclusion that limited programs beget more choice. From the record so far, it could be argued that limited choice mainly leads to more limited choice."[39]

FLORIDA'S VOUCHER PROGRAMS, TEXAS'S PROPOSALS, WEST VIRGINIA AND ARIZONA'S UNIVERSAL ESA

The Milwaukee voucher program is the best example of a politically risky pseudo-experiment, but there are others. School choice expansion was a hot topic of the 1995, 1997, and 1999 biennial sessions of the Texas legislature, and again in 2011, 2015, and 2017. Some proposals narrowed eligibility to low-income children assigned to selected regions' lowest-performing schools. So, only if the government says that a TPS is broadly ineffective can its assignees, after years of unengaging schooling, have some state funding follow them to a better-fit schooling option. The proposals said private schools had to accept vouchers as full payment.

In 1999, Florida enacted such a program, later deemed unconstitutional. Students were voucher eligible if their assigned TPS got a grade of F in at least two out of four years. Choice advocates lauded the program even though the education malpractice that made children eligible may have left them too academically deficient to stay in their new school. Many Edgewood (San Antonio) voucher users had to return to their assigned TPS because they could not keep up with their private school's curriculum. And though "half of Florida's fourth-graders can't read at a basic level,"[40] less than 6% of Florida's schools received an F.[41] The 51 U.S. school systems have not improved much since those 1999 statements. However, while every state still suffers terribly low performance, states such as Arizona, Florida, and Indiana that implemented multiple, targeted choice expansions improved their performance more than states that did not.

Like the effect of the Milwaukee program, the Florida effects spread restriction-laden parental choice. In a front page *Education Week* article, Darcia Bowman (2000) said that "more policymakers are borrowing a page from Florida's book and linking their choice plans to the performance of public schools."[42] That likely reduced the probability of system transformation through universal parental choice, churn, and rivalry.

The most promising choice expansion developments are (1) West Virginia's nearly universal Hope Scholarship, worth up to a $3,600 per year education savings account deposit[43] for students who opted out of their assigned TPS, which took effect in Fall 2022, and (2) Arizona's just-enacted universal

ESA with an annual deposit amount starting at $7,000.[44] Close behind are Indiana's program expansions and Florida's recently enacted flexible ceiling on voucher eligibility, though not nearly the "blowout" asserted by the *Wall Street Journal*.[45] Eligibility for vouchers of about $7,000 is still means tested, but Florida's family income eligibility limit rises when demand from eligible families falls short of the number of vouchers available.

Since that combination of a rising cap on voucher use and flexible means-test criteria is new, it qualifies as an experiment, but again, not an OEI experiment. With the fate of the 1999 Florida program as a cautionary tale, we'll see if it survives legal and electoral challenges.

THE INDIANA VOUCHER PROGRAM

Since it is tantalizingly close to OEI relevance, it may be big enough to yield transformational incremental change. Probably because it continues to target children from low-income families, we have not heard it referred to as an experiment. Nearly half of Indiana's schoolchildren are eligible, but only the poorest—those least able to take advantage of topping off (allowed!)—are eligible for the maximum voucher of $4,500. The voucher amount available to families closest to the income eligibility limit is half of the maximum. In existence only since 2011, there hasn't been enough time to determine if the program is large enough to eventually transform the Indiana school system. With a larger, more widely available ESA or voucher, the market bulldozer (Hess, 2002) will definitely fire up.

MORE EXAMPLES OF FAULTY ANALYSIS AND WISHFUL THINKING

As noted earlier, it is quite common for analysts to acknowledge that too few people have choice to create much competitive behavior[46] but then ignore that fact. Even economists—scholars who study market systems—sometimes use the term "experiment" carelessly. Two especially shocking examples of careless analysis appeared in a journal article written and peer-reviewed by economists. A 1997 article (Lamdin & Mintrom, 1997, p. 235), and another in 2019 (Ford & Andersson, 2019), surveyed parental choice studies. There is virtually no resemblance between the universal voucher plan Milton Friedman proposed as a replacement for the TPS monopoly on public funding and the privately financed, partial tuition vouchers sporadically available to some low-income families, but the authors equated them! "The nature of some of these [privately financed vouchers] programs allows studies of essentially Friedman-like voucher arrangements" (Lamdin & Mintrom, 1997, p. 235). "Friedman's theoretical idea . . . became a reality in Milwaukee" (Ford & Andersson, 2019, p. 159). Such errors may be one reason that economist Caroline Hoxby (2006) lamented that: "It is a struggle to keep [sound] economics in the discussion of school choice" (p. 7).[47]

In 2011, Grover Whitehurst and Ellie Klein created the "Education Choice and Competition Index."[48] "The intent of the ECCI is to create public awareness of the differences among districts in their support of school choice," which they hope will "provide a framework for efforts to examine the impact of choice and competition." Ease of market entry/exit is the key to competitive behavior, but the discussion of the index and the scoring rubrics makes no mention of entry/exit barriers or other essential elements such as price change or pursuit of profit. That's also true of an article about the index written by Aaron Churchill (2015) of the pro-reform Thomas Fordham Institute.

Another noteworthy Whitehurst-Klein analytical deficiency is the index's assumption that the presence of other schools necessarily yields meaningful competition. Public school choice can exist officially without creating much rivalry, much less genuine competition. Schools (TPSs) that must aim to serve all children cannot plan to differ greatly, and TPS leaders typically have no tangible reason to behave competitively. With just choice from the district's uniformly comprehensive schools, nearly all families agree on which TPSs are the best choices. That means that the probability of gaining an open seat in a preferred TPS is very low (i.e., little availability). Akin to the W-K error, David Armor (1997) wrote a report titled *Competition in Education: A Case Study of Inter-District Choice*.

The rare cases where conditions might have supported an assessment of openness and rivalry in delivering instruction were largely ignored because they didn't fit into the gold standard assessment mind-set where policy effects had to be found by comparing school choice program participants and unsuccessful applicants. For example, the early years of the 1998–2008, privately funded tuition voucher available to every Edgewood District (San Antonio) family created some entrepreneurial opportunities, though with the uncertainty created by a probably only temporary, partial leveling of the playing field.[49]

We can tell from the Edgewood experience, and other evidence (Hess, 2002), that large gains to TPS students don't accrue from formal, TPS strategic competitive effort, and that a substantial private-sector response cannot be expected from a temporary boost in demand. We have to rely on older, direct schooling-related evidence and limited foreign evidence, alongside broad, indirect evidence.

Economist Helen Ladd (Fiske & Ladd, 2000) coauthored a widely cited description of New Zealand's policy of universal public school choice. There are no profits, no market-determined prices, and 96.5% of the children attend public schools. Enrollment is only one of many determinants of each school's funding. The central government determines the supply of schools. New Zealand definitely did not have an OEI. The popular schools' space shortages forced parents to use unpopular schools that might have otherwise closed, and the shortages led to the partial reimposition of attendance zones. She said that space shortages persist because the government won't "invest in new school facilities while others [schools] remain under-utilized" (p. 250). Specialization was minimal because "local goals were secondary to those imposed from the center in the form of the National Education Guidelines" (p. 298).

Despite the near total absence of market forces, she repeatedly made statements such as (1) "New Zealand's foray into the realm of *full parental choice and competition*" (emphasis added; p. 250); (2) "a system of parental choice and market competition" (p. 292); and (3) "self-governing schools functioning in a competitive environment" (p. 297).

Journals, talk shows, and the popular press contain countless mistakes, including many by choice advocates, and few if any subsequent rebuttals or corrections. The misstatements indicate what many activists believe, and the misinformation that policy makers and the general public learn from them. Here are a few[50] examples:

1. The *Wall Street Journal*'s Jon Hilsenrath said there is "a fierce national debate over free-market competition in public schools," which is even more shocking if a lot of people believe "free market competition" exists "in" or between public schools.[51]
2. At almost the exact time that Milton and Rose Friedman (2004)[52] asserted the distinction between the typical "charity vouchers" and the transformational, market "bulldozer" (Hess, 2002) vouchers that Friedman (1962) envisioned, the *Wall Street Journal* repeated the widespread analytical error that Milwaukee had "a real voucher program."[53]
3. G. Carl Ball used phrases like "market-driven," "the competitive way," and "provide the customer the opportunity to evaluate the competition" to describe public school choice—choice among different branches of the same producer (Ball, 1990, pp. 54–55). The socialist countries proved that consumers' ability to shop at any state-owned store did not produce competition or improve the quality of their goods and services.
4. A right to attend another TPS does not establish any of the key elements of markets, but Tom Peters said public school choice is "a surrogate for competition" (Peters, 1990, pp. 57–58).
5. In 1986, the National Governors' Conference endorsed the concept of public school choice as a way to "unlock the values of competition in the marketplace" (Viteritti, 1999, p. 57).

A book edited by Joe Nathan (1989) includes more faulty analysis of public school choice, including public school choice that the authorities can veto.

1. Nathan and Edward Fiske (p. 5) applaud what Cambridge, Massachusetts, calls "controlled competition." Parents exercise public school choice as long as their choices advance racial diversity goals. The authorities vetoed all three top choices of 15% of Cambridge parents. Since Cambridge's limited public school choice is even further from an OEI than ordinary public school choice, Tony Wagner's opinion of the Cambridge schools is no surprise. Wagner, a resident of Cambridge and a prominent educator, said, "School choice has not produced significant improvements in the schools. The majority of the 13 [Cambridge K–8 schools] seem virtually interchangeable and are mediocre" (Wagner, 1996, p. 71).
2. Adam Urbanski (p. 228): "Competition among public schools would be more fair and more productive than competition between public and private schools."
3. Herbert Walberg (p. 69) complains about bureaucracies "un-subjected to market competition," and then says choice limited to the schools owned and run by the government education bureaucracy will solve that problem.

Even strong critics of the status quo take its key elements for granted.

1. John Chubb and Terry Moe (1990a) said that "district- or state-wide open enrollment systems and magnet schools" would achieve meaningful competition. Their controversial book demonstrates in great detail that bureaucracy significantly inhibits educational achievement, and that bureaucracy is an inherent part of democratic control. Then in their final chapter, Chubb and Moe lobby for a choice program run by a bureau[54] of a democratically elected government. They believe a "market system" is perfectly consistent with bureaucratic control of the choices, including price controls.
2. John Witte and Mark Rigdon said that the Chubb and Moe plan would mean "complete autonomy for all schools" (Witte & Rigdon, 1993).
3. Dr. David Salisbury, as president of the Sutherland Institute, described some choice programs, including the Milwaukee and Cleveland voucher programs, and said, "These educational choice initiatives are based on the free market principle that competition and consumer choice produce excellence in educational services."
4. The fallacy that a little bit of choice is enough to create meaningful competition took center stage in the Utah governor's boardroom.[55] The

February 17, 1997, meeting included education experts, activists, and Utah lawmakers.
5. Alan Bonsteel (1997)[56] said the Milwaukee voucher program provided America with "one of its first experiments in a system of open competition and freedom of choice in education, modeled after the highly successful GI Bill of Rights." But there's not much of anything open about Milwaukee's education industry, which lacks all of the key elements of competitive markets. The GI Bill was not limited to secular schools like the Milwaukee program was in 1997. The GI Bill's target population of military veterans greatly exceeded the 1.5% cap in effect in 1997.
6. Chester Finn and Diane Ravitch[57] were former high officials in the Reagan and Bush Education Departments, respectively. At the time, both were choice advocates. They labeled the Cleveland and Milwaukee low-income voucher programs "the most exciting reform" and charter schools the next most exciting, yet they admit that neither has changed the schools of the vast majority of children.
7. Helen Ladd, Ted Fiske, and Joseph Viteritti say that charter schools (Chapter 4) are "a market-based reform strategy,"[58] and that "real competition" (Viteritti, 1999, p. 221) exists with unlimited charter schools. Lewis Solmon, Michael Block, and Mary Gifford (2000) characterize charter schools as "A Market-Based Education System in the Making."

CONCLUSION

There is confusion about how to evaluate the effects of parental choice as a reform catalyst, and about what kinds of facts are relevant evidence. That confusion is an existential threat, at least to the political feasibility of private school choice, and perhaps to prosperity and civilization.[59] Absence of choice is the aberration, but choice advocates often assume the burden of proof and then support so-called experiments that cannot deliver it. Choice advocates should point out that "there is *no* historical experience indicating that government has a comparative advantage in the *production* [italics in the original] of goods and services" (Gintis, 1995, p. 503).

If the current dire circumstances are not sufficient to quickly implement the key elements of an OEI, what we need are genuine OEI experiments, not further study of limited movement among the schooling options of a static system. After a more detailed treatment of chartered public schools, Chapter 5 identifies and discusses the evidence that is relevant to the OEI issue.

NOTES

1. Howard Fuller, "The Case for Radical Reform," *Monthly Letter to Friends of the Center for Education Reform* 49–50 (December 1998–January 1999): 3. Also, Kevin Chavous, keynote address to the August 2010 School Reform Summit in Cleveland.

2. https://www.wsj.com/articles/experimentation-works-and-the-power-of-experiments-review-test-test-and-test-again-11584313983

3. Epple et al. (2017) do not note the low relevance—because of major restrictions—of the few seemingly large-scale programs. The West Virginia Hope Scholarship that took effect Fall 2022 may qualify if the $4,600 maximum amount that follows a child who opts out of the assigned school induces significant entrepreneurial initiative.

4. Are the West Virginia Hope Scholarship amounts large enough?

5. Only Epple et al. (2017) attempt to identify and examine large-scale programs, still restriction laden. In research by EdChoice, the leading school choice research organization, the top 25 are virtually all narrowly targeted, restriction-laden expansions of school choice.

6. https://www.brookings.edu/blog/brown-center-chalkboard/2022/09/01/apples-to-outcomes-revisiting-the-achievement-v-attainment-differences-in-school-voucher-studies/

7. Hess (2002) provides an excellent metaphor. We've seen the "pick axe," not the "bulldozer." And https://www.schoolsystemreformstudies.net/wp-content/uploads/Opinion-Forum/Interpretation.pdf

8. Milton Friedman and Rose Friedman, "The Voucher Challenge," *The School Choice Advocate*, January 2004, 1.

9. https://www.brookings.edu/blog/brown-center-chalkboard/2022/09/01/apples-to-outcomes-revisiting-the-achievement-v-attainment-differences-in-school-voucher-studies/

10. https://www.nytimes.com/2017/02/23/upshot/dismal-results-from-vouchers-surprise-researchers-as-devos-era-begins.html

11. www.buckeyeinstitute.org/perspect/2000_8Persp.htm; also see Frederick Hess, "Solve School Problems, but Do Not Oversell," *Washington Examiner*, November 30, 2010.

12. For example, much has been made—by choice opponents and proponents alike—of early negative effects attributed to a highly restriction-laden Louisiana program (Mills & Wolf, 2017).

13. https://www.cato.org/blog/more-school-choice-not-always-step-forward

14. https://www.schoolsystemreformstudies.net/wp-content/uploads/Opinion-Forum/Interpretation.pdf

15. Actual programs (like Milwaukee and Florida) and proposed programs, typically, though not universally, prohibit privately funded voucher add-ons. That means that private schools cannot charge voucher students more than the value of the voucher; a requirement that amounts to a price control.

16. Nearly all current private schools are nonprofit, which is a key reason to not judge the likely performance of a reformed school system through studies of existing schools. OEI conditions would attract many profit-seeking schools.

17. The unfortunate use of the term "experiment" spread from Milwaukee (Greene, Peterson, & Du, 1997) to the Cleveland low-income voucher program (Greene, Peterson, & Howell, 1997), some privately funded voucher programs like the one in Indianapolis (Weinschrott & Kilgore, 1998), and most recently (luckily not so) Hegarty (2003), describing the Milwaukee voucher program.

18. https://www.edchoice.org/wp-content/uploads/2015/06/4-Simple-Steps-to-Become-an-Expert-on-ESAs.pdf#page=4

19. Jon E. Hilsenrath, "Novel Way to Assess School Competition Stirs Academic Row," *Wall Street Journal*, October, 24, 2005, A1.

20. https://www.edweek.org/ew/articles/2001/02/07/21peterson.h20.html

21. Rene Sanchez, "Riley Launches Attack on School Vouchers," *Washington Post*, September 24, 1997, A6.

22. https://www.edchoice.org/school-choice/programs/wisconsin-milwaukee-parental-choice-program/

23. You might wonder why banning top-offs would matter much with eligibility restricted to low-income families. Low-income families often find top-off money, even within their own limited ability to pay, and they will find charity-funded scholarships.

24. https://www.the74million.org/article/analysis-what-wisconsins-governor-gets-wrong-about-how-much-milwaukees-school-voucher-program-costs-and-how-much-its-helping-students-in-and-out-of-the-classroo/

25. https://onlinelibrary.wiley.com/doi/full/10.1111/ssqu.12689

26. https://papers.ssrn.com/sol3/papers.cfm?abstract_id=3349453

27. https://www.tandfonline.com/doi/full/10.1080/15582159.2019.1673954

28. Barack Obama, "Transcript: Full Interview between President Obama and Bill O'Reilly," Fox News Politics, 2014.

29. Carnegie Foundation for the Advancement of Teaching, *School Choice: A Special Report* (Princeton, NJ, 1992).

30. For example, see Joy Kiviat, "Vouchers Improve Academic Outcomes," *School Reform News*, April, 2000, 6–7, and McGroarty (1996, p. 177–187), a detailed discussion of the Milwaukee voucher program.

31. https://papers.ssrn.com/sol3/papers.cfm?abstract_id=3388304

32. "74 percent of the parents who chose to use vouchers did so because of the disciplinary guidelines and general atmosphere of private schools": Nina H. Shokraii and John S. Barry, "Two Cheers for S. 1: The Safe and Affordable Schools Act of 1997," *The Heritage Foundation Issue Bulletin* 232 (May 14, 1997): 5.

33. Chester Finn and Diane Ravitch, *Wall Street Journal* editorial, September 7, 1995. Note that Professor Ravitch now (2022) argues that it was an unexciting reform, which is correct, but not because choice cannot be an exciting reform.

34. https://www.aei.org/research-products/report/cpr-scholarships-using-private-school-choice-to-attack-concentrated-poverty-crime-and-unemployment/

35. https://www.schoolsystemreformstudies.net/nation-at-risk-vi/

36. Mark Walsh, "Giuliani Proposes a Voucher Program for New York," *Education Week*, January 27, 1999, 3.

37. Howard Fuller, "A Research Update on School Choice," *Marquette University Current Education Issues* 97, no. 3 (October, 1997): 1.

38. Clint Bolick, "Voucher Advocate Says 'Milwaukee Plan' Should Be Exported," *Church and State*, May, 1992, 16–17.

39. Robert Enlow, "Limited Choice Is an Ugly Frog," *Wall Street Journal*, July 6, 2007.

40. "Victory in Florida," *School Reform News*, June 1999, 1, 4.

41. Fourth- and eighth-grade math, reading, and science NAEP scores reported in *Education Week*, January 11, 1999.

42. Darcia H. Bowman, "States Giving Choice Bills Closer Look," *Education Week*, March 1, 2000, 1, 24. The Louisiana statewide program is a current example.

43. https://www.edchoice.org/school-choice/programs/hope-scholarship-program/

44. https://www.federationforchildren.org/arizona-expands-school-choice-to-all-students/

45. https://www.wsj.com/articles/floridas-school-choice-blowout-11593212280

46. Isabel V. Sawhill and Shannon L. Smith, "Vouchers for Elementary and Secondary Education," in *Vouchers and Related Delivery Mechanisms: Consumer Choice in the Provision of Public Services* (Brookings Institution Conference, Washington, DC, October 2–3, 1998), 150–154. Even Milton Friedman refers to the Milwaukee and Cleveland programs as experiments: "Freedom and School Vouchers," *Chronicles*, December, 1998, "Polemics and Exchanges."

47. https://nzinitiative.org.nz/.../56-school-choice-the-three-essential-elements-aug-2006

48. https://www.brookings.edu/the-education-choice-and-competition-index/

49. http://faculty.business.utsa.edu/jmerrifi/evp.pdf

50. Some additional examples are discussed in greater detail in Chapters 6 and 12.

51. Jon E. Hilsenrath, "Novel Way to Assess School Competition Stirs Academic Row," *Wall Street Journal*, October 24, 2005, A1.

52. Milton Friedman and Rose Friedman, "The Voucher Challenge," *The School Choice Advocate*, January 2004, 1.

53. *Wall Street Journal* Editorial Board, "An Idea Has Consequences," *Wall Street Journal*, May 17, 2004, A20.

54. For a detailed discussion of the inconsistency between the findings and policy recommendations of Chubb and Moe (1990a), see West (1992).

55. "Free to Choose: A Legislative Briefing on Education Reform and School Choice," *Sutherland Speeches* 8 (November 1997): 1–17.

56. Page 5 of *A Choice for Our Children*, edited and largely written by Bonsteel and Bonilla (1997).

57. *Wall Street Journal* editorial, September 7, 1995.

58. Statement by Helen Ladd at a Brookings Institution Panel Discussion, February 24, 2000, based on Fiske and Ladd (2000).

59. Thomas Jefferson said, "If a nation expects to be ignorant & free, in a state of civilization, it expects what never was & never will be," which we believe will be proven correct if ignorance is allowed to persist/grow.

Chapter 3

Chartered Public Schools
Mostly Chance, Not Choice

> If you don't look facts in the face, they have a way of stabbing you in the back.
>
> —Winston Churchill

The key points of this chapter are that (1) even the "strongest" existing charter laws—highly conducive to independent public school formation—do not establish an OEI or schooling markets; (2) poorly conceived charter law assessment practices and hype about charter law—another case of hype about restriction-laden choice expansion—can poison the well for OEI-based school system reform; (3) every charter state has rules that are a plausible cause of the quite common charter scandals, something that represents an existential political threat to chartering and to school choice expansion in general; and (4) an existing "strong" charter law plus price decontrol would yield an OEI.

BACKGROUND

Thirty years after Minnesota enacted the first charter law, 44 states and the District of Columbia allow chartered public schools (CPSs). The CPS political bargain was to earn exemptions from some of the traditional public school (TPS) rules by promising much stricter accountability for results[1]—greater autonomy for increased accountability. Actual CPS autonomy and accountability varies widely by state. In some states, only school districts can authorize CPSs, which typically yields few CPSs, and those CPSs have very little de facto autonomy.

When we wrote this in early 2022,[2] about 3.3 million children (~6%) attended about 7,500 CPSs. Growth has slowed, so that may still be true as you read this. Indeed, despite much unmet demand, charter enrollment growth "came to a near halt in 2017."[3] Among CPS supporters, the near halt was widely seen as shocking news, but it is totally consistent with economic theory. The major growth impediments include (1) much basis for uncertainty, (2) funding inequity, (3) price control, (4) the open enrollment impediment to specialization, (5) a ban on profit in nearly every charter state,[4] and (6) dependence on donors. As growth impediments, those factors are especially significant together.

Despite significant regulation, some states have innovative CPSs offering a wide variety of instructional approaches—what chartering pioneers envisioned. But for immense, unrecognized informal regulation in the form of price control and a ban on selective, school-mission-based admissions (both are part of all 45 charter laws)—and the widespread dependence of CPSs on donors produced by inequitable funding and price control—instructional diversity would be even greater. Just the recognized formal regulation was enough to create cries of, "Regulations are Strangling Charter Schools."[5] Indeed, regulation is eroding autonomy and instructional diversity.

CPS operators must persuade parents to opt children out of the assigned TPS. So, a CPS needs to be choice worthy. That *should* yield accountability to parents, but often it does not. Low-performing and poorly managed CPSs can stay "popular" when—as is often the case—the available alternatives seem much worse: (1) return to a terrible assigned TPS, (2) pay more for housing to live in the attendance zone of a better TPS, or (3) make sacrifices to finance private school tuition. Indeed, *U.S. News and World Report* found[6] that CPSs with significant problems were able to stay in business, something that has been a persistent problem.[7] To maximize demand and benefits to CPS students, and because of donor preference, CPSs often concentrate in the areas where TPSs are most likely to be terrible, which can make a godsend out of even a low-quality CPS seat.

For the reasons cited above, and the shortages (wait lists) that result from mandating zero tuition and political determination of CPS per-pupil payment rates (price control), accountability may arise only from charter authorizers' power to close choice worthy CPSs for malfeasance or noncompliance. Popular CPSs have been closed.[8]

Authorizer activity and supply-demand imbalance depend upon critical charter-law specifics that vary widely among the states. For low-cost, CPS-delivered instruction, the politically set per-pupil public funding level can yield wasteful excess capacity and pressure to compete through frills that are worth less than their cost. But what is most common is that the politically set per-pupil payment yields fewer seats than are sought at the mandated tuition price of zero.[9]

The resulting persistent shortages—often lengthy wait lists—cut accountability to customers, sometimes to zero. Short of a stampede, removals by unhappy parents are quickly replaced from the wait list. The wait list can keep customer dissatisfaction from yielding revenue loss, which greatly reduces accountability to parents.

THE WACKY WORLD OF CHARTERING

A need: "restoring sanity in charter school policy."

—Jeanne Allen, Center for Education Reform[10]

In most publications, school choice has been synonymous with charter schools.

—Dr. Priscilla Wohlstetter[11]

Dr. Wohlstetter's innocuous observation is stunning, and sad, because it is arguably true that a CPS seat is mostly not a choice at all. Many families are not close enough to even a single CPS. And a nearby CPS is often not very useful. For many children, the instructional approaches of the nearby charters are not a good fit, and a good fit may have a wait list. Wait lists are common in every charter state and are often lengthy, even in the states with multiple CPS authorizers, no caps on the number of CPSs, and only small differences between TPS and CPS per-pupil funding.

The often-lengthy wait lists yield a very low probability of gaining admission via a lottery. A godsend aspect is seen when "lottery-based admissions"[12]—so memorably depicted in the film *Waiting for Superman*[13]—yield tearful faces. So, as a New Orleans parent famously observed,[14] having a nearby CPS often yields only school chance, not a school choice.[15] In New Orleans, and some other cities, controversy about lotteries reimposed school assignment, not based on attendance area, but on submitted preferences and a computer program.

With open enrollment requirements impairing schools' ability to specialize in instructional approaches that serve a particular set of children especially well, but others especially badly, and lottery-based random selection of applicants, we lose much of the potential of choice expansion to better match the strengths of educators with the learning needs of diverse children. Many families enter a lottery without regard to instructional fit (Henig, 2008, p. 116), just hoping for a free alternative to a very low-performing TPS.

An application process that allows selective admission of the best-fit students would yield greater benefits from each school's limited capacity. We can attribute the inability to capture that benefit to our sad history of discrimination based on race and to the terrible propensity of political control to yield equal treatment of unequals. As Thomas Jefferson noted, "there is nothing more unequal than the equal treatment of unequal things."[16]

Caps on what schooling can cost—price control—further impair production of specialized instruction. Price control arises mostly from unvetted, inaccurate equity assumptions (Chapter 9) and largely unrecognized efficiency losses associated with central planning (see Merrifield, 2019).

IMAGINING MARKET FORCES—AGAIN

Quality erosion[17] is a well-established (DiLorenzo, 2005; Hirsch, 1943; Murphy, 1996; Reisman, 1998; Rockoff, 1984; Rothbard, 1994; Schuettinger & Butler, 1979; Sowell, 2004)[18] but virtually unrecognized outcome of persistent shortages (the widespread CPS wait lists). Add the shortage-caused, sharp attenuation of accountability to customers to the frequent desperation to escape an assigned TPS, and sometimes the profit motive to cut corners, and you have a solid basis for the actual widespread scandalous behavior perhaps seen among the very large number of alleged cases.[19] Given the political significance of scandal and the perception that there is much more school choice conveyed by charter law than is actually the case, shortage-induced quality erosion threatens much more than chartering. It is an issue that arguably very seriously threatens the political feasibility of choice expansion.

That, and poorly chosen, alleged "poster child" examples of market-based determination of what is taught, where, how, and to whom, threatens the feasibility of an OEI as a key element of school system reform. Because school systems are not sufficiently open anywhere, and are thus low performing everywhere,[20] events that threaten the political feasibility of an OEI lower voters' capacity to recognize and reject devastatingly bad policy ideas. Yes! Without well-educated electorates, government of the people and by the people will eventually oppress and impoverish the people, sometimes gradually, sometimes suddenly. There are many modern riches-to-rags examples (Venezuela, Argentina, Greece), places where people unknowingly voted in policies with terrible track records. There are many older examples (Hubbard & Kane, 2013), but then there was less basis for the people or their sometimes-benevolent rulers to have known better.

Since *The School Choice Wars* appeared in 2001, we've seen the school choice poster child change from the Milwaukee voucher program that lacks essential elements of a high-performing industry[21] to places with high concentrations of CPSs such as Washington, DC, and New Orleans that even more so also lack the key elements discussed in Chapter 2. We see in chartering an example of a key point of Thomas Sowell's (2018) *Discrimination and Disparities*, that a single factor can be more than enough to produce totally different outcomes.

Jeffrey Henig's (2008) acclaimed *Spin Cycle* said the "charter school issue came to be framed in terms of markets vs. government" (p. 10), something he repeated in a 2019 op-ed.[22] Diane Ravitch said that "charters are supposed to disseminate the free-market model of competition and choice." *But a CPS is a mixture of school choice and chance because key provisions of charter law suppress market forces.*

More from Henig: "Charter [public] schools emerged as the surrogate to vouchers as the battleground on which the market vs. government conflict would be staged" (p. 42), "seen as an opportunity to show that market processes could perform better than public monopolies" (p. 57).

Henig did not object to CPSs being seen as a basis for market forces. He noted that there hadn't been enough time to render a verdict (p. 118). Charter analysts still debate "to what degree should market forces determine success."[23] Many do not trust market forces to produce quality control. The lack of trust exists despite the assumed presence of market forces through a charter law (Feng & Harris, 2020), but their continued absence despite a charter law is a far better reason.

ECONOMISTS DROP THE BALL

We can forgive Henig and Ravitch for not seeing that even the most CPS-friendly charter laws[24]—of which there are typically just three to five—still lack the basis for market efficiency. They are not economists. "Economist" is synonymous with price theorist, which means that economists are duty bound to explain how freedom to charge what the market will bear—what folks will pay—yields strong incentives to innovate, cut costs, and discover and enter underserved niches.

History's episodes of broad and narrow price control have shown that price formation and adjustment to eliminate shortages or surpluses are an essential information-conveying and incentive-creating process (Hayek, 1945; Schuettinger & Butler, 1979). But every CPS law curbs that critical process by forcing political determination of the per-pupil payment to CPS operators, and no charge to enroll (zero tuition, no "skin in the game"). Unfortunately, economists' attention to charter law has yet to include more than this rudimentary economic analysis of charter law found in *The School Choice Wars* (2001):

> Economist Scott Milliman co-authored an article that claimed Arizona's charter school law had "initiated a free market in public education."[25] Even though CPS law regulates market entry, CPS and their "competitors" have the same owner, and a dominant "producer"—traditional districts—has a nearly 90% market share. Milliman reached the conclusion that CPSs are "market-driven" even though CPSs are nearly always non-profit operations that cannot turn away customers, or even decide the price of their services.

Whether an economist agrees or disagrees with the basic rules present in all charter laws, he or she is duty bound to explain the consequences. And to make good decisions, everyone else must recognize those consequences. Epple et al. (2005), in a National Bureau of Economic Research working paper, recognized the key features that all charter laws have in common (open admissions and price control), but provided only statistical analyses of student test scores.[26]

And we cannot forgive, for example,[27] the editors of the April 2012 special CPS edition of the *Economics of Education Review* for omitting such an overview analysis from that edition's lead article. The edition's articles, mostly by non-economists (!?), focused on statistics-based, low-value, no-economics TPS-CPS comparisons critiqued later in this chapter. Likewise, that special edition's few authors that are economists also cannot be forgiven. They failed to note that constraints shared by every charter state's CPSs precluded seeing key market forces in action.

A search for exceptions yielded none. Top economics journals only published analyses of CPSs devoid of price theory, and thus devoid of economic analysis. They only presented statistical analysis.[28] Only two noted the presence of wait lists, but not the standard explanation for persistent shortages, or typical shortage consequences. One (Vanderhoff) used wait-list size as a measure of school quality even though quality is not one-dimensional and shortages are not just a function of demand. An unexceptional instructional approach can yield a long wait list by being more costly, because with that higher cost, little is supplied at the government-set price.

Vanderhoff also made the choice-yields-competition assumption even though TPSs cannot fear losing students to a full CPS. Likewise, the CPS chapter in Derek Neal's (2018) *Information, Incentives, and Education Policy* focused on the statistical benefits (lottery-based random assignment of applicants to CPS) of "over-subscribed" CPSs; there is no mention of the economics of "over-subscribed" (persistent shortages) goods and services. Every economic analysis of charter law should note that, mostly, the no-charge-to-enroll constraint would likely keep lots of innovation from even being fully developed. Innovation is much less urgent to a CPS operator of a sure-to-fill school, with the maximum possible per-student revenue without costly innovation effort.

And the sum of per-pupil public funding and donations may not be enough to cover the cost of an innovative instructional approach, especially initially when key inputs may not be widely available. So price control will keep many ready-to-try instructional approaches from getting off the ground. The ability to charge what the market will bear, combined with the potential for profit, may be necessary to motivate much more of the drawing-board activity needed to discover innovative practices. We cannot know what might have been.

Please don't assume that equity precludes permission for CPS operators to charge what the market will bear. Poorly grounded assumptions can be terrible things. Please wait until after Chapter 9 to consider reaching that conclusion.

So, indeed, as Bryan Hassel speculated,[29] "it seems likely that there is a large reservoir of entrepreneurial educators and non-educators who would be willing to engage in school start up, *if* it were not such a nightmare." Hassel, a non-economist, assumes that regulation is the deterrent, and indeed it has become an even bigger problem than at the time of Hassel's article (2003). But likely the bigger reason for the failure to fully tap into that likely large reservoir of entrepreneurial educators is the possible inability to cover expenses of many possible innovative approaches, even without additional costs arising from regulation. The other part of the nightmare is having to be donor dependent for innovative practices that will continue to cost more than the per-pupil public funding after time for standardization and cost-cutting based on experience and competition among providers for key inputs.

CPS operators' inability to use tuition to supplement the sum of per-pupil public funding and donor money also creates a lot of likely innovation-restraining uncertainty. Costs can change a lot faster—perhaps through regulation—than either the political process's or donors' willingness and ability to respond with increased funding capacity.

A likely key source of cost uncertainty is the aforementioned open enrollment requirement that is only rarely cited, even indirectly, as the key regulation that it is. The cost uncertainty arises because a CPS operator cannot know if/when a parent frustrated with the disabled/special education services of the assigned TPS will demand that a CPS admit them and provide appropriate services.

An above-average, weighted student formula–based payment for such children may not be enough for a CPS set up, or interested in being set up, to pursue a certain non-disability-related specialized mission: a particular niche. Market-based pricing also assures that a CPS can properly fund such children, on or off their own premises, and provide sufficient incentive for some CPSs to focus on such children.

The open enrollment requirement spreads a major inefficiency from TPSs to CPSs: that every school pretends to be ready to serve every child. The far superior alternative to a costly act of self-deception and futility is to use price decontrol to foster a system with a great choice for every child. But every charter law demands an open admissions policy, despite the recognition, even by some choice opponents, that a basis for selective admissions is essential (McGhan, 1998). The open enrollment requirement is a key reason for the creeping "isomorphism" lamented by the Center for Education Reform,[30] that CPSs are becoming more alike and more like TPSs.[31]

Note that many innovative practices—maybe the vast majority—that attracted enough donor support to get off the ground remain donor dependent. That's a key reason why those innovative CPSs have such long wait lists. Increased public funding would help stretch donor funding. But it is unlikely to be widely forthcoming from our mostly increasingly fiscally stressed state and federal governments. And additional funding would likely mostly yield new CPSs with wait lists rather than shorter wait lists for existing CPS. That is, increased per-CPS-pupil public funding would likely cause more places to have CPSs than it would shorten wait lists. Each place would still be massively underserved by popular alternatives to assigned TPSs and tuition-charging private schools.

CPSs harm the private sector and the pursuit of private school choice (Ravitch, 2010, p. 121). CPSs enroll children that would have used private schools (Finn, Manno, & Vanourek, 2000), leading, for example, to "transformation of black private schools into CPS"[32] and reports that CPSs are "killing private schools." Edgar Huffman said his school faced bankruptcy after he lost half of his students after passage of CPS legislation. "We basically had no choice but to go charter."[33] Independent public schools of choice/chance (CPS) strengthen the barrier to private schools created by public schools' monopoly on public funding.

CPSs YIELDING USEFUL EVIDENCE

We should certainly celebrate and tout the innovative, effective schooling approaches made possible by CPS autonomy in some states as a small taste of what is likely, generally, in any state where we further increase the ability and incentive to innovate. There is a lot of room to increase both. Allowing tuition top-off of per-CPS-pupil and weighted student formula–based public funding—price decontrol—are *the* key steps.

Allowing CPSs to charge what the market will bear ends donor dependence, school chance, and shortage-induced quality erosion, while providing more resources to purveyors of popular CPS-based instructional approaches that may be widely popular even when a large tuition copayment exists. It can be quite expensive to adequately engage some types of students. And we know that some parental "skin in the game" will improve school system performance (Coulson, 1999). Price decontrol frees up donor funds to provide means-tested copayment support (see Chapter 9). Low formal barriers to CPS formation and permission to operate a CPS for profit are essential partners of price decontrol.

The political embrace of the more-accountability-for-autonomy offer is another example of strong high-level concern about the usefulness of political/bureaucratic management, that the accountability to political authority that's often mistakenly seen as the only viable accountability may actually be, mostly, very counterproductive.

Another example of that concern are the longtime efforts to insulate public provision of schooling from pressures arising from local politics. We still see the effects of those efforts in accountability-suppressing, special-interest-empowering, off-cycle, unique-polling-place, low-voter-turnout elections for school board seats and bond proposals. More recently, we see proponents of a portfolio management approach[34] lamenting the effects of local politics, including *incredible* observations such as, "In a political world, the most logical choice is often the least likely" (Osborne, 2017, p. 136), and, "It is political suicide to be clear about the reforms you favor" (p. 189). When legislators seriously consider adding CPSs to their school systems, they admit that the political process is a likely source of serious education problems.[35] Within the groups seeking a CPS charter, it is a strong conviction. They would not undertake the always-arduous pursuit of CPS status unless they thought the avoided rules were quite counterproductive.

CPS studies can document the level and persistence of CPS achievements to indicate whether insulation from politics is possible in a government-run institution. Several scholars concluded that the prospects are poor. Sheldon Richman argued that "autonomous public school is an oxymoron" (Richman, 1994), a contradiction. In effect, Caroline Hoxby also reached the conclusion that politics will remain a major factor. She said CPSs just amount to new school districts (Hoxby, 1998). In New Jersey, "the state has defined each charter school as a kind of district unto itself";[36] likewise in Texas. Earlier, we noted the onset of debilitating regulation.

The evidence supports the view that an autonomous public school is a fantasy,[37] even in Arizona and Indiana that have, or have had, the strongest charter laws. For that reason, and because such strong charter laws are not stable[38] or the norm,[39] there is little hope that charter legislation that has the key provisions common to all existing charter laws will capture the benefits of an OEI, or even significantly change the school system.

We have not yet mentioned the vast majority of what is widely seen as useful evidence, or at least a series of important attempts to create insightful findings. That technical brilliance—intensive, meticulous nonsense—has been deployed to compare CPS students to TPS students.

CPS VS. TPS—WRONG COMPARISON

As Emmanuel Felton of the Education Writers of American noted in 2017,[40] "After 25 Years, [there is] No Shortage of Charter School Research."[41] But even when the studies manage the technical brilliance required by the mistaken, key underlying assumption that CPSs should be judged, collectively, by their ability to do better what we expect from TPSs, the findings of the TPS-CPS comparisons are dangerously misleading. Note that the key mistaken premise (we should compare TPS and CPS), as well as a key reason why the premise is mistaken, is in the final report of "The Evaluation of Charter School Impacts."[42]

- "On average, charter middle schools that held lotteries were neither more nor less successful than traditional public schools in improving math or reading test scores, attendance, grade promotion, or student conduct within or outside of school."
- "Charter middle schools' impact on student achievement varied significantly across schools."

Given the diversity in what is allowed across states under the charter label, it makes no sense to compare average outcomes of CPSs, or even TPSs, for the entire United States. The second bullet indirectly explains why it doesn't make much more sense to compare average outcomes within states. CPS diversity within states can still be quite significant.

Many CPSs do great things with the additional freedom that CPSs have in some states. Some fall flat on their faces. Many of the CPSs that were TPSs are little changed by their adoption of CPS status. The net effect has been zero,[43] something choice opponents are glad to trumpet as an indictment of school choice, generally,[44] even when only school chance, not choice, is present.

As the director of a key source of those comparisons (Center for Research on Education Outcomes [CREDO]), Margaret Raymond, noted,[45] charter advocates need to seek faster closure of low-performing CPSs. But common denominators of charter law are at least partly to blame for low-performing CPS persistence. Because of the often-terrible immediate CPS alternatives, a low-performing CPS can remain popular, especially if caps on the number of CPSs, or other market-entry impediments, prevent the creation of new CPSs capable, through greater efficiency, of wresting customers from lower-performing CPSs. Indeed, David Osborne documented many of the challenges of closing low-performing CPSs.[46]

Long-term donor commitments—now necessary for much CPS formation—to what can turn out to be low performers explain their persistence. As Andrew Coulson noted,[47] donor support of CPSs is not necessarily correlated with available measures of CPS performance. That's a key reason why it's important to eliminate CPS donor dependence.

By the way, having several times noted the problematic nature of CPS donor dependence, we must note that donations to a CPS are okay, both for donors and for a CPS, *as long as the CPS is not dependent on them*, that loss of donor funds is not a death sentence. A CPS might prefer to hold down tuition rates by raising money from donors, but with price decontrol they can survive through a tuition increase, if that becomes necessary.

Likely the key reason to *not* judge charter law by whether average CPS outcomes—within or between states—are better than average TPS outcomes is that what our 51 K–12 school systems need most is a menu of schooling options as diverse as how children learn and what best engages them in a learning co-production process.[48] That's especially important because it is common to define "fair" CPS-TPS comparisons as shackling TPSs and CPSs equally, to statistically impose TPS constraints on CPSs to make the comparison fair.

We must focus on building better school systems, not on fairness to an inefficient process (assigning children to a TPS). Self-selection that results from choice—typically deliberately ignored (!?) by academic study—is a major benefit (Pondiscio, 2019) of being able to choose from among options that differ in ways that effectively address student diversity.

Much more than better delivery of the mainstream pedagogy shackled by the political imperative to treat unequal children equally, we need for charter law to foster efficient alternatives to the mainstream pedagogy. One size does not fit all even when delivered by America's best TPSs. And the political process created an incentive system that yields some terribly low-performing TPSs, leaving behind the vast majority of children assigned to our many, virtually dysfunctional TPSs.

We need for charter law to yield schooling that complements and improves good TPSs, and to provide diverse escape options from the hopelessly dysfunctional TPSs.[49] CPSs can improve good TPSs, even without creating strong competitive pressures, by providing exits for children not suited to the TPS mainstream pedagogy. TPS classrooms become more teachable—less differentiated instruction needed—when the TPS mainstream outliers depart for schooling that fits them better.

Those outliers would have access to the extra genuine alternatives that CPS could provide if we allow market-based tuition change to inform and motivate education entrepreneurs, that is, by allowing CPS operators to charge what OEI competitiveness allows. Again, please withhold judgment on equity concerns until after Chapter 10. And certainly recognize that the current equity strategy has been terrible, especially for the least advantaged.

THE CORRECT CHARTER LAW SUCCESS MEASURE

Since the key issue for states considering charter law enactment or revision is the potential for significant school system improvement, such improvement is what we should directly test for. That is the correct criterion for any potential major policy change. More and better school system performance measures would be helpful.

Until we create better measures, we can start by seeing if differences in charter law over time, and between states, explain some of the differences in states' National Assessment of Educational Progress (NAEP) scores, despite the drawbacks of the NAEP exams[50] as "the Nation's Report Card."[51] To do that effectively, the 50-state-plus-DC data set needs to include measures of *all* of the factors that could credibly, significantly affect performance on a NAEP exam.

I suspect that most charter laws have not measurably affected overall school system performance. It may be that even the strongest charter laws haven't positively affected enough test scores to have a measurable systemic effect. If true, it is another critical fact to face before it stabs us in the back. It would not be a reason to eliminate charter law as an escape hatch, limited though it might be, or to abandon choice expansion as a transformation catalyst. It is a reason to introduce full-fledged market forces through charter law revision, or by relying on other policies to achieve the desperately needed transformational school system change.

CHARTERING—UP OR MALAISE

Even if some current charter laws make some school systems significantly better, a charter law—weak or strong—may directly or indirectly forestall the much more productive OEI-oriented transformations we have been arguing for. Such a school system uses *truly* market-driven price change and the profit motive to create the dynamic menu of schooling options that is as diverse as the engagement factors present in the schoolchildren population.

Like other attempts at choice expansion that create few if any market conditions (Feng & Harris, 2020), disappointment and confusion created by charter law could reduce the political feasibility of an OEI. Though some charter laws certainly yield an improvement over TPS-only situations, allowing CPSs could easily become a huge, perhaps permanent detour rather than a step toward an OEI. Quentin Quade's 1996 observation is still correct: CPSs "can be a detour, and a devastatingly bad one." They may already be.

More recently, and for other reasons, Fordham Institute's vice president, Robert Pondiscio, author of *How the Other Half Learns: Equality, Excellence, and the Battle Over School Choice* (2019), came to a similar conclusion: "It's a strange and dangerous moment in the charter-school movement."[52] But if the leaders of the CPS movement confront the factors handicapping CPSs and revise key elements of chartering, they might win an escape from the current malaise and make chartering the starting point of the school system reform we desperately need. The shifting politics of chartering prove that standing pat is not an option.[53] Moving forward is the only option.

Even if the leaders of the charter movement do the right things, a market-based tuition levy may prove to be politically incompatible with CPS status as public schools. Whether evidence and persuasion can eliminate the key devastating constraints anywhere remains to be seen. The next chapter explores the evidence generated when full-fledged market forces are actually present.

NOTES

1. For example, https://www.edweek.org/ew/articles/1998/06/10/39chart.h17.html

2. https://data.publiccharters.org/digest/charter-school-data-digest/how-many-charter-schools-and-students-are-there/

3. Center for Education Reform, "National Charter School Law Rankings and Scorecard," 2018, https://a5f2y4y9.stackpathcdn.com/wp-content/uploads/2019/01/CER_National-Charter-School-Law-Rankings-and-Scorecard-2018_screen_1-30-19.pdf

4. In the strong charter law states (Washington, DC; Minnesota; and Indiana in 2019), where CPS formation is easiest, a ban on profits loses most of the benefits of the openness, that is, low entry barriers to TPS alternatives.

5. https://www.edweek.org/ew/articles/2017/02/08/regulations-are-strangling-charter-schools.html

6. Thomas Toch, "The New Education Bazaar," *U.S. News and World Report*, April 27, 1998, 34–36.

7. https://credo.stanford.edu/sites/g/files/sbiybj6481/f/closure_final_volume_i.pdf

8. Robert Maranto and Scott Milliman, "In Arizona, Charter Schools Work," *Washington Post*, October 11, 1999, A25.

9. A market-based tuition levy may prove to be politically incompatible with CPS status as public schools. In every charter state, the law currently asserts the price control at P = $0. Whether evidence and persuasion (later in this chapter) can eliminate that devastating constraint remains to be seen.

10. https://www.edweek.org/ew/articles/2017/02/08/regulations-are-strangling-charter-schools.html

11. Endorsement blurb for Mark Berends, Joseph Waddington, and John Schoenig (eds.), *School Choice at the Crossroads: Research Perspectives* (New York: Routledge, 2019).

12. https://fordhaminstitute.org/national/commentary/achilles-heel-charter-growth-overregulation

13. https://en.wikipedia.org/wiki/Waiting_for_%22Superman%22

14. http://dcschoolreform.org/news/parents-can-inform-meaningful-school-change

15. The exact same term—"school chance"—has been applied to Washington, DC: https://blogs.edweek.org/edweek/civic_mission/2014/01/turning_school_chance_into_school_choice.html. Note that chance is widespread even in places—DC and New Orleans—with the highest concentration of CPSs.

16. https://www.goodreads.com/quotes/178043-there-is-nothing-more-unequal-than-the-equal-treatment-of

17. Lower-quality schooling can occur through many channels: (1) less teacher training; (2) lower building condition; (3) shoddy curriculum—perhaps updated less often; and (4) poor condition, maybe outdated materials.

18. All the seller's motives "now work in the direction of reducing the quality of his product" (Reisman, 1998, p. 239). Rockoff (1984) found that "quality deterioration was the main form of [price control] evasion" (p. 62). Murphy (1980) notes that "the only unambiguous implication of a price ceiling is that product quality is reduced" (p. 289).

19. http://charterschoolscandals.blogspot.com/ and elsewhere.

20. Based on PISA scores, the world's best school systems are only about 10% better than the U.S. system, repeatedly declared—bipartisan and nonpartisan—to be so bad as to constitute an existential threat ("Nation at Risk"), https://www.schoolsystemreformstudies.net/nation-at-risk-vi/. https://www.schoolsystemreformstudies.net/nation-at-risk-vi/

21. "The Milwaukee program, however, was invested with too much symbolic pressure as being the national experiment with choice" (Henig, 2008, p. 62).

22. Jeffrey R. Henig, "Teach for America's Defenders and Detractors Are Both Wrong," *Education Week*, July 17, 2019, 28, https://www.edweek.org/ew/articles/2019/06/26/teach-for-americas-defenders-and-detractors-are.html.

23. Lynn Schnaiberg, "Charter Schools Struggle with Accountability," *Education Week*, June 10, 1998, 1, 14. https://www.edweek.org/ew/articles/1998/06/10/39chart.h17.html

24. Based on Center for Education Reform rankings, typically three to five states receive a grade of A, a constantly changing three to five.

25. Robert Maranto and Scott Milliman, "In Arizona, Charter Schools Work," *Washington Post*, October 11, 1999, A25.

26. https://www.nber.org/papers/w21256.pdf

27. For the sake of brevity, I am using Henig and the *Economics of Education Review* editors, and the economists who authored articles in the *EER* CPS special edition, as examples of what is widely true. At the end of the chapter is a list of all of the sources that I could recall influencing the content of this chapter.

28. J. Schwankenberg and J. Vanderhoff, "Why Do Charter Schools Fail? An Analysis of Charter School Survival in New Jersey," *Contemporary Economic Policy* 33, no. 2 (2015): 300–314; A. Abdulkadiroğlu, J. D. Angrist, S. M. Dynarski, T. J. Kane, and P. A. Pathak, "Accountability and Flexibility in Public Schools: Evidence from Boston's Charters and Pilots," *Quarterly Journal of Economics* 126 (2011): 699–748; J. D. Angrist, P. A. Pathak, and C. R. Walters, "Explaining Charter School Effectiveness," *American Economic Journal: Applied Economics* 5, no. 4 (2013): 1–27; K. Booker, S. M. Gilpatric, T. Gronberg, and D. Jansen, "The Impact of Charter School Attendance on Student Performance," *Journal of Public Economics* 91, nos. 4–5 (2007): 849–876; E. A. Hanushek, J. F. Kain, S. G. Rivkin, and G. F. Branch, "Charter School Quality and Parental Decisionmaking with School Choices," *Journal of Public Economics* 91, nos. 4–5 (2007): 823–848; J. S. Hastings and J. Weinstein, "Information, School Choice, and Academic Achievement: Evidence from Two Experiments," *Quarterly Journal of Economics* 123, no. 4 (2008): 1373–1414; S. A. Imberman, "Achievement and Behavior in Charter Schools: Drawing a More Complete Picture," *Review of Economics and Statistics* 93, no. 2 (2007): 416–435; S. Loeb, J. Valant, and M. Kasman, "Increasing Choice in the Market for Schools: Recent Reforms and Their Effects on Student Achievement," *National Tax Journal* 64, no. 1 (2011): 141–164; T. R. Sass, "Charter Schools and Student Achievement in Florida," *Education Finance and Policy* 1, no. 1 (2006): 91–122; L. C. Sutton and R. A. King, "School Vouchers in a Climate of Political Change," *Journal of Education Finance* 36, no. 1 (2011): 244–267; J. Vanderhoff, "Parental Valuation of Charter Schools and Student Performance," *Cato Journal* 28, no. 3 (2008): 479–493; D. M. Welsch, "Charter School Competition and Its Impact on Employment Spending in Michigan's Public Schools," *Contemporary Economic Policy* 29, no. 3 (2011): 323–336; D. Epple, R. Romano, and R. Zimmer "Charter Schools: A Survey of Research on Their Characteristics and Effectiveness," 2015, https://www.nber.org/papers/w21256.pdf

29. https://www.educationnext.org/friendlycompetition/

30. https://www.edweek.org/ew/articles/2017/02/08/regulations-are-strangling-charter-schools.html

31. https://www.aei.org/op-eds/a-new-front-in-the-school-choice-fight/

32. Hugh Pearson, "An Urban Push for Self-Reliance," *Wall Street Journal*, February 7, 1996.

33. *School Reform News*, November 1998, 12.

34. Jeffrey R. Henig, Katrina E. Bulkley, and Henry M. Levin, "Can 'Portfolio Management' Save Urban Schools?," *Education Week*, October 4, 2010.

35. A general version of this concern is in Shlaes (2019, p. 14).

36. Leslie G. Pfaff, "The Right to Choose," *The New Jersey Monthly*, September 15, 2000.

37. Finn, Manno, et al. (1997); Lynn Schnaiberg, "Charter Schools Struggle with Accountability," *Education Week*, June 10, 1998, 1, 14; Thomas Toch, "The New Education Bazaar," *U.S. News and World Report*, April 27, 1998, 34–36; Lynn Schnaiberg, "Firms Hoping to Turn Profit from Charters," *Education Week*, December 10, 1997, 14.

38. The states with the "A" laws change constantly.

39. The number of "A" states has stayed small, 3–5 out of 40+.

40. https://www.ewa.org/blog-educated-reporter/after-25-years-no-shortage-charter-schools-research

41. The most prominent examples: (1) https://www.brookings.edu/blog/brown-center-chalkboard/2019/06/07/charter-schools-good-or-bad-for-students-in-district-schools/; (2) https://credo.stanford.edu/; (3) https://ies.ed.gov/ncee/pubs/20104029/

42. https://ies.ed.gov/ncee/pubs/20104029/

43. https://credo.stanford.edu/; https://credo.stanford.edu/sites/g/files/sbiybj6481/f/closure_final_volume_i.pdf

44. http://www.nea.org/home/33177.htm

45. https://credo.stanford.edu/sites/g/files/sbiybj6481/f/closure_final_volume_i.pdf

46. https://www.progressivepolicy.org/wp-content/uploads/2012/06/06.2012-Osborne_Improving-Charter-School-Accountability_The-Challenge-of-Closing-Failing-Schools.pdf

47. Andrew Coulson, "The Other Lottery: Are Philanthropists Backing the Best Charter Schools?," Cato Policy Analysis #677, June 26, 2011, https://object.cato.org/sites/cato.org/files/pubs/pdf/PA677.pdf

48. https://www.edweek.org/ew/articles/2016/08/24/we-must-diversify-charter-school-options.html

49. "Failed school" turnaround effort has a terrible track record; see Chapter 4 of Smarick (2012).

50. The primary drawback of NAEP as a measure of school system performance is that, for the sample of students taking the exam, it is a no-stakes exam. Students' scores yield no repercussions for the test takers—something more likely to lower scores the older the student.

51. https://www.nationsreportcard.gov

52. https://fordhaminstitute.org/national/commentary/no-apologies-no-excuses-charter-schools

53. https://www.aei.org/multimedia/the-shifting-politics-of-charter-schooling; https://www.wsj.com/articles/a-ruse-to-block-new-yorks-new-charter-schools-teachers-union-suny-authorizer-john-liu-eric-adams-11644961144; https://www.wsj.com/articles/charter-school-sabotage-biden-teachers-union-public-school-achievement-gap-hispanic-black-students-charter-schools-program-rules-11648224610

Chapter 4

Fallacies About School Choice

> Whatever the dire circumstances, there are always those who would rather risk peril than leave familiar surroundings.
>
> —Cartoon character Nacho Guarache (Leo Garza)[1]

This chapter is about the truly wrong aspects of the school choice debate. Choice advocates created some of the fallacies, and they are partly responsible for the persistence of all of them. *The subsection titles of this chapter state fallacies*. The 22 years since the publication of *The School Choice Wars* (2001) have made some of the fallacies less prominent, but all of them are still troublesome. Sadly, it is a long chapter.

ONLY THE SCHOOLS OF THE POOR ARE BAD

This fallacy arises partly from the natural assumption that the best schools are at least good at what they aim to do. The other key culprit is the correlation between perceived school quality and neighborhood socioeconomic status, which is at least reinforced—perhaps largely caused—by competition for homes near the better schools. The more affluent families win that competition, leaving the poorest families concentrated near the worst schools, which makes them worse.[2]

That correlation misled many scholars to believe that (1) "the most significant determinants of educational success are the student's socio-economic background and familial context" (Hess, 1998, p. 13); (2) school characteristics are not the cause of academic deficiencies;[3] and (3) "social measures that target the home and neighborhood environments of disadvantaged children might prove more effective than educational remedies" (Vanourek, 1996). Because statistical analyses explain data variability, the proper interpretation of such findings is that schools' impact on intellectual growth is consistent—consistently bad, since academic outcomes are appalling where socioeconomic conditions are the worst, rising to dismal where socioeconomic conditions are good.[4]

Indeed, major deficiencies in suburban TPSs are well documented and not rare,[5] but they are often hidden[6] from a school's students and their parents, or ignored/denied. Parents will not readily accept that they did not do right by their children, that the preferred choice—probably chosen through typically costly relocation—was still not very good.

In state after state, Lance Izumi found that the best schools are "Not as Good as You Think."[7] Former assistant secretary of education Chester Finn Jr. (1995) said that "millions of middle-class children [are] emerging half-ignorant from suburban schools." In 1996 and 1994, no state had more than 41% proficiency in any subject.[8] But even with some improvement, by 2019, several states still had proficiency rates in the 40s. And the top 2019 performances—Minnesota and Massachusetts—fourth-grade math proficiency rates just over 50%—were still dismal. Nationwide, at the 12th-grade level, the reading proficiency rate was 37%, math 25%.[9]

Chester Finn Jr. and Theodore Rebarber[10] cited the results of an especially informative National Assessment of Education Progress (NAEP) test question. It asked 11th graders how much a borrower would owe after a year on a one-year, $850 loan with a 12% interest rate. Only 6% of the 11th graders knew to multiply $850 by 1.12, or to find 12% of $850 and add it to $850. There aren't very many effective schools if 94% of the nation's high school juniors can't make that basic calculation.[11] In a 1992 survey of adult literacy, just 11% of U.S. high school graduates could restate in writing the main point of a newspaper article (Finn Jr., 1995).

The fallacy that the affluent typically attend effective TPSs is dangerous because:

1. It favors modest changes in the status quo and implies that we should copy the better schools.[12] Transfers to better schools are seen as rescues, even though transferees are usually only helped a bit. The fallacy produced plans such as the 1990s' Texas voucher proposals and the Florida program,[13] which focused on children enrolled in "low-performing" schools. In that kind of program, parental choice means that you can use some of the money earmarked for the education of your child if the government thinks your assigned TPS is bad enough. In Florida, children became eligible for a voucher when two to four years of education negligence and malpractice was bad enough to make the government confess inadequacy.[14] In 2020, "eight of the nation's fifty private school choice programs are failing schools programs."[15]

2. Parents able to relocate, or who can afford private school tuition, put their children in a top school and assume that best at least means generally good. A better comprehensive suburban school is not necessarily a significantly better fit for a particular child, and it may still be widely low performing, perhaps seeming to achieve better aggregate results because of better family support.

Opinion polls reflect a false sense of security. A majority believes that most TPSs are inadequate but that the well-publicized defects of the government-run system don't exist in their own schools.[16] According to the Manhattan Institute's John Miller, that's a big reason for the lopsided electoral losses of voucher proposals.

> Most suburbanites are happy with their kids' school systems. They admit the country's deep education crisis, but they just don't believe the problem affects them personally.[17]

Perception and reality must differ. Most suburbanites cannot be in effective schools when the country is in a persistent, deep education crisis.

Most of the private school sector is also inadequate. The public and private sectors have similar standardized test scores after adjustment for differences in student characteristics.[18] An available and affordable, but relatively resource-poor, private school may be a better fit than a family's assigned TPS, but better fit doesn't make it high performing, even narrowly defined according to a specialized mission. The private school would certainly be better if it had similar per-student resources. Families with the financial means to choose from the existing school menu still end up using low-performing schools quite often.

3. It reduces the political pressure for systemic reform. The most quality-conscious consumers are usually the most politically influential citizens (Hirschman, 1970). If a reasonable substitute is within their means, they leave. Their departure weakens the political pressure for reform. The fallacy also has the unintended consequence of voters in the best districts with the best schools believing they don't need choice expansion. They believe that parental choice is only for poor people who live in districts with the worst schools, which causes universal parental choice to be a heavy lift politically.

Like other caps on participation, limiting choice to low-income families undermines the potential for an OEI,[19] and it further concentrates poverty.

Quentin Quade's eloquent attack on the propensity to cap parental choice program eligibility still deserves much more attention:

> There is no logic which says school choice should stop at any particular income level or any municipal boundary line. One thinks in such incomplete categories only if still an intellectual captive of the status quo, perhaps seeing the virtues of choice just as a corrective of today's worst educational results, rather than as the natural, parent-serving social policy it is when seen in its own right. That, no doubt, is why some of today's most-heralded advocates of school choice continue to speak of it as "good for the poor but not for all." There is no true line between rich and poor as regards the merit of school choice.[20]

We need to do much more than upgrade inner-city, low-income-area schooling to the current suburban standard. We need to improve nearly everyone's menu of schooling options.

"FREE" AND COMPREHENSIVE IS ENOUGH

Comprehensive choice includes private schools, and all children are eligible. But the rare prominent comprehensive proposals[21] yield price control effects and discriminate against the children for whom the assigned TPS is a poor fit.[22]

Even Quade's (1996, p. 35) eloquent plea for choice with no out-of-pocket cost overlooked the discrimination issue. His definition of no financial penalty allows less public money for private school users (discrimination)—say $7,000 per voucher or education savings account (ESA) versus $13,000 per TPS student—*if the ESA fully covers the tuition*. Private school students still suffer a financial penalty because discrimination reduces (1) private schools' access to resources, and (2) the incentive and opportunity to open new schools and the incentive to compete. The latter falls further if the tax dollars that follow transferees don't come from their school district's budget.

Comprehensive proposals that limit private school eligibility to schools that accept tax dollars as full payment (they prohibit top-off/add-ons) further reduce parents' choices and undermine openness. They limit choice because it costs parents a lot to buy slightly more schooling than the public funds will allow. Again (it's a vital point), without the option to top-off public funds, privately *or from third-party assistance*, a $6,001/year private school would cost families $6,001 more than a $6,000/year private school. A $6,001 jump in buyers' education outlays to buy another dollar's worth of services has nearly the same effect as an explicit price (tuition) ceiling at the tax dollar amount.

Choice advocates should demand the right to supplement the public funds with private funds, as necessary, to achieve a good schooling fit. Unfortunately, they are often opposed or silent on this *critical* issue. For example, Daniel McGroarty (1996) said prohibiting what is commonly called a top-off or a copayment is "a sensible move to prevent the ratcheting up of tuition costs" (p. 98), and Gabriel Sahlgren (2013) said allowing copayment would promote "cream-skimming" (p. 143), common views among choice advocates that reflect much confusion about children, economics, and reform. For example, "cream" implies the widespread existence of uniformly brilliant children. But the vast majority of actual children have strengths and weaknesses and unique engagement factors. And a brilliant child is only cheaper to educate when the goal is being at TPS grade level, which means average for a particular age.

Higher tuition costs are likely only in the short run, especially if the level of per-pupil public funding is—as recommended throughout this book—nearly the same, regardless of where families enroll their children. The greater profitability of a private school that would result from the tuition increase that could result from greater demand would attract many entrepreneurs. The long-term net effect on tuition of the increased demand for private schooling, and the subsequent supply increase, is uncertain.

Competition may force many schools to accept the public funding amount as full payment with a much different effect than if the government requires it. With public per-pupil funding the same no matter which school the child attends, top-offs are parents' only out-of-pocket cost (means-tested top-off assistance is likely), certainly much less than private school users' costs without public support.

Some choice advocates' stated interest in keeping private school tuition from rising is contrary to their desire to improve the system. Higher prices triggered by increased demand are a key to new school formation. Note that the formation of new schools will then lower tuition levels, perhaps back to their initial level, but probably not that far.

A net tuition increase is likely for the private schools operating now. Tuition revenues don't cover the costs of many current private schools. Their ability to extend current subsidies to a larger student population is very limited, probably limited to the unused capacity of existing facilities. Increased resources per student are probably necessary for most private schools to expand facilities and to become more competitive in teacher labor markets.

There are five major reasons to allow add-ons. (1) Equity: everyone pays school taxes, so everyone should enjoy the benefits even if they want to buy more than the tax dollars will let them. (2) Freedom: it maximizes the range of choices, and the decision to add on does not harm anyone else. Add-ons allow some children to learn more without other children learning less, and society benefits when anyone learns more. (3) Parental involvement: parents choose more carefully when there is an out-of-pocket cost. (4) Increased school funding, where needed the most without higher taxes. (5) Efficiency: *price movement is a primary market mechanism.*

Without add-ons, price (tuition) changes can only reflect political forces. When parents cannot top off or get a charity to do it for them, prices cannot move to reflect market forces. *Price movement is how markets signal relative scarcity, motivate producers and consumers, and allocate resources. A price control—the effect of prohibiting copayment—is an extremely debilitating, anti-competitive factor!* We are shouting. Persistent shortages and continued reliance on oxymoronish central-plan optimization are a really big deal.

Financial penalties accompany choice expansion unless each child gets the same amount of public funding no matter which school they attend. The amount can vary by child, perhaps according to a weighted student formula (WSF). The public funding amount cannot cover the full cost of every possible useful education option, so the freedom to top off enlarges the menu, and it increases total spending on education. It also allows the introduction of new practices that are expensive at first but eventually become widely affordable. It also raises consumer vigilance, and it establishes the critical decentralized planning mechanism of price flexibility. A phase-in of nondiscrimination in public funding is acceptable if the final policy is certain at the outset.

CHOICE WILL OCCUR FROM THE EXISTING SCHOOL MENU

School system reform discussions suffer greatly from this fallacy: the static world fallacy. The status quo is deeply ingrained even among its critics. Many analysts cannot imagine a system much different than what we have now. Many speak as if the excess capacity of existing private schools defines the upper limit on choice expansion. Such intellectual captives of the status quo assume that the overwhelming majority of children will always have to attend TPSs organized into school districts, so that anything bad for the public school system is ultimately bad for children. They assume that the private sector will remain largely nonprofit and church run, with a few extremely select, expensive schools.

The February 1998 *Mobilization for Equity* newsletter plainly reflected this fallacy. Private schools don't have "enough [empty] seats. The majority of students will be forced to remain in the public system *regardless of how voucher programs are implemented* [emphasis added]."[23] That's dangerous nonsense! Choice expansion driven by current public funding levels would cause new schools to form quickly, some in former TPS buildings. Quite soon, children would stay in a TPS only when their parents want them there.

There are many other less blunt examples of the static world fallacy. Based on empty seats in Catholic schools, Peter Cookson (1993a) said, "You could get some competition quicker if you included private schools in a choice plan, but it wouldn't be much more competition" (p. 252). Stan Karp said, "This [the free market] meant [turn the education system over to] the local Roman Catholic Archdiocese,"[24] which Karp guessed had about 1,000 vacant slots. Linda Darling-Hammond said, "Vouchers are a smokescreen,"[25] a distraction from critical equity issues because there are only a "limited number of slots worth choosing." Robert Lowe and Barbara Miner said a voucher system would force parents "to compete for a few select schools."[26]

The assumption of restricted access also underlies Ann Lewis's (1996) certainty that "vouchers might help some students and some schools" (p. 5) but won't change the system. Restricted access to choice is an underlying assumption of anti–choice expansion campaign literature (Fondy, 1998). Particularly telling excerpts include:

- "Vouchers reward those who have not elected to attend public schools" (Lewis, 1996, p. 2).
- "The vast bulk of the voucher money would subsidize those who are already in private schools" (p. 3).
- "Vouchers abandon the many for the few" (p. 3).
- The American Civil Liberties Union believes that "for most students, vouchers offer a choice between a religious school and a failing public school." Vouchers "single out a few for special privileges."[27]

David Berliner and Bruce Biddle (1995) believe choice expansion "sets up a two-class educational system" (p. 178). They apparently believe that choice expansion will only cause a slight expansion of the private school sector, while most children remain in TPSs harmed by losing students, even though per-pupil funding of the TPSs stays the same or goes up. Many others repeatedly imply the same conviction.

The potential magnitude of reform through choice expansion is completely lost on the victims of the static world fallacy. They don't realize that choice expansion can remake entire school systems. With its nearly level playing field among schools, an OEI will contain only choice worthy schools.

If choice opponents are right about "public school abandonment," an OEI will not contain government-operated schools for very long. Non-religion-based and for-profit schools will comprise a much larger share of an OEI's private school sector than they do now.[28] In an OEI, private schools will no longer suffer the major handicap of having zero-tuition competitors. Private schools won't have to charge more for a much more cheaply made service.

The existing array of schools is no basis from which to evaluate the components and effects of an OEI. For that reason, it is worth repeating an important point of Chapter 3. The attractiveness of policies that use choice expansion to change the school system does not depend on whether existing private schools produce better academic outcomes than TPS.

Choice advocates like Denis Doyle and Douglas Munro recognize the power of choice to remake the system, but their actions frequently overlook that objective and thereby make that outcome less likely. For example, Doyle and Munro (1997) administered a questionnaire to people leaving Baltimore to see if choice would have prevented their departure. Even though the questionnaire defined "choice" as a restriction-laden program unable to trigger large changes in the menu of schooling options, many survey respondents said that even such limited choice would have prevented their departure.

CHOICE EXPANSION ONLY HELPS THE RICH

That is a typical assertion of anti-choice literature: "Poor parents cannot afford to pay the difference between a voucher and a private school's full tuition" (Fondy, 1998). However, even when per-pupil public funding of TPS leavers is much less than the per-pupil funds of TPSs (a mistake), the claim is only partially true, and not nearly as important as it is asserted to be. Charities will provide means-tested copayment (top-off) help. Many private schools are inexpensive enough that the demand for small vouchers or ESAs usually exceeds availability or private school capacity, whichever is less. Many low-income families make the major sacrifices needed to move a child to a private school, and many more want to.[29]

With the high level of nondiscriminatory, universal public funding advocated throughout this book, the claim that choice expansion would only aid the rich is utterly false. Universal choice funded with current K–12 public funding (nondiscrimination) would put all but the elite prep academies within the reach of every family with little or no top-off required.

Most private schools would have much more money per student. That, and the competitive pressures would greatly improve private schools, and TPSs may also respond to the competitive pressures. Since low-income families are often in below-average TPSs, they have the most to gain from the certain improvement and greater availability of private schools, and possible gains by TPSs. Since rich people already have access to elite prep academies, an OEI will help low-income families the most. The lowest-income families would get more tuition assistance than they pay in school taxes, so the truly rich would have to continue paying more in school taxes than they'd get back.

EVERY SCHOOL SHOULD ACCEPT ANY CHILD

Choice opponents assert that choice expansion gives choice to private schools,[30] because private schools can practice selective admissions. Supposedly, private schools will take only the easiest to educate and dump the rest in TPSs. It is an utterly false and disingenuous claim, but it is often politically effective because choice opponents depict specialization as discrimination. It is a disingenuous claim because many public school systems[31] use private schools as a "dumping ground for dummies" (McGroarty, 1996, p. 102) by paying private school tuition with public funds, another violation of choice opponents' demands.

The only discrimination in an OEI is by parents as discriminating consumers. They will choose a school that best suits the unique abilities and preferences of each of their children. Except for elite schools, sellers only rarely exercise their right to refuse service to someone. The shortages that are possible in the early stages of an OEI will quickly disappear, just as they do in any market when demand rises and prices are flexible.

What's important is that every child has access to a high-quality education. Competing schools of choice as a group, but not individually, are better suited to that objective precisely because market forces compel them to specialize. Market pressures push schools into particular niches. TPSs try in vain to address a broad spectrum of education interests and abilities. TPSs need the right to exclude (McGhan, 1998), that is, to direct poor-fit students to more appropriate services. Specialization opportunities need to be extended to TPSs, not taken from private schools.

Choice opponents' ability to turn TPS inability to specialize—a major shortcoming—into a political asset does not change the fact that it is a major handicap. Forcing every TPS—and CPS—to accept any child is a big mistake. Specialization, which makes a school's services a better fit for some children but less suitable to others, is a cornerstone of high productivity. Because private schools can specialize and TPSs cannot—TPSs must strive to serve every child in their attendance area—the private schools that accept TPS castoffs often serve them better for less than is spent on the mainstream TPS students. Private schools' ability to specialize in particular subjects or teaching styles significantly raises the productivity of the private sector.

Limited, restriction-laden choice programs maximize the danger that private schools will acquire some of the handicaps of TPSs (such as inability to specialize). An OEI will yield the opposite effect. Private schools and TPS will acquire some of each other's advantages. Private schools will have more resources per student, and TPSs will acquire some of the flexibility and freedom of a private school.

Choice opponents' claim that private schools, not parents, will exercise choice has two more false premises. The first is another result of the static world fallacy, and both are harsh backhanded criticisms of TPSs. Many choice opponents assert that the existing excess capacity of private schools limits parents' ability to exercise choice (the static world fallacy). Choice opponents misinform their listeners by implying that space shortages are permanent. Private schools would supposedly have to discriminate because they could accept only a small fraction of the likely flood of applicants.

The second false premise is choice opponents' claim that typical restriction-laden choice programs will allow private schools to dump hard-to-educate children on TPSs. It means that parents seeking typically more cheaply produced private school services will be forced to settle for more costly TPS services. When the least desired service costs the most, inefficiency is the reason. Once again, choice opponents' defense of the public school system is thinly disguised condemnation. It is a much more devastating criticism than choice advocates' arguments for choice expansion that don't depend on TPS dysfunctionality, which, sadly, is not unusual.

The dumping claim is disingenuous because TPSs already dump children in private schools, and it's another misleading aspect of narrowly targeted, restriction-laden choice expansion. Certainly, the claim contradicts OEI fundamentals such as specialization, competition, and the profit motive.

When schools specialize,[32] the easiest to educate student varies from school to school, and high achievers are easier to educate only when there are low expectations. *Like teacher talent and student ability, school quality is not one-dimensional!* Specialization will also respond to the reality that most children excel in some subject areas more than in others. Having specialized schools greatly reduces the cost of having much-needed, nonstigmatizing ability grouping, *by subject*—different from controversial, stigmatizing, and counterproductive tracking that falsely implies that children are uniformly high, medium, or low achievers.

In an OEI, high achievers are definitely not among the cheapest to educate. The parents of high achievers demand challenging instruction for their children no matter how far above each subjects average they are. Furthermore, parents of high achievers may demand highly customized attention. That's likely a major reason why their children are high achievers.

The profit motive means that it will not matter if some children cost more to educate than others as long as they are still profitable. That is another reason to allocate virtually 100% of current school spending through parental choice. The resulting high minimum level of per-pupil funding will allow entrepreneurs to profitably serve virtually every mainstream child with little or no private add-on. The mainstream children of specialized schools will include many now labeled "special ed."

Contracting Out Is Real Privatization

The public's well-founded belief that businesses outperform bureaucracies underlies the political support for the concept of privatization. Supporters are driven by images of businesses cutting costs or improving their product to compete for market share. Unfortunately, like the terms "parental choice" and "school choice," the term "privatization" covers a lot of possibilities, and the effects expected by supporters will not result from some of those possibilities.

Contracting out services, selling public assets to businesses, and load shedding (the government sheds responsibility for a service) are different forms of privatization. Contracting out was the dominant mode because it offended the fewest special interests (Ascher, Fruchter, & Berne, 1996, p. 615; Carpenter & Hall, 1971). Since the places that implemented that mode didn't privatize school ownership, privatization was a means, not an end, or as Emanuel Savas (1987) put it, contracting out is not "*real* [emphasis in the original] privatization" (p. 278). Marketing mistakes by reform advocates and resistance from incumbent school personnel compounded the disappointment with privatization efforts.

Competition in the management service market—where the TPS authorities are buyers—doesn't reduce the dominance of TPSs in the delivery of instructional services. The rise in the number of producers of education services is small, and the TPS authorities and the contractors they hire are at most semi-independent. Differences may provide parents with some choice, but it is hard to imagine ferociously competitive behavior between TPS authorities and firms hired by them. Furthermore, the barriers to entry remain. The market is not more contestable.

Contracting out the delivery of instructional services usually changes a government-owned, government-run monopoly into a regulated, privately run government monopoly. Poorly conceived contract language creates problems by misdirecting contractors' efforts, or by causing an overly narrow focus on specific evaluation criteria such as standardized test scores.

It is probably fortunate that the management contracts haven't included cost reduction in the performance criterion.[33] Contracted managers lack many of the cost-cutting options and perspectives of owners. There are major differences between the conditions and incentives of contracted managers and competing school owner-operators. Contracted managers are paid by the authorities that hired them, not by the children and parents they serve. Carol

Ascher's statement about performance contracting in the 1960s and early 1970s is still correct:

> Performance contracting was never meant to increase parents' voice in schooling. Indeed, families remain noticeably absent from the stories of these experiments. They described accountability in terms of companies and school districts. (Ascher, Fruchter, & Berne, 1996, p. 622)

Contracted managers have a strong incentive to narrow the curriculum and focus their efforts on politically relevant factors. Other suboptimal, even counterproductive, practices are common, including focusing teaching on particular standardized exams, or whatever measuring devices will officially determine the contractor's performance and compensation.

Competing owner-entrepreneurs face relentless pressure to cut costs and improve their services. Those dynamic factors are at the core of differences "between competitive market and political 'command-and-control' mechanisms of service delivery" (Bradford & Shaviro, 1998, p. 52). Contracted managers have no comparable pressures to motivate them. Their stockholders may demand cost-cutting measures, but the additional, much more important pressure from price-cutting competitors is lacking. Competitors also provide the critical cost and quality basis for comparison.

A contracted manager's most important initial competition is their predecessor's track record. The frustration that precedes the drastic step of contracting out management leads to contracts with short-term, static goals. Calls for *real* privatization and contracting out school management are dramatic statements of frustration with administrative and political processes. Peter Hutchinson, president of Public Strategies Group Inc., defined success as "turning the district's performance around,"[34] ending decline and bringing the district closer to normal, which is still "Nation at Risk" awful. Catching up is easier to define in a performance contract, and it is much less ambitious than continuous pursuit of a rising standard of excellence.

If the contracted managers succeed initially and turn some schools around, rise to national norms widely seen as dismal, or just outperform the district employees who preceded them, the better nearby TPSs become the new standard. There are no education entrepreneurs to compete with, and direct rivalry with TPSs can occur only if there are no attendance areas.

Once contract objectives are met, there is little incentive to modify practices already deemed successful. Tampering with successful practices is risky, and without real competition, the potential return on improvements is much lower. Education entrepreneurs from other places are only potential competitors, and then only in a very limited way. Potential competitors cannot continuously contest customers. They are limited to periodically contesting the renewal of the incumbent manager's contract with the school authorities.

The politics that created the problem, and convinced the authorities that they could not fix it themselves, will infect the contract's terms. The contracted manager often has little discretion in politically sensitive areas like personnel, curriculum, and student distribution or in potential areas of specialization. Putting those policies off-limits greatly reduces the potential for improvement. Such restrictions were a major factor in the nonrenewal of Education Alternatives Inc.'s (EAI) contracts for Baltimore and Hartford. EAI had to keep the existing curriculum, as well as teachers who were openly hostile to the new policies.

Alternative Public Schools (APS) believed it had the authority to choose its own staff. The Pennsylvania affiliate of the National Education Association (NEA) filed a lawsuit that reversed the APS's decision to terminate the union contract and dismiss all the incumbent teachers.

Uncertainty about contract longevity can create other problems. Political support is fragile, and the range of politically acceptable behavior changes with current events and elections. Early termination clauses like the Hartford/EAI contract—termination with only 90 days' notice—necessitate constant attention to political correctness.[35] Even if contracted managers have the authority to make politically sensitive decisions, they may not exercise it. Politically sensitive criteria like test scores receive too much attention, to the detriment of other important but less measurable or interpretable education outcomes.

Because the payback time for many capital investments is longer than the contract period, contractors may operate with less capital than owners. The approach of the renewal date and the contracted manager's estimated probability of nonrenewal directly affect investment decisions. Despite the nonrenewal, early-termination risks, EAI made some major investments. When the contract expired, EAI unsuccessfully sought a $3 million reimbursement.

Privatizing management has fewer potential benefits than private ownership, and the political risks for advocates are significant. Glitches and resentments accompany transitions to new managerial regimes, so it is not at all surprising when contracted managers cannot quickly produce the significantly better test scores that are the political process's primary contract renewal criterion. Contracting out management services is a time-consuming, deceptive detour off the road to genuine reform of the entire system.

Confusion about privatization and well-publicized but poorly explained disappointments reduces the political feasibility of OEIs. Attempts to duplicate them in different settings can tarnish success stories, and problems that should be interpreted narrowly give all forms of privatization politically costly image problems. When frustration with the political process prompts the authorities to try private enterprise, choice advocates should demand a level playing field for privately *owned* schools. To literally privatize schooling, the authorities should sell school facilities to independent education entrepreneurs, a step that does not preclude public subsidy of schooling costs.

CHOICE EXPANSION IS A GAMBLE

A symptom of the confusion about parental choice, and an underlying premise of choice expansion "experiments" and pilot programs, is the implicit assumption that we could make things worse. Evidence from restriction-laden choice, which is all the modern direct evidence we have, indicates that TPS users typically benefit,[36] at least from fewer differentiated instruction challenges, and perhaps from competitive pressures.[37] And there is no basis to expect an OEI to harm children; if anything, the opposite.

The only apparent basis for the fear of possible harm is that choice expansion will produce unpredictable change. A key finding of a November 14, 1997, conference at the Federal Reserve Bank of New York is a typical example: "participants *cautioned* [emphasis added] that the existing evidence [from restriction-laden parental choice programs] is insufficient to justify expanding choice proposals to the student population as a whole."[38]

Some of those conference participants noted the poor design of the alleged experiments, but they ignored the frustration and disappointment with the current system, a strong theoretical case for use of decentralized planning approaches, and the spectacular track record of that approach in hundreds of industries, including when applied to education (Coulson, 1999). Looking at an even larger body of marginally relevant findings, Epple, Romano, and Urquiola (2017) reached the same conclusions.

The certainties arising from the status quo are much worse than the uncertainties associated with leveling the playing field and price decontrol. Failure to implement an OEI guarantees major losses. Failure to effectively respond to the repeated "Nation at Risk" warnings[39] has already been very costly. The significant further delay required to generate, design, implement, run, and evaluate a valid experiment will be even more costly.

The funding and governance policies that strongly favor TPS have resisted change, but other kinds of change are huge problems. Public school system policy makers regularly try new rules, curricula, and teaching procedures in a desperate search for the magic set of commands that will make teachers successful at making one size fit all.

Policy makers conduct unplanned, uncontrolled experiments. The futile, desperate search yields constant upheaval. The unending parade of hoped-for centrally planned answers to central-planning failures is a major source of the low achievement problem. Denis Udall noted that "teachers are in a virtual state of panic, caught between crushing district mandates and the need to raise standardized test scores."[40]

A gamble?! What actual—as opposed to theoretical or potential—education outcome of the status quo would the general public miss? The actual outcomes of the 51 U.S. school systems are quite often the number-one political concern of Americans.

Choice opponents repeatedly say that the gains of the choosers came at the expense of students left behind in schools with less money and fewer active parents, evidence of competitive and sorting effects notwithstanding. But literally hundreds of studies[41] show that large funding increases produced little if any academic improvement. Choice advocates cite that evidence to contest calls for more public school system funding, but they do not exploit a legitimate interpretation of greater significance. The system's failure to respond favorably to additional resources is solid evidence of a totally dysfunctional system.[42] Productivity (achievement/cost) falls whenever per-pupil funding rises, and vice-versa.

Citizens have to establish semipermanent political organizations to seek high standards and accountability. Colleges[43] and businesses[44] spend rising millions on remediation. Polls show that a majority of families would use the existing, often struggling private schools if they could afford the tuition. Rising numbers of parents are rejecting an expensive TPS education they have already paid for, as well as relatively inexpensive private schools many of them could afford, in favor of the difficult task of homeschooling.

The supposed relative virtues (Ascher, Fruchter, & Berne, 1996; Levin, 1991) of a TPS-favored education system are only theoretical—unrealized to any great extent in TPSs, and not systematically absent from private schools. Even limited choice expansion *actually* yields the social gains that only our "common schools" (TPSs) are *supposed to* deliver (Schneider et al., 1997, pp. 86–90). Free public schools exist largely to provide economic opportunity to low-income families, but the least advantaged children end up in the worst TPSs.

Wide disparities in funding and other measures of resource allocation (like teacher experience) exist in public school systems even where court rulings demand equal funding. Despite the expense and agony of busing, neighborhood schools are still relatively homogenous by race and socioeconomic status. The only common outcomes instilled by the common experience intended from TPSs are high rates of nonproficiency, much of which is below the basic skills level. The extremism that receives so much attention, including in parental choice debates, was mostly learned in TPSs, or despite their best efforts to instill common values.

The existing debate is whether the public school system is "a disaster"[45] or a gold-plated disaster,[46] whether existing private schools or CPSs are any better, and in either case exactly what reforms are appropriate. Most parental choice opponents admit that many TPSs—yet *all* have children assigned to them—are not choice worthy. Probable TPS "abandonment" is one of their key objections to parental choice proposals. Even an ardent defender of the current governance and funding mechanisms—David Berliner—notes that the 51 U.S. K–12 systems are not capable of being effective. "It is clear that our system is not designed to produce masses of high-achieving students before the college years" (Berliner, 1993, p. 638).

Restriction-laden choice expansion proposals are a gamble.[47] They jeopardize the political feasibility of an OEI. The statements that many choice expansion advocates make about alleged experiments, and other indicators, threaten the choice expansion cause, however narrowly or broadly we define it.

OVERVIEW

This chapter discussed several troublesome fallacies. Facts contradict much long-standing conventional "wisdom." Fallacies are also a significant part of the next six chapters, but there is more room for informed disagreement. Chapters 6–11 criticize incorrect perspectives rather than ignorance, misunderstanding, and denial of reality. The next chapter is an especially good example of inappropriate perspective. It discusses the fear of increased regulation of private schools, an issue that choice expansion advocates need to thoroughly reexamine.

NOTES

1. *San Antonio Express-News*, August 30, 1998

2. A 1997 Doyle and Munro study (*Reforming the Schools to Save the City* [Baltimore, MD: The Calvert Institute]) found that expected change in school quality was a major reason for Baltimore's population decline, largely through relocation to suburbs. Numerous recent studies (see the Tennessee, Texas, and Georgia studies and journal articles at https://www.effective-ed.org/in-the-media) indicate that areas with the lowest-quality TPSs typically see "flight" to areas with better schools in the large difference between the number of preschool-age and school-age children.

3. Hess (1998); Vanourek (1996); Doyle (1997); Viteritti (1999, p. 14); Troy Segal, "Saving Our Schools," *BusinessWeek*, September 14, 1992, 70–78; Rene Sanchez, "Riley Launches Attack on School Vouchers," *Washington Post*, September 24, 1997,

A6; Milton Friedman, quoted in West (1996, p. 7); Paul T. Hill, "The Innovator's Dilemma," *Education Week*, June 14, 2000, 33. The mistaken idea that the major problems of the system exist primarily in inner-city schools is deeply ingrained. Consider, for example, the title of *Education Week*'s January 8, 1998, special issue: "The Urban Challenge." Titles like *An Imperiled Generation: Saving Urban Schools* (Carnegie Foundation for the Advancement of Teaching, 1988) are common. *Selling Out Our Schools* edited by Lowe and Miner (1996) contains repeated references to "problems in urban public schools" and "hundreds of fine suburban school systems" (Kozol, 1992, p. 13). Ann Bastian (1986, p. 18) talks about the "crisis in urban education" and says the "real places in crisis [are] 25 or so major urban systems, plus some hundreds of decaying industrial suburbs and dying rural districts."

4. As noted previously, "Not as Good as You Think," https://www.schoolsystemreformstudies.net/wp-content/uploads/Opinion-Forum/Interpretation%20of%20Evidence%20%E2%80%93%20Misleading%20Findings/NAGAYT%20-%20Izumi.pdf

5. The evidence is direct and indirect. The appalling tests scores, including the embarrassing international comparisons, are based on the entire student population. Growing expenditures on remediation by businesses and colleges are not limited to inner-city high school graduates. Direct evidence of troubled suburban schools includes (1) Singal (1991); (2) an *Education Week* report, "Dollars Don't Mean Success in California District," December 3, 1997, on the troubles of a California school district with $12,100 per student; (3) in San Antonio, Texas, community college-bound high school graduates must take the TASP test to determine if they can begin college courses without remediation. Thirty students from San Antonio's wealthiest district, the suburban Alamo Heights District, took the TASP test in September 1992. Of those 30 students, 22, 15, and 16 required math, English, and reading remedial courses, respectively. (4) See Greene, Peterson, and Du (1997) for a description of Milwaukee's dismal secular private schools; (5) Kamrhan Farwell, "Money Doesn't Always Equal High Test Scores," *The Press Enterprise*, August 10, 1998, is about several California school districts; (6) exploding remedial education spending by businesses, community colleges, and universities; (7) Clowes (2000, p. 7); and (8) Lance Izumi's "Not as Good as You Think" series.

6. See Chapter 4 of Lieberman (1993) for an explanation of how parents are deceived.

7. https://www.schoolsystemreformstudies.net/wp-content/uploads/Opinion-Forum/Interpretation%20of%20Evidence%20%E2%80%93%20Misleading%20Findings/NAGAYT%20-%20Izumi.pdf

8. 1994 and 1996 NAEP data reported in *Education Week*, January 11, 1999.

9. https://www.nationsreportcard.gov/

10. "The Changing Politics of Education Reform," Chapter 9 in Finn and Rebarber (1992, p. 189).

11. Because of its consistency with other indicators of educational achievement (remedial education spending by colleges and businesses, other standardized tests), the inference derived from this terrible result survives the criticism of the NAEP test that scores are low because students have no incentive to try hard. See Murphy (1996,

pp. 139–148) for more examples that illustrate that student achievement is utterly unacceptable nearly everywhere.

12. Numerous funding equalization lawsuits further eroded incentives and system performance. Hoxby (1996).

13. Jessica L. Sandham, "Florida OKs 1st Statewide Voucher Plan," *Education Week*, May 5, 1999, 1, 21. A similar proposal was rejected by the 1999 Texas's legislature.

14. A metaphor may help illustrate the incredible absurdity of such policies. Imagine having to pay a restaurant until the owner (not you) decides, only after at least two years, the food isn't good enough. Then even if the owner admits the establishment is "low performing," you can only take some of your money elsewhere.

15. https://www.federationforchildren.org/school-choice-america/programs-qualifications/

16. In "Up from Mediocrity," *Policy Review*, Summer 1992, 80–83, Finn calls it the "complacency problem." The phenomenon is also discussed in Ball and Goldman (1997, p. 231). It's similar to the public's attitude toward another major political institution, the U.S. Congress. People think little of the U.S. Congress, but congressional incumbents rarely lose an election.

17. John Miller, "Why School Choice Lost," *Wall Street Journal*, November 4, 1993.

18. https://nces.ed.gov/nationsreportcard/pubs/studies/2006461.aspx

19. For vouchers as a general tool of government policy, that principle is well established. See C. Eugene Steurle, "Common Issues for Voucher Programs," in *Vouchers and Related Delivery Mechanisms: Consumer Choice in the Provision of Public Services* (Brookings Institution Conference, Washington, DC, October 2–3, 1998), 15.

20. Quentin L. Quade, "Watch Your Step! If School Choice Is So Great, Why Don't We Have It?," *Network News and Views*, January/February, 1996.

21. For example, California's 1993 and 2000 parental choice ballot initiatives.

22. CEO America lobbied for a tax credit program (Linda Morrison, *The Tax Credits Program for School Choice*, National Center for Policy Analysis, March 1998) that has the explicit aim "to discourage non-government schools from raising their tuition and fees"; that is, limiting private schools' access to resources.

23. "School Vouchers on Trial in Milwaukee and Cleveland," *Mobilization for Equity*, February 1998, 1, 3.

24. Stan Karp in Lowe and Miner (1996, p. 32).

25. Linda Darling-Hammond interview in Lowe and Miner (1996, p. 12).

26. Editors are interviewed in Lowe and Miner (1996, pp. 14–15).

27. Nadine Strossen, president of the ACLU, statement posted on the Freedom Channel website, August 8, 2000.

28. That assertion is supported and discussed in greater detail in the context of the "Court Opinions on Church-State Issues Are Key Factors" fallacy a few pages below.

29. The Goldwater Institute, "The Top Ten Myths about School Choice" (Phoenix, AZ, Mimeographed, 1994). The findings are based on data from Phoenix, Indianapolis, Atlanta, San Antonio, and Milwaukee. In each, there are long waiting lists for

half-tuition grants available only to low-income families. The latest privately funded partial low-income voucher program attracted 1.25 million requests for 40,000 vouchers.

30. For example, that assertion is a centerpiece of virtually every piece of "No on Prop 174" literature. For example, consider this line from an anti-174 handout titled "It Hurts Kids, It Hurts Taxpayers": "Voucher schools would choose which kids get in." According to Wagenheim (1998, p. 12), "Under a voucher plan, it is schools that will do the choosing, not parents or students." Also see the July 29, 1997, letter written by the National Coalition for Public Education and the comments of Elliot Mincberg with People for the American Way posted on the Freedom Channel website.

31. Janet R. Beales, "Educating the Uneducatable," *Wall Street Journal*, August 21, 1996.

32. https://ciaotest.cc.columbia.edu/olj/cato/v25n2/v25n2i.pdf

33. Education Alternatives Inc. (EAI) sought cost savings because they get to keep half of each dollar saved, but the primary performance criteria are test scores. Elizabeth Gleick, "Privatizing Lives," *Time*, November 13, 1995, 88.

34. Peter Hutchinson, "The Five C's," *Education Week*, September 17, 1997, 37, 39.

35. Nancy Gibbs, "Schools for Profit," *Time*, October 17, 1994, 48.

36. See this, https://www.nber.org/papers/w26758, the latest in a long line of articles that document TPS gains.

37. https://www.edchoice.org/school-choice-bibliography/#testscores

38. FRBNY, *Economic Policy Review* 4 (March 1998).

39. https://www.schoolsystemreformstudies.net/nation-at-risk-vi/

40. *Education Week*, July 8, 1998, 41, 43. Several articles in a special "Insight" section (June 1, 1997) of the *San Antonio Express-News*: "Schoolhouse Blues," said the same thing. Constantly changing programs are taking teachers out of their classrooms and creating low morale and panic.

41. Hanushek (1996); American Legislative Council, *You Can't Buy Higher Grades: 50-State Report Card on American Education Funds*, April, 2000.

42. For more detail, see Lieberman (1993).

43. In a 1997 survey, three-fourths of the college deans reported an increase within the last decade in the proportion of students requiring remedial or developmental education; Arthur Levine and Jeannete S. Curetin, "Collegiate Life: An Obituary," *Change*, May/June 1998, 14–17, 51. In Texas, spending for remedial education increased dramatically from $38.6 million in the 1988–89 biennium to $172 million by the 1998–99 biennium, a 346% increase; Jeff Judson, *The True State of Texas Education* (San Antonio: Texas Public Policy Foundation, 1998). Nationwide, "30% of first-time college students take remedial courses because they can't read, write, or do math adequately. At community colleges, the percentage is often much higher—and it's rising"; David Wessel, "The Outlook," *Wall Street Journal*, November 19, 1998, A1.

44. In the April 1998, *School Reform News* (p. 7): "According to *Training* magazine, 20% of the companies it recently surveyed taught their new hires reading,

writing, arithmetic, or English—even though 2/3 of them already sported high school diplomas."

45. California governor Gray Davis, quoted in David Broder, "Reforming Education a Tough Assignment," *San Antonio Express-News*, March 2, 1999, 7B.

46. See the findings of the U.S. Congress cited in Kirkpatrick (1997).

47. John Merrifield, "Myth: Any School Choice Is Welcome School Choice," Chapter 10 in *School Choice Myths*, ed. Corey DeAngelis and Neal McCluskey (Washington, DC: Cato Institute, 2020).

Chapter 5

Government Regulation Issues

Many conservatives and libertarians prefer the status quo to the effect they expect from mainstream choice expansion proposals. They oppose prominent proposals because they're afraid that choice expansion would cause the regulatory maze that hobbles CPSs and TPSs[1] to quickly engulf private schools, a maze that is so stifling that many private schools won't accept TPS leavers (Sude, DeAngelis, & Wolf, 2018), and state and local school authorities sometimes refuse federal dollars because of the new rules they would bring.[2]

Local authorities may also oppose choice proposals because they may threaten the perceived high value of their TPSs. The high cost of not resisting the temptation to take federal education money yielded an April 26, 2017, executive order[3] to back off and move toward restoring state primacy in school system governance. Here, in the fear of regulation, we have shades of wrong, misleading, and irrelevance.

The largely misguided fear of increased regulation of private schools is self-reinforcing. It drives away the best private schools and the most conservative choice expansion supporters, which leads to weaker proposals and weaker results from choice expansions.

In one case, what we believe is excess fear of regulation caused a set of conservative groups to offer a modest tax credit proposal[4] that *specifically aimed* to change the status quo as little as possible! The tax credit plan's two main objectives were to (1) prevent private school tuition from rising, and (2) minimize impact on TPS funds. The stated goals amounted to helping existing private school users, transferring a few more children to private schools, and keeping the school system the way it was. Restriction-laden programs are more vulnerable to regulatory encroachment because they don't leverage market forces, and they leave most of the status quo in place as a natural constituency for regulation and opposition to transformational choice expansion.

The key premise of conservative opponents of parental choice is "the crucial principle that control follows subsidy."[5] Llewellyn Rockwell said proposals like California's Prop 174's $2,600 voucher are an enemy of religion

(Rockwell, 1998), and they would hurt private schools (Rockwell, 1993) because the government will attach debilitating conditions to the money.

The theory underlying such views is that the debilitating conditions would arise gradually as the private schools became addicted to the money.[6] Charley Reese said that "the long-term result [of choice expansion] will be that private schools will become as bad as government schools."[7] According to Quentin Quade, a sharp critic of that attitude, people who hold that view "believe that any tax dollars, *no matter the distribution method*, will ultimately and inevitably become a vehicle for state dominance and loss of independent identity."[8]

In the Reese scenario, private schools and TPSs become more similar as private schools acquire the handicaps of TPSs. When private schools become more like TPSs, longtime private school users suffer losses, and the benefits to choice program users gradually disappear.

When the enacted choice expansions and the proposals that get the most attention are restriction laden, the outcomes of choice expansion may be just what conservative critics like Rockwell and Reese fear. An OEI is much less likely to have such effects. In an OEI, all schools must be choice worthy to enough users to make the school viable, and private schools would benefit greatly from no longer having to charge more than TPSs for more cheaply produced services—their biggest handicap.

An OEI would make TPSs and private schools more similar by spreading some advantages of private schools to TPSs. A leading policy approach to an OEI outcome—bankable, nonrefundable education tax credits (see Chapter 12)—minimizes the regulation risk. But the other approaches to an OEI still do not necessarily entail enough regulation risk to justify opposing them.

KEY ISSUES

When public funds generally enhance purchasing power or subsidize the purchase of specific goods or services, does this typically lead to significant restrictions on the behavior of the subsidized buyers or their suppliers? How burdensome are the resulting restrictions? How does the likelihood of negative effects compare to likely long-term improvements in K–12 education? Is the devil in the details? Will some versions of choice foster burdensome restrictions much more than other versions? Are there trade-offs involved in the resolution of the key issues?

Choice programs that would establish an OEI entail some risks. When tax dollars follow children to private schools, some private school users may regret some loss of autonomy by their school. In contrast, failure to adopt an OEI entails intolerable certainties. Failure to take that risk—minimized by the OEI versions of choice—means the status quo's effects continue, including the significant peril of many private schools. Many private schools, including some that are quite popular, are in serious financial trouble.[9] Private schools suffer considerable ill effects from having to compete with relatively lavishly funded, zero-tuition TPSs.

Catholic school officials explained that they have to keep tuition low to avoid becoming exclusive schools for the financially elite, and "the practical impossibility of maintaining the present system with only the present formula (low tuition + a $500 [elementary] to $700 [high school] per student subsidy) for support."[10] "Some school closings may be necessary."[11] "The parochial system is in a rapid state of decline and facing bankruptcy in the inner cities" (Cookson, 1993a). Indeed, private school enrollment is significantly lower now than when those quotes appeared in *The School Choice Wars* (2001).[12]

Quentin Quade (1996) argued that private schools "are damaged, often unto death, because they are deprived of the resources that would come their way if parents were free to choose without financial penalty" (p. 2). The examples include a popular private school that used an emergency loan to meet its payroll.[13] Failure to implement an OEI will endanger many private schools. According to Quade, the conservative critics of vouchers and tax credits "display a fundamental lack of proportion in assessing degrees of risk and immediate vs. remote dangers."[14]

Quade goes on to point out that vouchers and tax credits reduce the probability of federal interventions. "By diminishing the role of central state authorities, it [choice through vouchers or tax credits] would lessen federal capacity to intrude via such state agencies."[15]

EVIDENCE

Expansion of private school choice directly subsidizes education buyers, not education producers, a crucial point for two reasons. It maintains the church-state separation, and *control follows money much more often when the government buys something directly*. So, the history of control following money is largely irrelevant to choice expansion, especially expansions that would yield an OEI.

The regulatory strangulation of CPSs is an example of the government buying something directly, and mostly school chance, not choice. Public dollars flow straight to the schooling producers. "The regulatory overburden that plagues most charter schools and authorizers" demonstrates that "the charter sector [already] needs a regulatory overhaul."[16] It needs such an overhaul even though CPSs have not been around that long. But the absolute *need* for such overhauls will not change the primacy of regulation for CPSs. Since price control curbs CPS governance and accountability via market mechanisms, CPSs must suffer governance by central planning and detailed regulation. Choice expansion through tax credits, vouchers, or education savings accounts (see Chapter 12) directly supports customers, not producers.

There is an empirical basis for a serious concern for the fate of private schools on the current unlevel playing field, but much less so for concern that subsidy of consumers of schooling will make private schools into de facto public schools. Australia provides public support to all schools, and the private sector "is remarkably free of regulation" (Boyd, 1987). In the United States, experience with other major *purchase subsidy programs* doesn't support the fear of government control.

There is no basis to predict damage to private schools large enough to justify denial of even modest, widespread benefits to the other K–12 students. Nearly every example[17] of purchase assistance produced no new regulation of the subsidized buyers or their suppliers. The examples include food stamps, social security, Aid to Families with Dependent Children (AFDC = "welfare"), training vouchers, housing vouchers, and especially the GI Bill support that was spent at private universities, including church-affiliated colleges.

Some control followed a buyer subsidy for only a few *federal* programs. However, *state* governments have the larger role in K–12 policy, and they can regulate private schools even if they don't accept state money. States derive their authority to regulate from compulsory attendance laws.[18]

The regulation of colleges is the most often alleged example of control accompanying tax dollars. Admitting students subsidized by federal grants or loans forces compliance with antidiscrimination rules. Though Bast and Harmer (1997, p. 6, note 15) and Kirkpatrick (1997, p. 97)[19] argue that compliance is not burdensome—course offerings and content are not affected—Hillsdale College and Grove City College feel they have to exclude federally subsidized students.

Home loan subsidies for veterans and first-time homebuyers are another example. Builders who cater to those homebuyers must comply with some building requirements. Though it may annoy builders and net benefits are doubtful, an undue burden isn't readily observable.

The greatest threats to private schools are (1) schools that don't charge tuition (public schools, especially CPSs), (2) highly restrictive choice policies that force schools to only reject applicants at random if the demand exceeds the space available, and (3) programs that ban copayment (private schools must accept the public funds as full payment). Universal choice programs that prohibit copayment largely curb services that cost more than the publicly funded amount. No one would pay thousands more for a few hundred dollars' worth of extra service.

The 1998 "Private School Plan" approved by the Houston School District[20] is a good example of the second threat. To get district money, a school must accept the $3,575 payment as full payment, and "schools have to meet state accreditation standards, *abide by state laws governing public schools* [emphasis added], and accept all students, regardless of conduct and academic performance"—virtually become a TPS. Students can attend the pseudo-private schools only if they are failing in a low-performing school.

Recall from Chapter 3 that the 1999 Florida program exemplifies the second threat and, along with Milwaukee, also the third (copayment prohibited = price control).

COMPETITION AND ETERNAL VIGILANCE

Parental choice policies that maximize openness to TPS alternatives minimize the risk of debilitating rules. And openness does not compromise other important reform goals. As upcoming chapters argue, the opposite is more likely true. When competition is weak, the authorities have to use rules to pursue what would otherwise have been accomplished through market-imposed discipline.

Competition from new firms is the key regulatory mechanism of most of the economy. Choice proposals that create the conditions described in Chapter 2 can benefit private school students enormously, including, especially, the many children who will transfer to the private schools that do not exist yet.

The likelihood of burdensome regulation is very small with any large-scale parental choice program. Choice proposals typically contain language that discourages new restrictions on private schools. In addition, a coalition large enough to enact significant parental choice can defend it against all but the most covert, marginal assaults. Examples like the Houston plan are important exceptions, but even the weak versions of parental choice are usually no threat to the autonomy of most existing private schools. A key reason is that most current private schools are church affiliated. Regulations targeted at them would violate the constitutional separation of church and state.

Secular private schools get no protection from the First Amendment, but they are scarce. Restriction-laden parental choice will keep their numbers small, and the small constituencies of secular private schools places them in the greatest jeopardy of increased regulation. However, in an OEI, secular private schools will have much larger constituencies, and pro-regulation forces will be much weaker.

Fear of debilitating regulation of private schools is a serious problem. It contributes to inertia. The current funding and governance process will survive anything but a well-conceived assault by united choice expansion advocates. Choice advocates must minimize the risk of increased regulation, resolve to maintain eternal vigilance against it, and convince disaffected conservatives and libertarians that alternate risks to private schools and the nation are a much greater threat. Support for an OEI version of parental choice is the best way to do that.

A move toward an OEI is self-reinforcing. By minimizing the risk of debilitating regulation, such a move will bring back some dissident conservatives. The return of dissident conservatives will help to reorient the parental choice movement to the critical objective: reform of the entire system. Only openness through nondiscrimination in funding children can accomplish that. While the fear of increased regulation receives too much attention, cost issues—the subject of the next chapter—do not receive enough attention.

NOTES

1. Joe LeConte, "Schools Learn That Vouchers Can Have a Hidden Cost," *Wall Street Journal*, January 26, 1999.

2. Gregory Fossedal, "Help for Schools? Try Deregulation," *Wall Street Journal*, March 27, 1996. That was before the subsequent more than doubling in the number of federal programs, all with conditions attached. https://www.cato.org/publications/policy-analysis/restoring-responsible-government-cutting-federal-aid-states

3. https://en.wikisource.org/wiki/Executive_Order_13791

4. Linda Morrison, *The Tax Credits Program for School Choice*, National Center for Policy Analysis Policy Report #213 (Mackinaw, MI, 1998), summarized in a April 27, 1998, *Wall Street Journal* editorial by Ronald Trowbridge.

5. Murray Rothbard, *Free Market* (January 1994), 1. Recall the CPS regulation discussion in Chapter 4. See also coauthor JM's Chapter 10 in DeAngelis and McCluskey (2020).

6. John Miller, "Opting Out," *New Republic*, November 30, 1992, 12–13; Sude et al. (2018).

7. Charley Reese, "Vouchers Are a Bad Idea," *Orlando Sentinel*, November 19, 1998.

8. Quentin Quade, "Must Tax Dollars Kill School Independence?," Blum Center website, https://www.marquette.edu/blum/taxkill.html, accessed August 8, 2000.

9. Quentin Quade, "Strap on the Armor and Go: Never Give In!," *School Reform News*, June 1998, 20, 16.

10. Jeff Archer, "Chicago Catholics to Reform Their School Funding," *Education Week*, January 13, 1999, 1, 14.

11. Jeff Archer, "Chicago Catholics to Reform Their School Funding," *Education Week*, January 13, 1999, 1, 14.

12. https://nces.ed.gov/programs/coe/indicator_cgc.asp. The published data do not include the likely significant Pandemic-induced decline in 2020.

13. Joe Klein, "Parochial Concerns," *Newsweek*, September 22, 1996, 27.

14. Quentin Quade, "Must Tax Dollars Kill School Independence?," Blum Center website, https://www.marquette.edu/blum/taxkill.html, accessed August 8, 2000.

15. Quentin Quade, "Must Tax Dollars Kill School Independence?" Blum Center website, https://www.marquette.edu/blum/taxkill.html, accessed August 9, 2000.

16. https://fordhaminstitute.org/national/commentary/betsy-devos-wrong-about-accountability-schools-choice

17. Bast and Harmer (1997); Quentin Quade, "Must Tax Dollars Kill School Independence?," Blum Center website, https://www.marquette.edu/blum/taxkill.html, accessed August 8, 2000.

18. Since attendance at a "school" is mandatory, the government must establish and enforce a definition of a "school." Milton Friedman, "The Only Solution Is Competition (Interview of Friedman by George Clowes)," *School Reform News*, December 1998, 20, 16–17.

19. The Supreme Court upheld the federal intervention because Congress had specifically stated that their intent was to aid particular *institutions* (emphasis in Kirkpatrick, 1997).

20. "Houston School District OKs Private School Plan," *School Reform News*, June 1998, 11.

Chapter 6

The Neglect of Costs

The status quo is unacceptable at any price, but that doesn't make cost irrelevant, either as a reform outcome or as a defect of the current system. The cost issue is especially important to households that have no school-age children and to families who believe that their suburban school is good.[1] Inflation-adjusted outlays of the public school system rose rapidly even when the decline in achievement was most rapid, and the official public-sector costs understate the full cost (Lieberman & Haar, 2003). Real growth in per-pupil outlays (172% from 1960 to 1990; another 39% from 1991 to 2018),[2] as well as non-monetary indicators such as student, teacher, and non-teaching staff growth (+96%, +252%, and +702% from 1950 to 2009, respectively)[3] and administrative support,[4] did not yield noteworthy, much less proportionate, achievement gains.

Only recently have *some* achievement measures, such as test scores, stopped falling. Having perhaps hit bottom, some test scores rose. Proficiency rates are still quite low. In addition, there is considerable suspicion that demographic changes such as reduced child poverty,[5] test-specific coaching, and changes in the tests are responsible[6] for the rebound. Indicators such as the high cost of remedial courses for college freshmen suggest continued deterioration in TPS effectiveness.[7]

Though expenditure statistics cannot include the information collection, communication, decision-making, contract enforcement, and access costs that parents incur, such "transaction costs" are important. Again, effects vary from typical restriction-laden programs that shuffle a few children among little-changed existing schools to the open education industry (OEI) version that can change the system. The latter has lower transaction costs, which are probably much lower than the transaction costs of the current system.

MORE MONEY?!

The incomplete official data[8] indicate that per-pupil expenditures average over $13,000 per year, triple the inflation-adjusted 1965 level.[9] There are many examples (urban systems such as New York, New Jersey, and Washington, DC) of school systems with per-pupil outlays well over $20,000 per year. Nearly all private schools spend less per pupil, which is still true after adjustments account for differences in public and private schools' obligations.[10] Literally hundreds of studies (the vast majority) fail to associate higher expenditures with better performance (Hanushek, 1997), though labor market studies find that there is a small significant effect on earnings. That does not mean that schools cannot use increased resources to improve, only that they usually do not.

In 1999, $100,000 to $200,000 in taxes supported a classroom of 20 children, and an average teacher cost less than half of the lower figure.[11] We've seen that approximately double in 20 years, with considerable variation by place and where the estimate is found (what is counted). That certainly represents a drop in productivity (Hoxby, 2004).

Still, many analysts assert that more money is the answer to the achievement crisis. They often pursue that by lawsuit (Hanushek, 2006). Choice opponents like Kevin Smith and Kenneth Meier (1995) probably still find it "hard to fathom how educational policymakers can realistically hope to improve student performance given the limited resources at their disposal" (p. 21). Calls for increased spending never specify existing per-pupil spending levels.

TPS–PRIVATE COMPARISONS

Achievement

Unqualified private school–TPS achievement comparisons are a major concession to OEI opponents such as Albert Shanker and Bella Rosenberg,[12] Kevin Smith and Ken Meier (1995),[13] and skeptics such as Donald Frey (1992) and Dan Goldhaber (1996). Standardized test scores "are a crude measure of success."[14] They do not reflect many of the advantages that private schools must have to achieve their high levels of parental satisfaction. Criteria such as moral climate, discipline, safety, and individual attention are especially important in the vast majority of relatively inexpensive private schools that have no snob appeal.

Parents who choose private schools for nonreligious reasons, quite often including sectarian schools, would not keep paying the tuition without large net benefits. Of course, choice opponents make comparisons that are least favorable to private schools. For example, Shanker and Rosenberg used 1990 National Assessment of Educational Progress (NAEP) data to point out that "students in *all* schools [public and private; emphasis in the original] are achieving at disastrously low levels."[15] Frey made a similar comparison.

The key qualification of the test score comparisons is private schools' financial handicap; they must compete against much better funded, zero-tuition public schools. The private schools that are most often compared to public schools are the secular schools that don't benefit from church subsidies and are therefore more vulnerable to financial problems. Comparisons underutilize and understate private schools' cost effectiveness advantages.

Cost

The private school sector's mix of low-price, church-subsidized parochial schools; expensive elite schools; and a few in between those extremes complicates direct comparisons. Also, analysts often overcorrect for TPSs being responsible for all children.[16] Expecting every school, rather than the whole system, to engage any child increases cost while reducing the quality of services to all students, for example, through huge distractions that arise from mainstreaming special needs children. We mostly should not compare TPS and private, especially when both are massively, unwisely shackled.

But choice advocates should make much greater use of cost comparisons (Savas, 1982, p. 102), especially cost differences between the TPS origin of school choice program participants and the church subsidy–adjusted cost of private schools chosen by the program participants. The latter cost is typically much lower. For example, Alabama Accountability Act (AAA) participants achieved at about the average for all Alabama students for about half the cost, even though most AAA participants were drawn from just the Alabama TPSs (Merrifield & Ortiz, 2014) formally designated as "failed."

Low-cost private schools typically produce equal or better measured performance even though cost data likely understate private schools' cost advantages. Public-sector cost data are incomplete (Lieberman, 1993), and efforts to control for differences favor public schools. Every attempt is made to completely factor out the special needs expenses of TPSs, with the result that comparisons do not favor private schools as much as they should. For example, the comparisons adjust the private school cost estimates to reflect that every TPS campus accepts nearly every child. The adjustments don't take into account that failure to specialize inflates costs. It costs more per child to offer special education services on nearly every campus.

Spreading special services over many campuses also creates greater mismatches between the service requirements of children and the skills available on a specific campus. Mismatches reduce the quality of services special needs children receive.

Parental choice and specialization would also cut costs and improve the quality of many of the elective courses offered to mainstream students. The use of attendance zones rather than choice to decide each school's users elevates the appearance of special needs children by raising the variability in student skills, interests, and learning modes seen on each campus. Specialized private schools chosen by their users serve special needs much more efficiently. The cost comparisons also overlook the greater level of parental satisfaction private schools achieve.

Private schools already serve children that TPSs don't pretend to serve adequately.[17] Taxpayers pay to enroll thousands of children in private schools, but school authorities, not parents, exercise choice.

THE COSTS OF CHOICE

Perception

Higher costs seem obvious to the people who think only in terms of very limited choice. Henry Levin and Cyrus Driver (1997) said that choice expansion—defined as a restriction-laden voucher program—would mean cost increases of up to 25% or more. Edward Fiske made an even more puzzling generalization.

Based on a study of Cambridge, Massachusetts's controlled choice,[18] Fiske (1991) said, "All parties must acknowledge that choice will cost more" (p. 196). It is debatable whether controlled choice is even real parental choice. It means that parents identify their three favorite TPSs before district officials choose the school in pursuit of racial balance,[19] which is not necessarily one of the most preferred three.[20] Certainly, controlling choice creates costly administrative functions that are unnecessary in an OEI.

Hold-harmless approaches to parental choice keep the TPS from losing money when students leave. Since the public money that assists the transfer from the assigned TPS does not come from the school district budget, hold-harmless approaches drive up costs by design. For example, Puerto Rico funded parental choice from the sale of some telecommunications assets. Participants used $1,500 vouchers for private school tuition or to move to a different TPS. Puerto Rican TPSs gain the $1,500 voucher amount when they accept a transfer, but do not lose $1,500 when someone leaves, an unintended incentive to drive turnover. Hold-harmless plans are expensive, they reduce competitive pressures (Hoxby, 1998),[21] however slight, and as the Puerto Rico example illustrates, they can create perverse incentives.

With tax revolts heard and seen often, choice expansion advocates must vigorously refute sweeping generalizations about choice expansion costs. But, rather than explain that administrative costs depend upon which version of choice expansion is adopted, choice expansion advocates often make another mistake. To deflect the accusations that choice adds costs, choice expansion advocates propose a lower level of public support for TPS leavers (discrimination) so that the savings cover the extra costs that mostly arise from limiting choice.

Through the school choice fiscal notes calculator, we can at least deal with concrete estimates.[22] The COVID pandemic's fiscal impacts may cause much-increased calculator use to optimize the fiscal savings potential of choice expansion, that is, use choice expansion to cut taxpayer burdens, likely with a positive effect on school system performance.

Reality

Studies of parental choice costs, like the findings of Levin and Driver, have only shown that restrictive versions of choice are at least as costly as the status quo. That's no surprise. Implementing restriction-laden private school choice expansions and public school choice doesn't eliminate any administrative functions, but it'll add some to track student movement and shift resources. In addition, limited flight from the least popular TPSs could raise capital costs by creating excess school capacity.

It would not require an expansion of the bureaucracy to establish the critical elements of an OEI. The authorities won't have to manage parents' OEI choices. In fact, an OEI will probably shed many of the administrative expenses that characterize the status quo.

District offices, if they don't gradually disappear entirely, will likely look more like the much smaller administrative apparatus of the Catholic school system than the much larger administrative structure typical of large urban districts.[23] An OEI will probably make schools smaller and more numerous, so choice expansion may not even permanently increase families' transportation costs.

Less restrictive versions of parental choice that maximize competitive forces can operate with the current level of public funding of K–12 education services, or less. An OEI would provide similar children with the same public funding—probably through the weighted student formula already in widespread use for TPSs—no matter which school they attend, so an OEI would achieve funding equalization (a court-mandated outcome in a growing number of states) without busing, formation of magnet schools, or creation of controlled choice.

Through school formation, exit, and pricing, an OEI tells the authorities when public funding is consistent with their goals. Changes in the number of sellers equalize the profit rates of markets with similar levels of risk, so education entrepreneurs will open more of the most profitable schools until they earn only normal profit rates. Families unable to add on with private funds, or with a third-party stipend, get good-fit schooling as long as the public funding level is enough to cause numerous schools to accept the public funds as nearly[24] full payment.

Overcapacity and low-value frills would signal that public support is excessive just as they did in the pre-deregulation airline industry. Most of the fares set by the Civil Aeronautics Board (CAB) were very attractive to the airlines. The CAB protected the regulated airlines from competition from new airlines, so the rivalry for passengers occurred through more frequent flights (overcapacity) and low-value frills that ended when deregulation created competition to lower fares.

The Outlook

In an OEI, private school pupils receive as much per-pupil public funding as TPS students. With current public K–12 spending, most private schools will have much more than they spend now,[25] even without money from copayment. Therefore, significant excess capacity is a very likely early, temporary outcome of an OEI publicly funded with as much money as TPSs spend now.

Because of typically strong condemnation of education cuts, the authorities may not react to evidence of overcapacity with funding cuts. However, since excess capacity reduces the pressure to increase funding, spending should at least rise less rapidly than before. Funding growth at less than the rate of price inflation is the most likely cost-cutting scenario.

There are three reasons why such a cost-cutting scenario is likely to accompany major improvements: (1) Rule compliance will consume fewer resources. Since high rule compliance costs are inherent in government operations, TPSs may have difficulty competing with private schools. Therefore, an OEI may reduce the number of children attending schools burdened by the expense of district offices. (2) The imperative to remain choice worthy will strengthen productivity incentives. (3) Each household's freedom to supplement their public funds with private money can cause education funding to rise alongside a reduction in taxpayers' burden.[26] Choice advocates must make that case.

OMITTED PUBLIC-SECTOR COSTS

U.S. Department of Education estimates of public school system expenditures per pupil suffer from several major omissions (Lieberman, 1993, pp. 118–122).[27] For example, the federal component does not include federal spending on education research and development, training, or remedial or compensatory programs like Head Start. Fees charged to parents and donations of time (parent volunteers, school board members, and meeting attendees) or money are not included.

The state component omits some pensions, employer contributions to social security, textbooks, administrative costs, school district labor relations, judicial costs, and noneducational agencies performing K–12 services. The school district figures do not include capital outlay, interest, capital equipment, and the rental value of already-paid-for facilities.

TRANSACTION COSTS

Economists believe that reasoned pursuit of self-interest underlies virtually all personal choices and societal outcomes. That means policies such as government ownership of school systems result from pursuit of self-interest by individuals in the context of political institutions. Inertia and special interest pressures underlie a rational explanation of public school system dominance of the K–12 system.

The current system began with the early 1800s combination of modest taxpayer support for private schools, a growing number of Catholic Church–run schools, and anti-Catholic bias. The public school system arose to deny public funding to Catholic schools.

TPSs spread and became deeply entrenched because they created powerful special interests and because private schools struggle to survive in an economic environment where they must charge hefty tuition for a less expensive product than TPSs offer for "free." The belief—despite mounting evidence to the contrary—that only government-run schools can produce the melting-pot effect of the "common school" (discussed in Chapter 10) bolsters inertia.

Some economists have sought out more contemporaneous explanations of why the key elements of a severely criticized status quo are so durable. John Lott (1987) said that governments run school systems to consolidate their power through indoctrination.

Byron Brown (1992) said that governments run school systems to reduce uncertainty and minimize transaction costs. Brown notes that schools do not specialize and offers an explanation consistent with the pursuit of self-interest. Brown said parents want a system of uniform attempts at one-size-fits-all because "school choices are lumpy (lots of all-or-nothing choices) and fraught with uncertainty" (p. 294). So, Brown says that parents demand "comprehensive uniformity" to eliminate the time costs and potential for error inherent in choice making from a diverse menu of schooling options.

Brown said the political process created "an *implicit* [emphasis in the original] contract between schools and their clients (students, parents, and taxpayers)" to use comprehensive large schools to address student diversity. According to that rationale, clients want schools to be "remarkably similar in substance and in means of production." Brown used private schools' failure to specialize much beyond religious instruction to support his assertion of clients' interest in comprehensive uniformity and disdain for specialization.

In light of differences in teacher strengths and students' engagement factors, Brown's published claim that a diverse clientele really does want a uniform product is truly incredible. It deserves more attention lest it become another justification of the public school system's monopoly on public funds.

Brown is wrong about the nature of the implicit contract between the public and school decision makers. We have 51 systems of uniformly comprehensive schools because parents would not tolerate assignment of children to specialized neighborhood schools. Significant specialization is feasible only if we end the funding discrimination against the children for whom the assigned TPS is a poor fit.

The Transaction Costs of the Current System

Comprehensive uniformity yields some simplification, but the benefits are small, and it creates offsetting burdens. Influencing decision making is difficult, and parents still expend much effort to exercise choice. Right now, most families have only TPS choice via relocation, so they must evaluate neighborhoods, commutes, and possibly job changes to choose a school. The perceived differences in TPSs are still big enough to make them the number-one basis for residential choice, and a top determinant of home prices.[28]

Some families conceal a false address to escape the dilemma between undereducated, perhaps physically threatened children and a costly move. Many middle-class families cheat to become eligible for low-income vouchers.[29] Most people take the law very seriously, so exercising "black market school choice"[30] creates a significant psychological burden. It's common enough that taxpayers fund detection and enforcement efforts.[31] Those huge transaction costs may top the savings that result from the greater ease of comparing uniformly comprehensive TPSs.

The alleged "implicit contract" (Brown, 1992) between school decision makers and their clients must adjust to change with virtually no communication on school policies. There isn't even much involvement in school elections. The provisions of the alleged implicit contract are certainly not clear to the authorities. The overlapping authorities keep changing their minds, adding new rules, including contradictory ones. "When federal, state, and local programs and things the general public wants the schools to do all arrive at the same time, it gets crazy" (Freiwald, 1996, p. 180). Contrary to the alleged implicit contract, the authorities pursue limited forms of specialization with growing numbers of magnet schools and CPSs, and other versions of public school choice.

The futility of participation in school policy making,[32] and all of the well-established reasons for low participation in political decision making, are better reasons for the minimal communication between clients and policy makers. The political process suffers from a lot of apathy because participants bear 100% of the high participation costs, but most will enjoy only a fraction of the benefits, and then only if their position prevails. Long ballots and frequent elections dilute awareness of most ballot propositions and public offices.

Because people naturally respond to the large number of issues and high participation costs by focusing their efforts where the stakes are highest for them, educators have especially high participation rates in school district elections. As a result, teacher union clout greatly exceeds their share of the electorate. Combined with the typically low voter turnouts of school district elections, teacher unions often have enough clout to pick the people that ostensibly represent the taxpaying public in collective bargaining. Union officials often sit across the collective bargaining table from public officials they elected, including recent union officials.

Issues that would arouse the "masses" to overthrow entrenched special interests define the real implicit contract—things like no big tax hikes, don't change attendance zone boundaries to lower my property value and assign my kids to worse schools, and don't assign my kids to a specialized school. Because of a poorly informed public,[33] the key issues are few and general. The controlling special interests do not have to endure much scrutiny or accountability.

Weak, perverse accountability may be why school board failure is common, and perhaps even the norm. "In district after district, they repeat a handful of practical errors" (Smoley, 1999). *Governing Public Schools* urged a reassessment of school board governance (Danzberger et al., 1992). And the 20th Century Fund authored a scathing assessment of school board governance;[34] more recently, see Chester Finn's 2006 call to "jettison one of the chief obstacles to reform."[35]

The problems cited in those reports often appear in the mainstream media. The *San Antonio Express-News*'s (November 15, 1995) editors stated this common viewpoint: "Career school board members put petty politics ahead of children and education. Entrenched politicians tend to keep superintendents' careers relatively short." Indeed, school district superintendent is a very hard, yet ultimately unnecessary job. It is tough to satisfy a diverse clientele with a uniform product, and school principals can run schools.

Eugene Smoley found that citizens are "suspicious of the board members they elect" (Smoley, 1999, p. 2). Donald Roberts (1990) was not as kind: "The weakest links in the American chain of poor public school performance may well be ill-prepared, poorly educated, shortsighted, parochial-minded, weak-willed local school board members" (p. 58).

The combination of the system's resistance to change, disappointment with K–12 outcomes, its periodic status as the nation's number-one political issue,[36] and frequent status as a state's number-one political issue do not support an assertion that participation is low because of complacency or satisfaction with the status quo. It suggests that large transaction costs probably frustrate efforts to bring about substantive changes.

Huge extra transaction costs lie elsewhere in the political/administrative process that governs school policies. According to the OECD[37] data cited previously, the 1994 U.S. systems contained three classroom teachers per four non-teaching staff, the lowest ratio of teaching to non-teaching personnel in the OECD's survey of its multi-country membership. Most of the OECD countries allow more school choice than the United States, and they have more school-based decision making, though none of them have an OEI. Choice and efficiency are correlated (Wolfram & Coulson, 2009).

The lopsided OECD data are not surprising. The U.S. K–12 system contains many layers of control—federal, state, local, union contract—and overlapping constraints. Much of the administrative structure exists to regulate, monitor, or comply with the actions of administrators and legislators in another part of the system. Carl Ball and Steven Goldman (1997) noted that

> education is composed of several separate systems that function without an overall plan. A great deal of resources and personnel are wasted as a result of unstable governance, lack of incentives to improve, structures that reinforce continuity, and the absence of quality controls.[38]

In the 1990s there was some interest in abolishing the Texas Education Agency (TEA), but debate of that idea ended when State Representative Christine Hernandez pointed out that most of the TEA was federally funded and necessary to comply with federal mandates.[39] There is no "overall plan" because the system is compliance driven, rather than performance driven (Ball & Goldman, 1997). Compliance issues require lots of paperwork, meetings, and enforcement effort. Lauro Cavazos, President Bush's (41) first secretary of education, made this observation:

> This top-down hierarchical structure is ineffective and inefficient. State and district administrators have limited contact with individual schools and virtually no association with students and teachers. (Cavazos, 1991, p. 357)

Together, federal, state, and district mandates leave little autonomy in schools and classrooms. Though a major aim of the rules is greater accountability to the public and policy makers, the combined effect is often the opposite. The maze of rules leads to costly reporting requirements, frustrating contradictions, and demoralizing micromanagement that denies educators many ways to excel. It also shields them from blame for failure.

Such autonomy is especially important in schools that match clients and educators via assignment, rather than by choice. If teachers had more control of the curriculum, methods, and textbooks they use, it would end some of the tension that results from principals, teachers, and parents (Sarason, 1990) not choosing each other. Less autonomy and freedom of choice generate transaction costs through uncooperative behavior, complaints, conflict resolution efforts, and lawsuits.

Union contracts are among the most significant restrictions. Taxpayers pick up the tab for whatever is agreed to, but the secrecy that shrouds the process means the general public has little opportunity to influence the key contract provisions before they attain the force of law. The collective bargaining process, and other aspects of establishing and maintaining worker organizations, is another significant source of transaction costs. Costly strikes, the ultimate in transaction costs, occasionally make big headlines.

Several studies assert that union contracts deter achievement (Lieberman, 1997, pp. 217–225, notes 14–20 on p. 288; more recently, Munk, 1998), and that they contribute significantly to hostility between teachers and school officials.[40] The compliance issues that union contracts establish often go beyond personnel policy, and the union presence makes it extremely difficult to dismiss unproductive employees.

Diane Ravitch, before her conversion to "status quo + money" cheerleader, put it more bluntly. Referring to TPSs that had resisted at least 15 years of intense reform efforts, including many that often had dangerous conditions, Ravitch (1994) noted the incredible fact that "somebody's children are assigned to those schools."

The difficulty dismissing unproductive employees imposes several large transaction costs. Giving troublesome employees glowing performance evaluations to get other schools to hire them devalues such information. That makes it harder to make personnel decisions, and unproductive people get a chance to mess up more schools. Performance evaluation skepticism reduces the mobility of experienced people and tilts hiring choices toward the inexperienced.

Another frequent, costly ploy is to pay unproductive employees to do nothing,[41] or shift them into administrative positions, sometimes new positions created just for them. In addition to the direct cost of their compensation, concealment of the practice usually requires the creation of an important-sounding job. At a minimum, the effect is another distraction for teachers, and it may mean more paperwork or another infringement on teacher autonomy.

Corruption is a final source of transaction costs. Public officials spend other folks' money, which is the least motivated type of expenditure. It creates a temptation to channel some into their personal bank accounts. There is much evidence (Segal, 2004; Wirt and Kirst, 1997) that costly safeguards are far from foolproof. The cost of nepotism, cronyism, and patronage is even harder to quantify. Since it probably affects who is hired more than how many are hired, the effect on quality probably exceeds the impact on expenditures.

The Real Reason for "Comprehensive Uniformity"

As noted above, policy makers cannot and should not assign children to specialized schools. The diverse interests and aptitudes within each attendance area, and politics' appearance-of-fairness imperative, demand a similar diverse menu from each school to which children are assigned based on where they live. The very limited types of specialization that exist in some public school systems exist outside neighborhood schools.

A restaurant analogy may help clarify this issue. Eateries are not as "lumpy"[42] as school choices, and the commitment is shorter, but picking a new eatery is "fraught with uncertainty" (Brown, 1992). Though restaurant patrons are clearly not against specialization or afraid to make choices, a system of taxpayer-funded neighborhood restaurants would cause the public to demand comprehensive restaurants to serve all major tastes, and they'd be uniformly comprehensive for fairness. You can't assign diverse people to any kind of genuinely specialized restaurant.

For most of the same reasons that we have very few broadly effective TPSs, we'd then have a lot of lousy restaurants that most people would attend only because taxpayer funding would give the government restaurants a considerable price advantage. The quality of the food would suffer immediately from chefs' inability to specialize.[43] Because every restaurant would have to try to prepare a similar diverse menu, chefs would have to prepare many meals far outside a manageable area of culinary expertise.

A restaurant analogy demonstrates another key point. You can address consumers' aversion to uncertainty without comprehensive uniformity.

Restaurants such as McDonald's, Subway, and Pizza Hut are part of franchises that are global in scope. A mix of franchises and independent restaurants provides diners with the genuine variety a diverse population demands, and a degree of certainty that mobile, risk-averse people want. The same mixture of franchises—public school systems and independent schools—would characterize an OEI. In fact, that mixture exists already, but on a very small scale because the private sector is tiny and dominated by church-run schools.

The Apparent Uniformity of Private Schools

What about the observation that private schools don't specialize much beyond religious instruction? There is a two-part answer: (1) Except for religion, there isn't much demand for subject-specific specialization at the lower grade levels, and the precarious competitive situation of private schools—having to demand a large payment for a less expensive service—precludes much subject-specific specialization at any grade level.

To hold tuition levels down, private schools have to concentrate on the basics. They focus on subjects that many parents will demand and on subject areas with enough qualified teachers that some will work for much less than TPS salaries.[44] In fact, instruction in religion is probably the only subject specialty area that is both cheap enough to produce yet valuable enough to convince a large number of families to incur thousands of extra dollars in school expenses. Church dominance of the private sector supports that belief. An OEI's equal taxpayer support of private school and TPS students will produce more subject area specialization, especially at the higher grades.

(2) Subject-specific specialization is not the only kind of useful specialization. Private schools' propensity to be much smaller than TPSs is a quite significant form of specialization. So is the greater level of parental involvement. Structure, flexibility, and focus on discipline are other present forms of specialization. Student ability differences, special needs, and use of technology are growing areas of specialization.

Lower Transaction Costs with an OEI

An OEI will reduce transaction costs in several ways. Families can then exercise choice without changing neighborhoods. When TPSs have private alternatives with roughly equal public funding, the TPSs may trim some overhead to increase funding for classroom activity. To the extent that government-run institutions actually require significantly more administration, TPSs will become increasingly rare as more efficient alternatives become more popular.

An OEI will not eliminate corruption, any more than it can fundamentally change human nature. Periodic episodes of fraud are inevitable, but chronically corrupt situations persist only with a captive audience. Now, only legal-political means can end corrupt political regimes. In an OEI, corruption sows the seeds of its own destruction by driving paying customers to more efficient schools.

The nature of education services, and the infrastructure used to deliver them now, is such that episodic corruption is likely to be less common in an OEI than in most other markets. School owners, and their parent/child clients, will greatly prefer a continuous long-term business relationship. Reputation will be a very large determinant of choice worthiness.

The difficulty of converting much of the physical capital required to deliver education services to other profitable uses encourages education entrepreneurs to adopt a long-term planning horizon, and it discourages hit-and-run episodes of fraud.

In an OEI, many school employees will learn that they can achieve more[45] by shopping the market than through collective bargaining. The greater payoff to individual professionalism will weaken the rationale for collective bargaining, and with it the reason for teachers to tax themselves to hire collective bargaining agents. Professionalizing teachers and empowering good teachers, rather than forcing them into collective bargaining situations that can hurt them, will eliminate a huge impediment to change and a significant source of transaction costs.

Another huge impediment to change is the confusion of the goal of education with the dominant delivery mechanism of TPSs. For much of the public, taxing themselves to support TPSs is synonymous with supporting the education of children. Chapter 8 discusses this issue, in particular, the effect on the many choice advocates who also believe it or accept it as a constraint.

NOTES

1. John Miller, "Why School Choice Lost," *Wall Street Journal*, November 4, 1993. Widely called the diversity excuse: "they lament the condition of public schools overall, but are quick to exempt the schools their own kids attend"; https://www.theatlantic.com/magazine/archive/2010/12/your-child-left-behind/308310/. Also refuted by Lance Izumi's "Not as Good as You Think Series": https://www.schoolsystemreformstudies.net/wp-content/uploads/Opinion-Forum/Interpretation%20of%20Evidence%20%E2%80%93%20Misleading%20Findings/NAGAYT%20-%20Izumi.pdf

2. A calculation made by Lamdin and Mintrom (1997) from raw data in the *Digest of Education Statistics*, National Center for Education Statistics, 1995, 82. For 1991–2018: https://nces.ed.gov/programs/digest/d20/tables/dt20_236.15.asp

3. https://www.edchoice.org/wp-content/uploads/2017/05/Back-to-the-Staffing-Surge-by-Ben-Scafidi.pdf

4. https://www.edchoice.org/wp-content/uploads/2017/05/Back-to-the-Staffing-Surge-by-Ben-Scafidi.pdf. Other types of staff "support" have also risen dramatically. According to an international comparison by the Organization for Economic Co-operation and Development (OECD), the United States is the only country with fewer teachers than non-teaching staff (a 3:4 ratio compared to a 5:2 ratio for the other countries examined by the OECD). See the 1995 OECD report: *Education at a Glance: OECD Indicators* (Paris).

5. https://fordhaminstitute.org/national/commentary/hypothesis-nclb-era-achievement-gains-stemmed-largely-declining-child-poverty

6. Steve Stecklow, "SAT Scores Rise Strongly After Test Is Overhauled," *Wall Street Journal*, August 24, 1995, B1, B12.

7. David Wessel, "The Outlook," *Wall Street Journal*, November 9, 1998, A1; https://cdn.americanprogress.org/content/uploads/2016/09/29120411/CostOfCatchingUp2-reportINTRO.pdf

8. Many costs are not included in the official estimates. For the lengthy list of excluded items, see Lieberman (1993, p. 119). For more detail, see Lieberman and Haar (2003).

9. $13,186 in 2019: https://usafacts.org/data/topics/people-society/education/K–12-education/spending-per-student-in-K–12-public-schools/

10. Robert Genetski, "Private Schools, Public Savings," *Wall Street Journal*, July 8, 1992; at least one third cheaper in the Chicago area.

11. For a more detailed example, see Jami Lund, "How Much Bureaucracy Is Carried by Classroom Teachers?," Evergreen Freedom Foundation, *Policy Highlighter* 9, no. 5 (March 31, 1999).

12. Chapter in Hakim et al. (1994).

13. "If regulation is ceded from democratic institutions to the market, public schools will mimic private schools" (Smith & Meier, 1995, p. 64).

14. Terry Moe in "Responses to a Harvard Study on School Choice: Is It a Study at All?," Pioneer Institute for Public Policy Research, *Dialogue*, 1995, 6.

15. Chapter in Hakim et al. (1994, p. 60).

16. Robert Genetski, "Private Schools, Public Savings," *Wall Street Journal*, July 8, 1992.

17. Janet R. Beales, "Educating the Uneducatable," *Wall Street Journal*, August 21, 1996.

18. https://newschoolsforneworleans.org/oneapp-is-now-nola-public-schools-common-enrollment-process-ncap-learn-whats-new-and-whats-stayed-the-same/

19. Cambridge's controlled limited choice persists, but in 2001 the objective changed to socioeconomic balance.

20. Most are "granted" their first choice, but 15% aren't allowed any of their three choices.

21. Hoxby (1998) found that "when competition has little fiscal implication, a public school is less likely to react."

22. http://school-choice-fiscal-notes-calculator.net/

23. Recall the OECD data cited in Chapter 2. OECD, *Education at a Glance: OECD Indicators* (Paris: OECD, 1995), 176–177.

24. Some scholars believe that public funds should never cover 100% of education expenses, even for low-income families. Having some out-of-pocket expense makes parents more demanding consumers. For examples, see the discussions in West (1994); Lieberman (1993); and Milton Friedman's views quoted in Amity Shlaes editorial, "The Next Big Free-Market Thing," *Wall Street Journal*, July 9, 1998.

25. David Boaz and R. Morris Barrett, "What Would a School Voucher Buy? The Real Cost of Private Schools," Cato Institute Briefing Papers #25, March 26, 1996.

26. The fiscal notes calculator, which includes a teacher salary impact component, predicted that a Texas ESA proposal would raise teacher salaries and total school system funding.

27. Omissions vary by state, and even by district within states sometimes.

28. See survey results cited in Wyckoff (1991); Hayes and Taylor (1996); and Yinger and Nguyen-Hoang (2011).

29. Mark Walsh, "Audit Criticizes Cleveland Voucher Program," *Education Week*, April 15, 1998.

30. Angie Garcia, "Vouchers Not Edgewood's Real Problem," *San Antonio Express-News*, December 6, 1998.

31. "Suburban districts are setting up elaborate programs to apprehend and expel the urban students who are sneaking into suburban schools in order to get a better education." David Boaz, "Five Myths About School Choice," *Education Week*, January 27, 1993, 36.

32. Individuals experience futility because organizations carry more political weight, and because authority is spread over several administrative levels. A. P. Dixon, "Parents: Full Partners in the Decision-Making Process," *NASSP Bulletin*, April 1992, 15–18, has documented that a feeling of powerlessness (futility) is the primary reason for the low level of parental involvement. Parental involvement is low now because of lack of support from educators, not lack of parental interest. Pierce (1993) reported similar findings.

33. See Lieberman's (1993) discussion of the impossibility of being well informed.

34. The Twentieth Century Fund, *Facing the Challenge: The Report of the Twentieth Century Fund Task Force on School Governance* (New York: Twentieth Century Fund, 1992).

35. https://www.educationnext.org/lost-at-sea/

36. The latest poll to confirm that long-standing fact is the Kaiser Family Foundation and Harvard University Survey cited in *Education Week*, October 21, 1998, p. 30. According to the Public Agenda Foundation, *Given the Circumstances: Teachers Talk About Public Education Today* (1996), "recent polls show that education has jumped to the top of the list of public concerns."

37. OECD, *Education at a Glance: OECD Indicators* (Paris: OECD, 1995): 176–177.

38. Similar sentiments are expressed elsewhere, including in considerable detail by Pogrow (1996).

39. Kemper Diehl, "Setting Out to Slay the TEA Dragon," *San Antonio Express-News*, December 12, 1993.

The Neglect of Costs 101

40. Ann Bradley, "Teachers' Pact Deters Achievement, Study Says," *Education Week*, October 1, 1997, 1, 13.

41. https://nypost.com/2020/08/15/nyc-pledged-to-ban-teacher-rubber-rooms-they-went-underground-instead/

42. Brown, like many other economists, uses the term "lumpy" to describe all-or-nothing choices, a situation where you cannot unpack and reassemble customized bundles of goods or services. For example, if you want to enroll your child in a program that is only available in one school, you have to accept all of the other characteristics of that school, including many you do not like. The program you want might come bundled with other school attributes you don't want.

43. It can't be because of low-quality chefs, because they'd be the same chefs as before the government set up the "public" restaurants. Over time, quality declines further reduced incentives because of the absence of profits and competition to motivate attentiveness to customer wants and risk-taking innovation.

44. The average is 73.5% according to Ballou and Podgursky (1997).

45. Even if a teacher realizes a lower salary (there may be none), they may value the changed working conditions more, including opportunities to specialize, smaller schools, better relationships with parents because parents have chosen the school rather than been assigned to it, etc.

Chapter 7

Fund Children or Institutions?

America's schools do not exist for teachers and other employees. Schools exist for the children.

—Robert Chase, president, National Education Association[1]

Systems are not sacred; children are.

—Ted Forstmann, CEO, Children's Scholarship Fund[2]

They [children], not the schools they attend, are our destiny.

—Hugh Price, president, Urban League[3]

Sacrificing . . . children for the sake of a process.

—Senator Joe Lieberman (D-CT)[4]

Our public school systems have a long history. Among Americans, only well-traveled people and education scholars can describe other school systems. Most citizens equate schooling with tax-supported schools staffed by government employees. They assume that the vast majority of children will attend public schools, especially TPSs. Education analyst and many-time New York City and State teacher of the year John Gatto noted that,

> among even the best of my fellow teachers, and among even the best of my students' parents, only a small number can imagine a different way to do things.[5]

The same is true for the district superintendents that I have spoken with, including those desperate for a "new system." They see not penalizing families for using private schools as public support for two school systems. Even conservative members of Congress such as Marge Roukema (R-NJ) see education funding in terms of systems, not support for children.

No matter how proposals of relief for private school costs are designed, the ultimate effect is to burden the taxpaying public with support of two school systems.[6]

Relief for private schools is not the reason to allocate school taxes through parental choice. Parental empowerment is a good idea because education outcomes take priority over the preservation of a long-standing process.

Choice opponents assert that we should support the dominance of public schools—their education finance monopoly—because the public schools dominate now.

> Voucher schemes will divert vital resources away from public schools. Nearly 46 million children attend public schools. America's tax dollars should be invested in public schools where 89 percent of school age children are enrolled.[7]
>
> With 90% of our nation's children attending public schools, we must commit ourselves to providing the world's best public education system.[8]

Providing a top public education system doesn't require an unlevel playing field between TPSs and alternatives that are better for *some* children. Indeed, the opposite is true. Quentin Quade (1996) stated the problem eloquently:

> When only one *means* is provided to achieve a good *end* [emphasis in the original], the means comes to be treated as an end-in-itself. When that happens, there is no effective way to evaluate and test the means, and criticism of it is portrayed as an attack on the end itself.

Charles Glenn said, "Blind self-righteousness persists among the public education establishment today."[9] That combination of narrow-mindedness and self-righteousness is a major part of the unproductive school choice debate and persistent education policy failure. We saw that during the pandemic with frequent prioritization of teachers' interests over students' interests.[10]

Even choice advocates often equate support for children with support for the public school system. That ends-means confusion and anti-market bias is also evident in the mainstream media. This passage from Walter Shapiro's article in *Time* is a good example:

> This [Friedman's voucher plan] extreme free-market proposal would literally destroy the public schools in order to save them. Few advocates of choice are willing to go that far.[11]

Note that "them" refers to the public schools. Friedman didn't want to destroy public schools or save them. His focus was the children, but Shapiro's focus was the public school system.

Choice opponents exploit the belief that support for children means supporting TPSs by asserting TPS ownership of school taxes. To them, it is not the per-pupil funding that matters. They want all of the money, even if it means less per TPS pupil. They insist on "no public funds for private schools." "Public money should be spent on public schools. We should not spend public monies on private institutions."[12] They oppose "private education at public expense."[13] Even though private school users pay taxes too, choice opponents want to limit public funding to the children enrolled in publicly owned, political process–controlled schools.

Choice opponents characterize parental choice proposals as attacks on the public school system—"vouchers harm public schools."[14] The opposite is more likely. Choice expansion helps TPSs by providing alternatives for the students not engaged by the mainstream pedagogy. The children who stay in the TPS—and their teachers—benefit from the exit of children for whom the mainstream pedagogy was not a good fit. That appears to be exactly what happened in San Antonio's Edgewood District,[15] where district schools improved despite no formal response to a privately funded universal voucher program. Unfortunately, choice proposals often reinforce that perception with promises not to harm TPSs.

An OEI will not be politically feasible until choice advocates sharply focus on the welfare of children. That requires political indifference to which institutions provide schooling (nondiscrimination). That means the public funding support for a particular child must be nearly the same whether they use a publicly or privately owned school. Since uniformity of any kind will serve a large share of the population badly (one size cannot fit all), barriers to choice are inconsistent with a focus on the welfare of children.

Anti-choice forces don't concede that keeping the public school system's monopoly on public funds is a higher priority than the welfare of children. The ends-means confusion is such that some may not even realize their policy proposals preserve a system that contains major barriers to private services that are already better for some children, and openness would improve those services. Public debate of OEI proposals would widely expose the focus on system preservation. Proposals to just transfer a few children to schools that are better fits for them do the opposite. *They implicitly sanctify the prioritization of system preservation.*

Chapter 7

THE SYMPTOMS

Choice opponents want us to believe that helping most children is synonymous with keeping the current governance and funding system and increasing its funding. However, disappointment with reform efforts makes it harder for choice opponents to reconcile their self-interest in a system in which they are powerful with the education needs of children.

Gradually, more people will realize "that the education establishment is waging a war against children" (Fox, 1997, p. 17). The COVID pandemic accelerated that process. Howard Fuller included a similar clause in his resignation (as Milwaukee Public Schools superintendent) statement: "In this city and other cities around the country, we don't put children first; we put systems first."[16]

Even some prominent Democrats have publicly agreed. Longtime U.S. senator Joseph Lieberman (D-CT) said the debate over parental choice is about whether we should do "what is necessary to put children first" or "preserve the status quo at all costs (sacrificing the hopes and aspirations of thousands of children for the sake of a process)."[17] Education scholar/analyst Joseph Viteritti (1999) noted that

> many charter laws have been written to put the demands of local school districts before the needs of children. To limit competition, the number of charter schools permitted to operate has been severely restricted. (p. 78)

What Dr. Viteritti said in 1999 is still true. The system is so deeply ingrained that even critics of the current system worry that parental choice will undermine the political support of TPSs. For example, Dan Goldhaber (1999) believes that the effect of "enhanced choice" on "support for TPS" is a critical issue. He said that the authorities should consider linking voucher value to public school spending so that people "who opt out of the public system still have some incentive to support it." The concern is troubling, but the challenge can yield a virtuous outcome. The same level of public funding should follow a child regardless of where the student enrolls. Nondiscrimination is the best thing to call it.

Choice advocates, like former Florida governor Jeb Bush, put the system first though he claimed otherwise.[18] As governor, he supported limited parental choice—only for children assigned to unacceptable TPSs. Governor Bush's own words contradict his claim that it is a "child-centered" program. "The whole point of this [Florida's voucher program] is to achieve the exact opposite result [failing schools are left behind]."[19]

Michigan's "Kids First! Yes!" November 2000 ballot initiative was another example.[20] Unless districts vote to support vouchers, only children in TPSs with high dropout rates are eligible for them, and the voucher is worth much less than the per-pupil funding of TPSs, which is state-sanctioned discrimination against children for whom the assigned TPS was seen as a poor fit. Both restrictions shortchange children to avoid appearing to harm TPSs.

Choice Opponents' Priorities

Choice opponents' priorities surface regularly. Former National Education Association (NEA) president Keith Geiger said that choice advocates should "quit talking about letting kids escape."[21] The 1996–1997 *NEA Handbook* says, "New approaches must not divert current funds from the regular public school programs" (Quade, 1997, p. 3). Longtime American Federation of Teachers (AFT) president Albert Shanker said, "I'll start worrying about kids when they start paying union dues."[22]

Former NEA president Robert Chase recognized choice opponents' growing credibility problem. Like longtime AFT president Shanker, Chase sought credibility with lip service to key concerns and widely shared beliefs such as the primacy of student welfare. Then he forgot the students and returned to the longtime NEA/AFT policy of maximizing TPS enrollments.

For example, there is widespread agreement that school infrastructure is in a sorry state and that public school performance is intolerable, yet Chase repeatedly refers to public schools as "cathedrals."[23] His most telling comment was that we should accept "our responsibility to redeem our institutions." Indeed, we've been committed to that. But decades of system-friendly reform frenzy have failed to produce the improvement we need. The public school system business plan—a central plan—will likely keep us from succeeding at it.

D. A. Weber, the former president of the NEA's California affiliate, was not as soft-spoken as Chase. Weber asserted that any threat to the public school system, even potential competition with only half the money per child (California's Proposition 174), is "evil" (Lieberman, 1994, p. 29). Weber said Prop 174 should not appear on the ballot because voting on a proposition to eliminate "education finance monopoly" (Quade, 1996) is an immoral act of the highest order. He contended that such a ballot proposition is no different than "voting on legalizing child prostitution" (Lieberman, 1994, p. 29) or to "empower" the Ku Klux Klan in some unspecified manner.[24]

Joan Buckley, an AFT officer, says letting children go to a school chosen by their parents is "abandonment."[25] Like then-AFT-president Sandra Feldman, Buckley is worried about what will happen to the public school system if children leave, not what will happen to the children if they have to stay. Reacting to the September 1999 court ruling against the Cleveland low-income voucher program, Feldman said, "Now we can make sure the money will be in the public schools."[26] Comments such as Feldman's, and titles like Robert Lowe and Barbara Miner's *Selling Out Our Schools* (1996), typify the focus on maximizing enrollment in the public school system, rather than maximizing the welfare of children. Those fears of free enterprise in open market settings also reveal pervasively bad economic education.

Similar statements were made about the court-terminated Florida voucher program, which is only barely parental choice and certainly does not threaten the dominant position of the public school system. Yet, Representative James Bush's (D-Miami) had this summary of the vote to enact the program: "It's like being at a funeral here today, a funeral for public education. . . . After two years, we will go to the cemetery and put public education in the ground, ashes to ashes, dust to dust."[27] We see the identical rhetoric now directed at Arizona's universal education savings account (ESA).

Of course, nothing of the kind actually occurred, nor will the Arizona ESA undermine the public education commitment.[28] For large-scale programs, the opposite is much more likely. The opposite actually happened in the small Edgewood District on the west side of San Antonio.[29] Moving the unengaged to better schools *for them* allowed the TPS teachers to focus on the mainstream student majority (lighten the "differentiated instruction" load) likely to remain in TPSs.

An incredible example of putting the system first comes from Berliner and Biddle (1995). They believe the "Nation at Risk" claim is "a manufactured crisis."[30] Their discussion of 24 Philadelphia TPSs noted that 80% of fifth graders can't read. That's a real crisis! Instead of celebrating that some children can leave, they regret that some parents school their children elsewhere. They regret one Philadelphia effect: it "has generated some remarkably fine private schools" that more parents are using.

Berliner and Biddle fear that "high-status private schools would surely become more numerous, the use of public education would become threatened in more communities, and the "Philadelphia effect" would become the American educational norm. For the benefit of assumed but unspecified future efforts to improve TPSs, they regret escape from the other Philadelphia effect: thousands of fifth graders cannot read.

Apologists for a dysfunctional status quo always ask for more time and more money. Those words appeared in *The School Choice Wars* (2001), yet over 20 years later, the "effect" persists[31] because public schools' monopoly on public funding persists, the epitome of the persistent education policy failure, the result of an unproductive school choice debate.

Misled by the Limited Choice Definition

Though it does not fully explain complaining about children fleeing unacceptable outcomes of a very reform-resistant system, a key premise of the Berliner and Biddle book is a conviction that parental choice will be very limited. That narrow definition of choice expansion was also evident in James Norton's article in the March 29, 2000, *Education Week*: "School vouchers provide opportunity for a selected group of students."[32] Norton was not describing a particular program. He thought he was restating a stylized fact about parental choice.

Joseph Viteritti (1999) pointed out that selective granting of choice

> rests on an assumption that many poor people will remain left behind in failing public schools when others are allowed to choose. It is a gravely cynical assumption. It accepts the premise that under a system of choice, failing institutions would be allowed to persist much as they do now. (p. 114)

Against Free Enterprise

Despite the great track record of free enterprise in open markets,[33] and the dismal failures of socialism and government management of nationalized industries,[34] anticapitalist bias is pervasive (poor economic education), and especially widespread in the ranks of choice opponents. Choice opponent Alex Molnar vilifies the market with Marxist-Leninist language:

> For the market to produce winners, there always have to be losers. Market values have eroded and debased the human values of democratic civil society. Will America . . . be further ensnared in the logic of the market?[35]

Former NEA president Bob Chase said the "market god will stop at nothing in the name of money. The market is eager to grab hold of the public schools."[36] In his convention keynote address, Chase said the "run-amok marketplace" was one of the "broader lessons of Littleton" (the Colorado public high school where two students killed several of their peers).

Chase and many others characterize the market as a "thing" or a "being" capable of thinking or planning. It is not! The market is only a process of voluntary exchange usually guided by rivalry and property rights established and enforced by society. Rival entrepreneurs want to earn income by being the best choice for the families that choose them, not "grab hold of public schools."

Market forces continuously improve goods and services all over the world, but Gerald Bracey said it is "revolutionary" to claim that market forces would greatly improve schools.[37] In contrast, Andrew Coulson's *Market*

Education (1999) demonstrated that the idea is not even revolutionary for education. Educator Tony Wagner (1996) called such claims "free market fantasies" (p. 70).

The Weber and Chase comments reflect a conviction that market forces—the results of voluntary exchange—are evil. Weber believes that allowing private school entrepreneurs to profit by luring children to their schools with choice worthy services is tantamount to child prostitution. I wonder what Weber thinks about his child's pediatrician who does exactly what he is afraid school entrepreneurs would do; that is, seek business through high quality services.

Arthur Levine's reluctant support for very limited choice expansion reflects a similar, though more soft-spoken sentiment. Levine limited his support to "rescue operation[s] aimed at reclaiming the lives of America's most disadvantaged children,"[38] again implying that it is wrong to profit by providing children the best education value their parents can find for them, and that government-run schooling is too important to end public funding discrimination against children who find a better fit outside of TPSs.

To Levine, "rescuing" especially disadvantaged children with choice is the lesser of two evils. Levine's willingness to support slightly reduced discrimination was "painful" for him, and "only in response to a desperate situation"; a last resort to "save the most disadvantaged children." Many educators still have not come even that far. Levine made it clear that he was outside of the mainstream of his education colleagues.

The introduction of *Education Week*'s 1997 "Quality Counts" issue[39] said it would be "sad for America to have to give up its current system" (level the playing field between TPSs and alternatives). Why? *Education Week*'s editors did not say what the public would supposedly miss if the education finance monopoly ended, or what the public would miss if a much larger share of the K–12 population no longer attended TPSs. Likewise for Jonathan Alter, a once prominent author and *Newsweek* writer. He revealed his anti-market bias with a warning that if the current reform efforts fail, they may have to try vouchers.[40] (Gasp!)

Accepted Discrimination

Any major difference in the taxpayer funding of private school and TPS students implies public institution ownership of school tax dollars, and that some students—the ones enrolled in privately owned schools—are less important than others. Choice expansion advocate Daniel McGroarty's response[41] to choice opponents' insistence on "no public funds for private schools" is common. He does not point out that school taxes exist to support the education of children. Instead, McGroarty said taxpayers could support private school users because that precedent was already set. Public funds already support some children in private schools.

Choice advocates go to great lengths to configure choice expansion in ways that will allow them to claim that choice won't harm TPSs and to publicize that feature of their proposals. The right response to that political hot potato is to point out that funding a school system—any system—is not in the best interests of children. Instead, parental choice proposals typically address concerns about TPS impacts by providing families that prefer private schools only a fraction of the public funds earmarked for their children (discrimination), and it's usually only low-income families. The result, as described by Joseph Viteritti, is that "the farther you get from an assigned public school (TPS), the more the funding goes down."[42]

Higher-income families bear a larger school tax burden, but choice expansion proposals often allow no public money for the schooling choices of the affluent. Even choice expansion advocates often implicitly assert that higher-income families should get a direct benefit from their school taxes only if their children attend public schools. They say that it is inequitable to help rich people[43] pay private school tuition.

The choice expansion proposals that ban private copayment all but ban private funding of formal schooling, a restriction that is as unenforceable in spirit[44] as it is counterproductive. It means that families can use a voucher, ESA, or tax credit funded with the school taxes they paid only if they promise not to buy more schooling than the public funding will buy—crazy.

CHANGING ATTITUDES

There is a mixed bag. Diane Ravitch, despite a history of documenting the failures of politically run schooling, reverted to a total bear hug for the public school system monopoly on public funding. Senators Corey Booker (D-NJ) and Elizabeth Warren (D-MA), who achieved prominence, in part, through choice expansion advocacy,[45] ended their drive to increase freedom to use private schools to briefly contend for the 2020 Democrat presidential nomination. The recent increased polarization of politics pushed them away from the Clinton and Obama positions and toward much weaker support for just freedom to use a CPS. Their advocacy had included longtime liberal support for private school choice.[46]

But there's also cause for some optimism about this part of the choice expansion debate. Even before the pandemic boost in public awareness of TPS practices such as teaching critical race theory and long closures, there was growing, though still semantic-sensitive, support for choice expansion.[47]

However, except in Arizona and West Virginia, where universal programs were recently enacted, strong public opinion poll support[48] for choice expansion has not yet yielded much actual choice expansion, even the narrowly targeted variety that continues to receive too much, insufficiently nuanced attention from researchers.

Already in the 1990s, a rising, though still small, number of choice advocates began to assert indifference to school ownership and focus on matching children to the best schooling environment, public or private. Increasingly, children are the direct focus of their comments. Robert Aguirre, a director of San Antonio's privately funded CEO programs, was unequivocally indifferent about instruction delivery. CEO voucher users can use them to enroll in another public school. When asked about the impact on TPSs, he changes the subject to the children.

Texas Justice Foundation president Alan Parker campaigns for choice expansion with universal child-based funding. Even public officials have begun to answer the typical demand of choice opponents ("Public money shouldn't go to private schools") with demands like Jersey City mayor Brett Schundler's "Public money for the [entire] public" (Schundler, 1998, p. 12; Wagenheim, 1998, p. 12). Texas legislator Kent Grusendorf (R) said that "publicly funded education was created for the benefit of our children and future generations—not for the benefit of any governmental institution."[49]

The mainstream media contains efforts to disentangle the good "end" of public education from the deficient means of public school systems with a monopoly on public funds. Robert Lutz and Clark Durant announced that "we need a fresh definition of public education, one defined by who is served rather than by who provides the service."[50]

Andrew Coulson's *Market Education* (1999) demanded that we "stop asking how state schooling can be tweaked to minimize its faults, and start asking: What is the best we can do for our children?" "For decades, government-owned schools in many nations have repeated a futile cycle of criticism, reform, failure to improve, criticism, and so on" (p. 365). Syndicated columnist William Raspberry cited a Coulson article[51] that made the same point and said, "In other words, the institution of public schooling [with high barriers to use of alternatives] is not the best mechanism for advancing the ideals of public education."[52] *Brilliant!*

INSTITUTIONAL INDIFFERENCE WITHOUT APOLOGY NEEDED

Choice advocates need to follow the lead of Quade, Lutz, Durant, and Coulson in even larger numbers. Education services and the ideal of public education are not the same thing as the public school system delivery mechanism. Choice expansion proposals are self-limiting, and ultimately self-defeating, as long as choice advocates worry about their impact on TPSs. Choice will only yield a limited escape hatch, not a reform catalyst, until many more choice advocates develop that attitude.

Taxpayer support of choice worthy schools, government-owned or privately owned, according to parental decisions, including the right to supplement public funds with private funds, raises equity issues that are a major part of the school choice debate. Those issues are the subject of Chapter 10. First, the next chapter discusses the roles and perspectives of the different levels of government.

NOTES

1. Robert Chase, *Vital Speeches*, May 1, 1998, 444–446.

2. Ted Forstmann, "School Choice, by Popular Demand," *Wall Street Journal*, April 21, 1999.

3. August 3, 1997, speech printed in Center for Education Reform, *Monthly Letter*, no. 38 (September, 1997): 6.

4. Nina H. Shokraii, "What People Are Saying About School Choice," *The Heritage Foundation Backgrounder* 1188 (June 2, 1998): 3.

5. John Gatto, quoted in David Harmer, *School Choice* (Washington, DC: Cato Institute, 1994), 61.

6. Representative Marge Roukema (R-NJ), quoted in Sharon G. Voliva, "Public Support for Nonpublic Schools," PrairieNet.org, accessed August 26, 1999.

7. Letter written by the National Coalition for Public Education, July 29, 1997.

8. Republican Main Street Partnership, *Defining the Federal Role in Education: A Republican Perspective* (Washington, DC: RMSP, 2000).

9. Charles L. Glenn, "Where Public Education Went Wrong," *Family Policy* 11, no. 5 (September–October, 1998).

10. https://www.aei.org/op-eds/do-schools-exist-for-students-or-teachers/

11. Walter Shapiro, "Tough Choice," *Time*, September 16, 1991, 55.

12. Texas Federation of Teachers, "The Choice Issue," undated, late 1990s.

13. Gerald Tirozzi, "Vouchers for Some Harm the Rest," letter to the editor, *Education Week*, February 10, 1999, 37.

14. Rob Boston and Steve Benen, "Vouchers Harm Public Schools, Violate Church-State Separation, National Watchdog Group Charges," Americans United for Separation of Church and State, July 29, 1997.

15. http://faculty.business.utsa.edu/jmerrifi/evp.pdf

16. Statement cited in Quade (1996, p. 35).

17. Nina H. Shokraii, "What People Are Saying About School Choice," *The Heritage Foundation Backgrounder* 1188 (June 2, 1998): 3.

18. Jeb Bush, "A Year's Worth of Knowledge in a Year's Time," *Heritage Lectures*, no. 648 (November 10, 1999): 3.

19. Jeb Bush, "A Year's Worth of Knowledge in a Year's Time," *Heritage Lectures*, no. 648 (November 10, 1999): 5.

20. "School Choice Legislation in the States," *School Reform News*, April 2000, 20.

21. *Larry King Show*, November 10, 1992, cited in Peter Brimelow and Leslie Spencer, "The National Extortion Association?," *Forbes*, June 7, 1993, 72.

22. Albert Shanker, *School Reform News*, December 1998, 11.

23. Robert Chase, *Vital Speeches*, May 1, 1998, 444–446.

24. That kind of view—fairly widespread—is a result of poor schooling. Weber and many others see markets and capitalism as a dreadful process, and indeed it is in many countries where cronyism and corruption distort and control markets. The difference between "good capitalism" and politically perverted capitalism is something that absolutely needs to be taught in the K–12 years. In non-politically-correct (driven by ignorance) schooling, how markets do work under general circumstances would be widely taught. Parents would insist when offered that schooling feature. Walberg and Bast (1993); Baumol et al. (2007).

25. Tiffany Danitz, "Private Vouchers Are Going Public," *Insight*, September 8, 1997, 14–16.

26. Nina S. Rees, "Fighting for a Good Education," a Heritage Foundation op-ed, September 7, 1999.

27. Mark Silva, "House Approves Bush's Program for Public Schools," *Miami Herald*, April 29, 1999.

28. https://www.salon.com/2022/07/01/schools-out-forever-arizona-moves-to-public-education-with-new-universal-voucher-law/

29. http://faculty.business.utsa.edu/jmerrifi/evp.pdf

30. Berliner and Biddle (1995). They say that everyone, up through and including the U.S. Congress, has been duped. The U.S. Congress's harshly worded indictment of government-run school systems is quoted and discussed in Kirkpatrick (1997).

31. https://thephiladelphiacitizen.org/struggling-philadelphia-school-system/

32. James H. K. Norton, "Solution or Problem?," *Education Week*, March 29, 2000, 47.

33. The countries with the greatest reliance on markets are the wealthiest and have the most rapid growth rates. See the data and discussion in Kim R. Holmes, "In Search of Free Markets," *Wall Street Journal*, December 12, 1994; *Wall Street Journal* Editorial Board, "Free to Grow," *Wall Street Journal*, September 3, 1996.

34. Kim R. Holmes, "In Search of Free Markets," *Wall Street Journal*, December 12, 1994; *Wall Street Journal* Editorial Board, "Free to Grow," *Wall Street Journal*, September 3, 1996; plus Shleifer (1998); Yergin and Stanislaw (1998).

35. Alex Molnar, "School Reform: Will Markets or Democracy Prevail?," in Lowe and Miner (1996, pp. 16–17).

36. Bob Chase, "Keynote Address to the NEA National Convention," Education Intelligence Agency, July 3, 1999.

37. Gerald Bracey, Fifth Annual Bracey Report, quoted in *Educational Leadership* 55, no. 7 (1998): 66.

38. Arthur Levine, "Why I'm Reluctantly Backing Vouchers," *Wall Street Journal*, June 15, 1998.

39. January 22, 1997, special issue.

40. Jonathan Alter, "Chicago's Last Hope," *Newsweek*, June 22, 1998, 30.

41. Daniel McGroarty, "Voucher Wars: Strategy and Tactics as School Choice Advocates Battle the Labor Leviathan," Milton and Rose Friedman Foundation, Indianapolis, *Issues in School Choice*, no. 2 (April 1998).

42. Education Policy Institute Update, January 14, 2000, summary of the January 12 Freedom and Equal Opportunity in Education Conference.

43. Private school tuition on top of school taxes is a trivial expense for only a tiny fraction of the population. According to 1996 Census Bureau data, it only takes an income of $75,316 to place a family in the top 20% of income earners, an amount that certainly does not make a family "rich," especially if they live in a major city. The *average* family income of the top 20% is $125,627.

44. "Rich" people can still purchase tutoring and after-school instruction.

45. https://www.forbes.com/sites/frederickhess/2020/01/14/what-cory-bookers-exit-means-for-charter-schooling/#658ead952b4f; https://www.wsj.com/articles/betsy-devos-is-on-a-mission-to-rescue-teachers-unions-hostages-school-reform-education-K–12-family-policy-change-11655845136

46. David Kirkpatrick, "School Choice Choir Has a Broad Range of Voices," *School Reform News*, July 1999, 9.

47. https://www.theatlantic.com/education/archive/2018/08/school-choice-gaining-popularity/568063/

48. https://edchoice.morningconsultintelligence.com/

49. Kent Grusendorf (Texas state representative–R), "Test Vouchers Before Flunking Them," *San Antonio Express-News*, April 29, 1995.

50. Robert Lutz and Clark Durant, "The Key to Better Schools," *Wall Street Journal*, September 20, 1996.

51. Andrew Coulson, "Are Public Schools Hazardous to Public Education?," *Education Week*, April 7, 1999, 36.

52. Andrew Coulson, cited in William Raspberry, "The Historical Case for School Choice," *Washington Post*, August 17, 1998, A19.

Chapter 8

Federal, State, and Local Roles and Perspectives

The roles and perspectives of different levels of government are an increasingly important part of the unproductive school choice debate and the resulting persistent education policy failures. President Bush (43) included private school choice in the initial draft of the No Child Left Behind (NCLB, 2001) legislation that passed without that provision. NCLB's successor, the Alexander-Murray-Obama Every Student Succeeds Act (ESSA, 2015), didn't assert choice expansion, but it supposedly provided states greater flexibility[1] in how to achieve school system reform.

The Obama administration supported chartering, but not in ways that would address its fundamental flaws and unleash it from the effects of political control—all described in Chapter 3, and the latter in great detail in Thomas Sowell's (2020) *Charter Schools and Their Enemies*.

Pro-choice-expansion Secretary of Education Betsy DeVos administered the ESSA, and the Trump administration proposed a federal tuition tax credit too late to perhaps have it enacted, by itself, by a Congress with Republican majorities in both houses.

Of course, primary responsibility for school system reform rests at the state level. The states with Republican control of all statewide offices and both houses of the legislature have shown, by their inaction on choice expansion, that teacher union/education establishment resistance may not be the most important political barrier to choice expansion, even through weak charter laws and/or narrowly targeted, restriction-laden private school choice.

Rural Republicans' unwillingness to defy rural district superintendents, and suburban Republicans' fear of alleged effects on suburban public schools, may be the key factors underlying the big gap between Republican state legislators' pro-choice rhetoric and what they will vote for.[2] Republican inaction probably persists because most people don't blame them. They blame teacher unions.

At the local level, it is widely taboo to even confess persistence of scandalously poor performance, especially by supposedly good suburban schools that are typically only not as bad as their inner-city counterparts. But a few of the United States' 13,452 school districts[3] have dared to confess that their attempt at one-size-fits-all leaves some children unengaged and poorly educated, and have proposed ceding their monopoly on public funding of K–12 schooling.

FEDERAL OPPORTUNITIES AND DANGERS

Regardless of the questionable constitutionality of the federal government's forays into the schooling industry, the U.S. Department of Education extensively intervenes in an area of policy that had been reserved for the states. The goals of federal involvement have been five-fold: (1) supplement, not supplant, state and local governments; (2) secure education's status as a national activity; (3) provide better management of federal education programs; (4) consolidate federal education programs to improve efficiency; and (5) improve educational quality (Alger, 2016). Vicki Alger (2016) argues that only one goal has clearly been achieved: securing education's status as a national activity.

With Alger's point in mind, the dangers of federal involvement are quite high. It is quite possible that federal involvement in state and local schooling has made things worse, in large part by further fragmenting the central-planning basis of what is taught, how, where, and to whom. Central planning is always fragile—easily disrupted—and, at its best, fails in theory and in fact. So it is very unlikely that a federal role beyond data collection, research support and dissemination, and cheerleading (bully pulpit) would lead to any kind of a system resembling an OEI.

With that as the backdrop for potentially positive things the federal government could do, actual federal involvement has indeed been counterproductive. Vicki Alger in *Failure: The Federal Misedukation [sic] of America's Children* (2016) outlines the myriad of programs, many of which overlap in goals, are wasteful, and, worse, are unproductive. All of them, of course, assert effort through the current system and have little hope of fostering an OEI.

That said, some uncertain opportunities presented themselves during the choice-minded Trump-DeVos administration vilified by status quo supporters. It proposed merging the Labor and Education Departments, and in the latter years of the Trump presidency, it offered a tax credit program that would have moved the system in the OEI direction.[4] Under the program, individuals would get an income tax credit for contributing up to 10% of their adjusted gross income, and they would be able to give to any program in the country.

Businesses would be allowed to give up to 5% of their net taxable income. States would have full discretion to determine the programs and students eligible for the scholarships.

The federal tax credit plan met with pushback from both sides of the political aisle. On the left: (1) JoAnn Bartoletti, director of the National Association of Secondary School Principals, called the proposal "particularly tone deaf."[5] "Mobilizing behind a scheme to further starve public schools and nine in 10 American students of the resources they need is not only unresponsive but insulting, and it reflects this administration's persistent disdain for public education."[6]

(2) Sasha Pudelski, the cochair of the School Superintendents Association, said, "Rather than attempt to meet the current unfunded mandates in federal education, like [special education], the Administration would rather throw money at a scheme designed to defund public schools further. This proposal is shockingly poor in both conception and design."[7] Note the language used in such rhetoric, such as "disdain for public education." Such verbiage clearly illustrates the conflation of the public education commitment and the public school system.

People who tend to be pro–tuition tax credit or pro-voucher also opposed the DeVos tax credit initiative. Neal McCluskey of the Cato Institute said that federal choice policies present dangers even though the feds are trying to "skirt the control problem" by "sticking with tax credits instead of vouchers, and letting states opt in."[8] Although truly a choice expansion advocate, the Cato Institute's McCluskey claims, "but not only is this unconstitutional—taxes are authorized to execute specific, enumerated powers, not to lightly engineer state policy—it won't, ultimately, prevent encroaching federal control. So, the conservative stance is that choice expansion is great, but not when done by the federal government."[9]

McCluskey, as well as others such as Corey DeAngelis, claim that as federal money travels to private schools, the federal government will begin to claim control over what or how things are taught: "What happens when, instead of a President Trump, we have a President Sanders or Harris and they don't like the policies of religious schools, or maybe how economics is taught? Suddenly lots of private schools and other options will be federally pressured to look very similar—shape up or credit eligibility goes away—and true choice will be curtailed."[10]

The political language concerning the federal tax credit proposal illustrates the essence of our unproductive school choice debate. Proponents focused on empowering the disadvantaged victims of poor-fit schooling options. As DeVos stated, it was a "bold" proposal to give "hundreds of thousands of students across the country the power to find the right fit for their education."[11] Her central point is that creating access to options for students and families who are underserved by their assigned TPS is a laudable goal of the federal government.

Her counterparts used rhetoric such as, "Secretary DeVos keeps pushing her anti–public school agenda despite a clear lack of support from parents, students, teachers, and even within her own party," and, "Congress has repeatedly rejected her privatization efforts."[12] Note how her opponents focused on the *system* by using terms such as "anti–public school" and "privatization" [of the system], rather than focusing on the welfare of the students, implying that student welfare requires public school system dominance.

The war of words probably boils down to the "public education" confusion discussed in Chapter 7. Choice advocates need to make a much bigger deal about the debate's key terms. The language used obfuscates key issues, often on purpose. It is worth repeating from Chapter 7 that public education is a commitment that hopefully all of us agree is vital to society, that *all* students have access to engaging formal schooling. We need to condemn the use of the term "public education" to refer to the government owned and operated public school system delivery process.

The judicial system delivered a mixed bag of decisions. Some specific choice expansions were struck down, but key court decisions provided critical general support for choice expansion. At the heart of many federal and state court cases are highly debated, archaic Blaine amendments adopted by many states over 100 years ago. Blaine amendments are state constitutions' clauses that essentially ban "any direct or indirect" payments to any schools or institutions controlled "by any church, sect, or denomination."

States instituted these amendments amid anti-Catholic bigotry in the late 1800s and early 1900s as an effort to ensure that public money did not support Catholicism or Catholic schools. Unable to single out Catholic school users, the Blaine clauses in state constitutions forced discrimination against all users of religious schools.

The newly asserted unconstitutionality of the Blaine amendments stems from two recent Supreme Court cases. In the first case, *Zelman v. Simmons-Harris*,[13] the court "held—by a vote of 5 to 4—that the funding of religious schools with taxpayer money through voucher programs does not violate the Establishment Clause of the United States Constitution."[14] Because *Zelman* opened up religious affiliated primary, elementary, and secondary schools to students who needed choice expansion to pay the tuition, proponents of choice expansion saw *Zelman* as a monumental victory.

Espinoza v. Montana Department of Revenue sealed the deal on Blaine amendments.[15] John Roberts wrote the majority opinion, stating, "[A] state need not subsidize private education. . . . Once a state decides to do so, it cannot disqualify some private schools because they are religious."[16]

The question, moving forward, is whether realistic, politically feasible federal involvement benefits can outweigh the costs. The concept of arena shopping, which stems from searching for the best level of government to achieve a policy entrepreneur's goal, could help choice advocates. For example, 1960s civil rights leaders took their case to Washington, DC, in an effort to end racial segregation, among other prejudices, nationwide, which culminated in the Civil Rights Act of 1964.

Federal action could move the needle in states if a robust education savings account, voucher, or tax credit system was set up at the federal level. Policy inertia would likely keep that from happening, as left-leaning policy makers would likely block it at the federal level, but such a policy might ignite a family-empowering schooling policy nationwide, forcing states to get on board.

Other tax credit initiatives, aside from the DeVos plan, provide for credits to businesses with pass-through income to dodge the U.S. government's $10,000 cap on state and local tax deductions. Business owners can earn a tax credit by donating to charities and, in particular, private schools, including religious schools, and voucher programs, to exceed the $10,000 cap and reap larger benefits. Carl Davis of the Institute on Taxation and Economic Policy opposes the IRS's proposal and calls it a "scheme" of "tax avoidance" for the wealthy.[17] However, Davis is only looking at this situation from the side of taxes and who pays what, rather than the outcome for students.

If wealthy people are giving, or investing, in voucher programs that allow students better fits for their schooling opportunities that governments simply oppose, then maybe these types of programs could lead us to a more OEI-centered policy focus. Such "schemes" may be more obscure ways of funding choice expansion without a straightforward tax credit or voucher policy. It could work behind the scenes, which may be needed given the anti-voucher, anti–tax credit, anti–education savings account sentiment.

STATE PERSPECTIVE

By failing to mention schooling, the U.S. Constitution left the states responsible for schooling policies. Driven largely by anti-Catholic bigotry, states shifted their public education commitment from a largely private system to a public funding monopoly for a public school system. Though all but Hawaii delegated much education policy making to school districts that often differ significantly according to informal categories such as urban, rural, suburban, wealthy, and poor, the governance and funding policies that need to be reformed to create an OEI are still state policies. And concerns about inequitable funding and especially poor performance by poor urban districts caused states to reclaim some of the policy-making authority, and funding responsibility, delegated to districts.

Embrace of Chartered Public Schools

That situation drove many states to allow CPSs as alternatives to TPSs. However, recall from Chapter 4 that the price control created by every charter law widely replaces the intended school choice with school chance. Because of the widespread debilitating shortages created by price control, chartering has not yielded an OEI. Nonetheless, chartering has become a frequent political happy medium that both right- and left-leaning policy makers embrace that has been helpful in urban areas, especially inner cities where TPS performance is worst.

Special Circumstances of Rural Areas

Even with OEI-conducive state policies, rural areas may not contain any brick-and-mortar schools of choice/chance. Low population densities make it hard for many schools to exist, as there are only enough schoolchildren for one. Private schools are very rare, and rural charters are far from ubiquitous: "Of the nation's ten most rural states, seven have no charter law; some state laws have provisions that make starting a rural CPS impossible or nearly so; rural charters get much less funding than district-run schools and face high costs related to transportation and buildings."[18]

Indeed, one rural charter school in north Georgia is simply the local public school that rebranded itself a charter school and is the only public school option in the county. Such a move is not exactly a robust action to expand school choice.

Not only do purveyors of TPS alternatives face practical challenges, but rural areas are treated differently when it comes to schooling, and will likely continue to be. "Often, small communities are cohesive and non-diverse in a myriad of ways, and inert. Also, rural means a lot of different things: the term includes hollows in the Appalachian Mountains, former sharecroppers' shacks in the Mississippi Delta, desolate Indian reservations on the Great Plains, and emerging *colonia* along the Rio Grande."[19] Since the current public school is often the largest employer in the community, "the existing district school is woven tightly into the community's fabric. New charters are often seen through narrowed eyes."[20]

Worse yet, from a schooling outcome perspective, the community identity associated with the local TPS is most likely held together not by what happens inside the classroom but by what happens on the field, court, or diamond. Need proof of a community's concern for its local school? Look where people are nearly every Friday night in the fall.

An OEI could undermine athletic programs and opportunities for students if many schools in a low-density area either split the athletes or centralized them into just one of the schools. Neither outcome would be politically pleasing to families, athletic or not. Unfortunately, athletics can be seen as more important than academics, and rural people who identity with the local TPS through athletics are unlikely to politically support an OEI, even if one is feasible in rural areas.

The larger issue, though, isn't rural areas' practical and political hostility to additional brick-and-mortar schools; it is how to address student diversity in light of the challenges presented by rural areas. Low population densities and the tightly woven, TPS-centric societal fabrics of rural areas may require a focus on virtual ways to address student diversity, perhaps including, especially, course choice[21] to achieve better schooling fit while keeping more children at least partially connected to their assigned TPS.

Resistance to Openness

Another important aspect of a state perspective is that resistance to establishment of the OEI conditions described in Chapter 2 will vary. Teacher union political clout varies considerably by state. Chapter 14 discusses how to weaken that clout. Terry Moe in *Special Interest: Teachers Unions and America's Public Schools* illustrates, with an immense amount of evidence, why many states, more than others, will struggle in moving toward an OEI.

In some states, the rural effect, or a Republican-in-name-only (RINO) effect, is the key change-blocking factor. The state-by-state variability in teacher union and RINO strength will dictate which paths to reform are most likely to succeed, and, from a national strategy perspective, in which states to pursue an OEI first.

Several states' TPS management policies during the COVID pandemic may be the best case for an OEI. Many states kept TPSs closed long after evidence had been marshaled to argue for a resumption of in-person learning, indeed, alongside open private schools. Some districts took the odd tack of self-righteously justifying their failure to teach. Virginia's Arlington Public Schools pointed to its "commitment to ensuring equity" to prohibit teachers from covering new material (since it couldn't ensure that every student had adequate internet bandwidth).[22]

That behavior further undermined the already dubious equity arguments for government-run, zero-tuition schooling. So, even as the pandemic wound down, the rural and disadvantaged students enrolled in a TPS (but often absent) disproportionately suffered the consequences of online lessons prepared by classroom teachers without talent or interest in online schooling, which often amounted to watching a video for a few minutes or sometimes nothing at all.

The more advantaged children had alternatives to such low-quality online lessons, including open private schools. Lacking school choice and other avenues to learning, the disadvantaged students who needed schooling the most were hurt the most by lengthy closures. And rural areas needed far less regulation during the pandemic than did densely populated areas, but the closure policies often applied to all.

The pandemic was likely a missed opportunity for major steps toward an OEI. As parents raged about the failure to open schools, especially in early 2021, as studies of the disease should have eased concerns about children and teacher safety, cries for school choice were heard. Parents wanted students back in school, but many areas had no open public schools. Such a scenario had parents wishing they had vouchers, tax credits, or education savings accounts (compared in Chapter 12) for access. States, particularly those controlled by right-leaning policy makers, should have seized the opportunity to capitalize on the pro-choice fervor growing across the country. After all, remote instruction by remote instruction amateurs had proven to be a massive disappointment.

LOCAL PERSPECTIVE

Though local may be the level of government with the most opportunity for some movement toward an OEI, primarily because there are so many school districts, local reform appears least likely to open the menu of schooling options to entrepreneurial initiative. With few, usually temporary exceptions, school districts have been unwilling to give up their monopolies on public funding or confess that a politically correct curriculum delivered by a system that does not reward merit will yield a bad fit for many children.

School districts typically don't even welcome a chartering process that falls well short of delivering OEI conditions. A key reason may be widespread teacher union dominance of school board elections.[23] In the states where the only charter-authorizing agent is the local school district, there are very few CPSs. The few school district–authorized CPSs typically mainly serve a population of students that the local district would rather not serve. A few districts authorize CPSs to serve the highest-performing students, to keep their best students from leaving.

However, the case needs to be made, locally, that pursuit of a local OEI is worthwhile. Empowering students with money to choose a TPS alternative leads to happier parents and students. No studies, to our knowledge, document widespread dissatisfaction with the opportunities created by school choice expansion. An OEI allows for self-sorting so that students are more likely to end up in academic situations where they can succeed, and the students would probably not sort themselves on socioeconomics, race, ethnicity, or sexual orientation.

The same is true for teachers. Currently, it is more than fair to say that, in the absence of a diverse menu of schooling options, teachers have an incredibly difficult job because we expect them to be everything to everyone through skilled differentiation of instruction. Regardless of students' talents, interests, or abilities, they are piled into the same rooms—sometimes randomly—and expected to perform at high levels.

A plethora of psychological research exists—documenting the obvious—that children learn differently. Since teachers teach differently, too, we need a sorting process—choice, aided by entrepreneurial initiative—to match teacher talent to student learning styles and other engagement-determining factors. Students *and* teachers deserve options for what best suits them. No parent would send their child to a general practitioner to set a broken bone.

One local district conspicuously tried to move the needle on choice. The conservative and affluent Douglas County, Colorado (a Denver suburb), school board adopted a merit pay plan, a new curriculum, and a voucher program. A court injunction halted the voucher program.

Michael Brickman noted that such a move, by a wealthy district, "draws attention to the false assumption that the average wealthy, suburban school district is fat, happy and complacent. That highlights what could happen if districts employ reforms to go from good to great, instead of from poor to passable."[24] That another lawsuit prevented implementation of the entire plan reveals the challenges faced by local policy entrepreneurs, but that should not obscure two important facts: (1) local policy entrepreneurs need state-level help, and (2) even without that, there are 13,452 local opportunities for school boards to address many of their own issues. After all, what level of government better knows the needs of students and teachers than that level that is closest to them?

CONCLUSION

Policy-making failure at the state and local level, in large part due to the unproductive school choice debate, added federal intervention, which created a three-headed—therefore fragmented and especially low-performing—central-planning process. One of the reasons that the process persists is the assumption that a decentralized planning process, which requires market-based price (tuition, salaries) formation for at least the TPS alternatives, is unacceptable from an equity perspective. The next chapter challenges that assumption.

NOTES

1. Not everyone agrees: Cato Forum—Neal McCluskey, "Ding, Dong, No Child Left Behind Is Dead . . . Or Is It?," Cato Institute, 2016; McCluskey, "ESSA Seems Ripe for Federal Control," Cato Institute, 2016.
2. https://www.wsj.com/articles/a-school-choice-shake-up-in-iowa-kim-reynolds-house-primaries-gop-11655496097
3. https://nces.ed.gov/programs/digest/d20/tables/dt20_214.10.asp
4. https://www.nytimes.com/2019/02/28/us/politics/devos-tax-credit-school-choice.html
5. Erica L. Green, "Betsy DeVos Backs $5 Billion in Tax Credits for School Choice," *New York Times*, February 28, 2019.
6. Erica L. Green, "Betsy DeVos Backs $5 Billion in Tax Credits for School Choice," *New York Times*, February 28, 2019.
7. Alyson Klein, "Betsy DeVos Pushes New Federal Tax Credit to Expand School Choice," *Education Week*, February 28, 2019.
8. https://www.cato.org/blog/even-something-great-school-choice-should-not-be-federalized
9. https://www.cato.org/blog/thanks-no-thanks-federal-school-choice
10. https://www.cato.org/blog/thanks-no-thanks-federal-school-choice
11. Erica L. Green, "Betsy DeVos Backs $5 Billion in Tax Credits for School Choice," *New York Times*, February 28, 2019.
12. Alyson Klein, "Betsy DeVos Pushes New Federal Tax Credit to Expand School Choice," *Education Week*, February 28, 2019.
13. 536 U.S. 639 (2002).
14. Laura S. Underkuffler, "The 'Blaine' Debate: Must States Fund Religious Schools?," *Cornell Law Faculty Publications* 575 (2003), https://scholarship.law.cornell.edu/facpub/575
15. https://www.wsj.com/articles/a-school-choice-landmark-11593558981
16. 591 U.S. ___ (2020).
17. https://itep.org/itep-urges-irs-to-end-salt-workaround-scheme-for-businesses/
18. "Utilizing Charter Schooling Strengthens Rural Education," Thomas B. Fordham Institute, https://fordhaminstitute.org/national/commentary/utilizing-charter-schooling-strengthens-rural-education
19. "Utilizing Charter Schooling Strengthens Rural Education," Thomas B. Fordham Institute, https://fordhaminstitute.org/national/commentary/utilizing-charter-schooling-strengthens-rural-education
20. "Utilizing Charter Schooling Strengthens Rural Education," Thomas B. Fordham Institute, https://fordhaminstitute.org/national/commentary/utilizing-charter-schooling-strengthens-rural-education

21. https://fordhaminstitute.org/national/commentary/fifty-state-strategy-course-choice; https://fordhaminstitute.org/national/commentary/course-choice-ideal-post-pandemic-policy-solution

22. https://www.wsj.com/articles/failure-in-the-virtual-classroom-11592776152

23. https://www.wsj.com/articles/the-parental-revolt-continues-school-board-elections-ballotpedia-curriculum-education-11654522470. "Union-endorsed candidates win roughly 70 percent of all competitive school board elections," Boston College's Michael Hartney discovered after examining school board races in California and Florida over an extended duration. His findings were published in January 2022 in the journal *Interest Groups & Advocacy*.

24. Rick Hess, "The Most Interesting School District in America? Douglas County's Pursuit of Suburban Reform," *Education Next*, September 19, 2013, https://www.educationnext.org/douglas-county-the-most-interesting-school-district-in-america/

Chapter 9

Equity and Equality

[There is] tremendous evidence that school systems based on compulsion are neither fair nor equitable.

—Paul Hill[1]

Equal access is an unfair, ineffective schooling strategy, and it's unenforceable. Many families earn advantages. Since taxpayers cannot fund schooling for all at a level that some families can provide for their children, pursuit of equality means a less educated population.

Middle- and upper-income family flight from the areas with the worst public schools—often really bad[2]—concentrates the families that cannot afford the higher housing costs around the better TPSs (Yinger & Nguyen-Hoang, 2011) around the worst TPSs. That makes those TPSs worse, which helps create and reinforce the income stratification of U.S. urban areas.[3]

Since no amount of school funding can make one size fit all, equity needs to be formally redefined to mean pursuit of equal fit (Rose, 2016), which requires a diverse menu of schooling options. Existing public funding, plus the entrepreneurial initiative of an OEI, will foster relentless pursuit of increasingly better fit.

The acquisition of knowledge by some doesn't hurt others. Quite the contrary, when families buy more education, other people usually benefit through increased rates of innovation and better decision making by businesses and governments. Despite that, many proposed school choice expansions would discourage private spending on education. Certainly, the current 51 U.S. public school systems' monopoly, or near monopoly, on public funding does that. Implicit in such disincentives is the incorrect premise that disadvantaged children benefit when advantaged children learn less.

A high minimum level of opportunity for equal fit for everyone is achievable and critical. That and equality in the eyes of the government define "equity" in this book. This book's stand for a nondiscriminatory, high level of public funding for every child would achieve that outcome. The current system, existing choice expansion programs, and most parental choice proposals do not.

EXISTING INEQUITIES

The current use of public K–12 money amounts to a caste system. The political process created different levels of per-pupil funding even though the public school system "is built upon the assumption that schools should educate all of the children and do so in approximately the same manner for each child."[4] Many states even mandate uniformity in their state constitution.

A particular child's public funding level—their education consumer caste membership—depends on several characteristics, including family income, school ownership (public or private), and "special *needs*" on both the high and low end of the academic potential spectrum. The status quo discourages private spending on formal schooling because families forgo their share of taxpayer support if they aren't satisfied with a public school.

Savage Inequalities

The title of a 1992 book—*Savage Inequalities*[5]—still describes our school systems, even in states under court orders to equalize funding. Even within districts, budgeting and personnel policies favor affluent neighborhoods.[6] For example, older teachers seek transfers to affluent neighborhoods, and more resignations occur in less affluent neighborhoods. So, the process reinforces itself because more teachers have to start their careers at the least desirable schools.

Some of the outrage about unequal funding of public school students takes the form of funding equalization and funding increase lawsuits. They've made some lawyers wealthy but failed to equalize funding or improve schooling outcomes.[7]

The system demands a titanic struggle to achieve an equalization mandate that doesn't even include students enrolled in private schools. And reality continues to elude the mandated outcome, in part because children are not the real subjects of efforts to equalize funding. Institutions like school districts and schools are the focus of equalization efforts.[8]

Unequal public funding by family income level is unintentional, but the other grounds for discrimination are intentional. The inequities are often large, and many are not rationalized or defensible. Private school users are largely ignored. Their parents pay school taxes, but most private school users receive no public funds.

To stay competitive with zero-tuition public schools, most private schools must keep tuition levels well below public schools' per-pupil funding. Therefore, even though the parents of private school students pay for schooling twice,[9] they typically receive less schooling resources than public school users. Private school users have only slightly higher average incomes than public school users. Most private school users make major financial sacrifices to enroll their children in low-budget private schools.

The most widely known choice expansion proposals reinforce the Robin Hood effect of taxation—taking much more from richer families—by means testing eligibility. The resulting double Robin Hood effect is often deliberate. Benefits for low-income families funded by taxes collected from everyone are often the key objective of choice expansion proposals. But every family deserves a direct return on their school taxes, especially the people who pay the most. Even regressive tax systems usually extract more money from wealthier families.

Rules that ban public-private tuition copayment are another reflection of the Robin Hood philosophy. The implication of such low-income-targeted choice expansion proposals is that the affluent can directly benefit from tax dollars that come disproportionately from their pockets only if they accept a service (TPS assignment) that many low-income families want to escape.

Prohibiting copayment also prevents charities from topping off public funding. That curbs low-income family access to instructional approaches that cost more than the per-pupil public funding level, approaches likely to be needed the most by lower-income families. And while many people assume that low-income families are unable to make tuition copayments, a 1999 privately funded tuition voucher program for low-income families that required a significant copayment received 1.25 million applicants.[10]

Special Needs

In principle, children with "special needs"—another "caste"—are an entirely appropriate focal point of special treatment. However, the implementation mechanisms are controversial. Gifted children have "special needs" too, yet they are largely ignored.[11] The status quo remains true to Admiral Hyman Rickover's (1959) words written over 60 years ago: "The system looks upon talented children primarily as a vexing administrative problem."

Thirty-four years later, Rexford Brown (1993) found that policy makers see gifted and talented programs as elitist and hated by bureaucrats because "they hate making exceptions; exceptions always screw up the system" (p. 109), a longtime general complaint about centrally planned industries.

Indeed, worth repeating as often as possible is that in policy making, the *appearance* of fairness is paramount. So, one frequent, bad outcome of policy making is equal treatment of unequal children, which was already lamentable in the 19th century when Thomas Jefferson noted that "there is nothing more unequal than the equal treatment of unequal people."

Public schools' comprehensive uniformity is another major source of "special needs" problems. The inability to specialize significantly makes special needs seem more common, it increases the stigmatization of the children who seem to have special needs, and it reduces the quality of the services for the truly needy. In an editorial about his son, newspaper editor Bob Richter put the problem and the solution in the proper perspective:

> Dedicated, well-meaning, lovely teachers who truly cared about him, but couldn't teach him because for the most part, they had little experience with blind children.
>
> He's now in a place where every teacher is a specialist and every kid is like him.[12]

The "special ed" label arises—sometimes even for gifted children—for the same reason as labels like "nerd" and "dweeb." In "one-size-fits-all" neighborhood schools, more children stand out; there is just one mainstream and more variability.[13] Delivering the same curriculum at the same level to everyone serves the appearance of the fairness imperative, but little else.

We label some gifted children as "special ed" and sometimes even medicate them because they can't cope with boredom or certain teaching styles.[14] Children with as much potential as mainstream students are stigmatized as learning disabled if the ways to realize that potential are not compatible with the official pedagogy.[15] Teacher micromanagement (more in Chapter 14), including "teacher-proof" curricula and precise timetables, sometimes preclude minor changes that would otherwise occur in our many engagement factor–diverse TPS classrooms.

The system's demand for special services for some, but without the appearance of special treatment, further impairs the ability to serve the children who need special services.[16] In addition, many "inclusive" practices hinder the education of mainstream children.

We don't have to help lower achievers at the expense of the higher achievers, but we do. There are also better ways to help the low achievers. Public schools are hurt by their inability to specialize or use ability grouping to any significant extent, or as Barry McGhan (1998) put it, public schools (individual schools, not the entire system) need the right to exclude (sort).

We spend a lot to help low-achieving, non-mainstream children realize their potential. Federal Law 94–142 entitles children to an individualized education plan, which led to greater per-pupil funding of special needs children, and which may underlie the rapid growth in the number of special needs children (Hess, 1998, p. 41). For example, already by the 1996–1997 school year, Texas had 50% more special education children than gifted and talented children,[17] still 30% more in 2020.[18]

In contrast, we spend very little to help gifted children realize their potential. For example, in 1996–1997, Texas spent $1.2 billion for special education and $174 million for gifted and talented, and many of the gifted and talented programs exist only in name. Officially, Texas has about 50% more special ed than gifted and talented children, so spending averages about 4.5 times more per special ed child. That is consistent with the Benbow and Stanley (1996) finding that public school systems spend more per lower-achieving student. "Higher achieving students have been lost in the shuffle." A 1993 *Newsweek* article had the same conclusion:

> They're the best and brightest, and they're bored. That's the conclusion of the federal government's first assessment in 20 years of education for the nation's smartest students. While other countries push their best students to do even better, Americans push them aside. Gifted programs are also viewed as elitist. Gifted programs are often seen as luxuries.[19]

Ingrid Eisenstadter said it was "A Stupid Way to Treat Gifted Children."[20] The Benbow and Stanley (1996) study found that,

> over the past three decades, the achievement of waves of American students with high intellectual potential has declined as a result of inequity in educational treatment.

The most recent (2018–2019) "State of the States in Gifted Education"[21] says (p. 2), "May the report serve as a call to action to adequately address the needs of the advanced learners in our nation," which is in agreement with this unsigned, undated gifted education case study[22] finding that "they [still] aren't getting as much attention as learning-disabled students."

THE OUTLOOK WITH AN OPEN EDUCATION INDUSTRY

In an OEI, schools of choice must specialize to survive. Specialization creates several mainstreams, so children are closer to the mainstream of their school, even the mainstream of an assigned TPS that would very likely see those furthest from the mainstream opt for alternatives. That means fewer special needs issues will arise, and less stigmatization will result from those that do. Children will have more peers with similar interests, aptitudes, and learning styles.

The availability of specialized services will spare many parents and educators the often counterproductive formal process of findings, labeling, and individualized education plans available through Federal Law 94–142.[23] Per-pupil public funding worth enough so that many schools will accept it as full or nearly full payment—recommended throughout this book—will further reduce the use of Federal Law 94–142. Specialization raises productivity, so schools will provide better services at a lower cost. On a much smaller scale, for a very narrow range of special needs, specialized private schools already do. The increased productivity means that public funding greater than the TPS per-pupil funding level would not be needed as often.

Supplemental private support through tuition copayment would yield better schooling for some children. And note that unequal access to the menu of schooling options is already a big part of the status quo, and that public funding of over $13,000[24] would eventually[25] give most children access to an existing private school, and then more access as entrepreneurial initiative responds to demand growth from families that were unwilling or unable to pay full tuition costs.

Twenty-seven states have average tuition levels below $10,000,[26] many well below. A few very costly schools inflate the statewide average tuition above what most schools charge. That, and very high averages in northeastern states, is responsible for the current national average private school tuition of $11,963.

Sadly, maximizing choice is not a primary goal of many choice advocates. They believe symbolism should take precedence over substantive improvement. For example, Coons and Sugarman (1999) strongly object to public-private shared financing of tuition because "conscious government finance of economic segregation exceeds our tolerance" (pp. 190–192). The main objection isn't the economic stratification that no system can eliminate, and that exists now with public support because of the larger property tax bases and higher home prices of more affluent districts and attendance areas of better TPSs. The primary objection seems to be that the policy *consciously* allows affluent families to benefit from the school taxes collected disproportionately from them to provide their children better schooling than everyone can afford.

> What is today merely a personal choice of the wealthy, secured entirely with private funds, would become an invidious privilege assisted by the government. (Coons and Sugarman, 1999, p. 191)

DESTRUCTIVE PARANOIA

Some people have been misled to believe that the size of the economic pie is fixed (another *huge* schooling failure!), so that higher-income families can only gain at the expense of lower-income families. They advocate taxation to reduce disparities in access to education services, and they oppose tuition copayment.

Efforts to move closer to equality than a high minimum level of support[27]—possible with current public funding levels—would have several *very counterproductive* effects. Prohibiting the use of private funds (copayment) to supplement tax dollars—which many parental choice programs do—doesn't help children from low-income families.

Some low-income families find the money to enroll a child in a better-fit school, and the disadvantaged children aren't better off when other children learn less. Extra education for anyone enlarges the economy for everyone. Higher productivity and the greater civic responsibility that results when any family invests more in schooling for their children is good for society.

There is also a freedom issue. Another name for most income is "earnings." Another is "compensation." Higher-income families earn the right to make extraordinary investments in their children. The rest of us should cheer them on. There are few, if any, more socially beneficial ways for them to spend their earnings. In addition, unless we ban tutoring, high-income families cannot be stopped from investing in their children.

The key reason (first stated in Chapter 1) to allow add-ons is worth repeating. It needs to be shouted from the highest rooftops. *Market-determined, flexible prices are a cornerstone of decentralized planning; they are the only nondisastrous way to identify and address underserved needs in what is taught, where, how, and to whom*. Price controls have major debilitating side effects like shortages or surpluses, black markets, reduced quality, deceitful practices, and *forced* discrimination, if only randomly through a lottery.

When copayment is illegal, most private schools' tuition levels can only reflect the political process. The resulting price uniformity and inflexibility greatly diminishes specialization opportunities and the potential to offer new programs that, like any innovation, are often quite costly when first introduced. Add-ons funded by the wealthy permit innovations that might otherwise not be developed to the point where they're widely affordable.

The prospect of temporary high profits motivates innovation, and purchases by the wealthy allow new products to get through the costly developmental first stage of the product life cycle. "Throughout history, innovations and improvements that have started out benefiting the wealthy have ended up with the poor as the major beneficiaries."[28]

Those effects of banning copayment are far too high a price to pay for a symbolic and futile pursuit of equality or certain definitions of equity and fairness. *The answer to complaints that low-income families cannot send their children to some schools is charity-financed copayment support for low-income children.* Since such funding needs only finance add-ons, a particular level of philanthropic funding would support many more children than it can now.

Consider the likely effect of price decontrolling CPSs. With CPSs able to charge what the market can bear, the donor money now used to sustain many CPSs—including many that are low performing—that cannot make ends meet with the public per-pupil funding would become available for means-tested copayment assistance. Price decontrol puts some skin in the game, while the reallocation of donor funding from CPSs to users of CPSs maintains schooling affordability for lower-income families.

There are also practical reasons to keep policy making from becoming preoccupied with fear of "wicked windfalls for the wealthy."[29] A top reason is that *there are very few families that are wealthy enough so that thousands of dollars per child per year in tuition is a negligible expense.*[30]

It is foolish to diminish the benefits of the vast majority just to deny benefits to a tiny minority simply to spite the most successful members of society. Limiting choice expansion reduces education purchases, and it preempts genuine competition. In addition, there are solid political reasons, including a significant array of controversial government programs, to believe that programs restricted to the poor are poor programs, if not immediately then eventually, for lack of influential political support.

Nondiscrimination in public funding also avoids the administrative cost of means testing.[31] William Clune (1994) said there is growing support for such an approach.[32] A high nondiscriminatory, publicly funded minimum—this book's proposed public policy approach to equity—was the mainstream position at least as early as 1905. Elchanan Cohn said that Elwood Cubberly "set down basic values and goals for the distribution of school funds by the states" (Cohn, 1974).

> *All* [emphasis added] children of the State are equally important and are entitled to the same advantages; practically this can never be true. The duty of the State is to secure for *all* [emphasis added] as high a minimum of good instruction as is possible, *but not reduce all to this minimum* [emphasis added]. (Cubberly, 1905, p. 17)

However, this book's proposed approach differs from Cubberly. This book interprets "all" literally. Cubberly did not. His comment was a reaction to inter-district differences in per-pupil funding of TPSs, so his definition of "all" didn't include the children enrolled in private schools.

This book's proposed approach to equity does not eliminate the redistributive effect of taxation. The children of low-income families will still receive schooling that costs more than their parents' school tax payments. Allowing higher-income families some direct benefit from their school taxes no matter what kind of school they choose for their children is just, and it ensures a broader base of political support and therefore better programs.

Certainly, the current 51 U.S. school systems have no genuine equity advantages over what we propose. Their approaches have been a disaster for our least advantaged families and increasingly so during the pandemic. With the need to have a computer and internet access for remote learning, which some families struggle to provide, we've seen a way for the appearance of fairness imperative of the political process to create a basis for even lower performance: "No one can have it unless it is definitely available to everyone. We've seen schools opt to limit—or even forbid—instruction out of a fear of lawsuits."[33] The pandemic also demonstrated another important basis for genuine choice: differences of opinion on handling risk such as virus exposure.

An OEI with a high minimum level of per-pupil public support, with donors providing means-tested tuition copayment assistance, is at least a good starting point for a school system design that yields high levels of efficiency and equity (best defined as "equal fit")[34] by any definition other than forced equality.

A chapter on diversity issues closes out the debate issues section of this book. It describes the significant differences between the status quo, allegations about the restriction-laden programs that dominate the choice expansion debates, and the likely outcomes of an OEI.

NOTES

1. Paul Hill in "Responses to a Harvard Study on School Choice: Is It a Study at All?," Pioneer Institute for Policy Research, *Dialogue*, 1995, 1–11.

2. For example, "An Education Horror Show: A Case Study in Public School Failure and Lack of Accountability," *Wall Street Journal*, July 7, 2019, https://www.wsj.com/articles/an-education-horror-show-11562532467

3. https://www.opportunityatlas.org; https://www.effective-ed.org/in-the-media

4. Laurie Bergner, "Work for Education Equity," *San Antonio Express-News*, November 30, 1993.

5. Kozol (1992).

6. Berliner and Biddle (1995, p. 178) explain how new teachers start at the least desirable schools and transfer out as soon as they have enough seniority. More recently, see DeRoche (2020).

7. https://www.econtalk.org/hanushek-on-test-based-accountability-federal-funding-and-school-finance/

8. For example, see McCarty and Brazer (1990).

9. Wendy Wagenheim, legislative affairs director of the Michigan ACLU, gave a rare public defense of the pay twice requirement (Mackinac Center for Public Policy, "ACLU Hypocritical on School Choice, Critics Charge," *Michigan Education Report*, Fall 1999, 5). She said paying for public schools while using private schools was the same as having to help pay for police even if you hired a private security service. The two are not comparable. A private education is a substitute for a public one. A private security service supplements and compliments police services. It is not a substitute for them.

10. Wendy Zellner, "Going to Bat for Vouchers," *BusinessWeek*, February 7, 2000, cover story.

11. Benbow and Stanley (1996); Barbara Kantrowitz and Pat Wingert, "Failing the Most Gifted Kids," *Newsweek*, November 15, 1993, 67; Ingrid Eisenstadter, "A Stupid Way to Treat Gifted Children," *Wall Street Journal*, July 12, 1995.

12. Bob Richter, "Special Students Lost in a Murky System," *San Antonio Express-News*, May 21, 2000.

13. An article by Benbow and Stanley (1996) found that there is an insistence that every student be taught from the same curriculum at the same level.

14. *Wall Street Journal* Editorial Board, "ADD a Campaign Issue," *Wall Street Journal*, March 27, 2000: "10% of the small male population is currently under the influence of Ritalin, a sort of cure-all for fidgety children." See also Turtel (2005).

15. "That there is a single best pedagogy" is a typical "faulty assumption" (King, 1996, p. 180).

16. Andrew P. Dunn, "What's Wrong with Special Education," *Education Week*, May 17, 2000, 36, 39.

17. Texas Education Agency, *Academic Excellence Indicator System: 1996–97 State Performance Report*, 1997.

18. https://rptsvr1.tea.texas.gov/cgi/sas/broker?_service=marykay&_program=perfrept.perfmast.sas&_debug=0&ccyy=2020&lev=S&prgopt=reports%2Ftapr%2Fpaper_tapr.sas, p. 22.

19. Barbara Kantrowitz and Pat Wingert, "Failing the Most Gifted Kids," *Newsweek*, November 15, 1993, 67.

20. Ingrid Eisenstadter, "A Stupid Way to Treat Gifted Children," *Wall Street Journal*, July 12, 1995.

21. https://www.nagc.org/sites/default/files/Revised%20NAGC_CSDPG_2018-2019%20State%20of%20the%20States%20in%20Gifted%20Education%20Report-FINAL.pdf

22. https://acasestudy.com/the-treatment-of-gifted-children/

23. Andrew P. Dunn, "What's Wrong with Special Education," *Education Week*, May 17, 2000, 36, 39.

24. Public K–12 education spending per public school student is over $13,000 (2018—most recent data available) (https://nces.ed.gov/programs/coe/indicator_cmb.asp). Children already enrolled in private schools are also entitled to public funding. That expense, plus the money for Federal Law 94–142, and for oversight and enforcement, data set maintenance, and K–12 education policy evaluation, will leave at least $10,000 per child.

25. After some time to establish new schools.

26. https://www.privateschoolreview.com/tuition-stats/private-school-cost-by-state

27. "Any choice plan must secure equal family opportunity to attend any participating school" (Coons and Sugarman, 1999, p. 191). The parental choice policy proposed by this book may satisfy Coons and Sugarman. Since Coons and Sugarman seem willing to accept a program if "the amount of the voucher were so large as to preempt all interest in spending for [formal] education by all but an insignificant number of families." Their view would seem to depend on how small a number is "insignificant" and whether "all interest" could be softened to allow for the kinds of modest add-ons the vast majority of families can afford. Recall that low-income families are waiting in line to supplement privately funded vouchers with their own money. The vast majority of families can afford some add-on.

28. Milton Friedman, in Bonsteel and Bonilla (1997, Chapter 27).

29. See the skillful assault on the paranoia about "wicked windfalls for the wealthy" in Quentin L. Quade, "Watch Your Step! If School Choice Is So Great, Why Don't We Have It?," *Network News and Views*, January–February 1996.

30. According to 1996 Census Bureau data, it only takes an income of $75,316 to place a family in the top 20% of income earners, an amount that certainly does not make a family "rich," especially if they live in a major city. The *average* family income of the top 20% is $125,627. Consistent with a Tax Freedom Day in early May (delineates how much of a year the average American must work just to pay their state, local, and federal taxes—see the Tax Foundation Website at TaxFoundation.org for more details), assume that taxes consume 35% of the income of the top 10%'s average family. That leaves disposable income of $81,657. Even for such a wealthy family, tuition for two children to attend private schools would consume around 10% of their disposable income.

31. Two examples of arguments for means testing: (1) Caroline Hoxby in Ladd (1996), and (2) Paul Wyckoff (1991).

32. Clune's title implies that equity means equality. Since equality can only be approximated at levels below what some parents would like to spend, I don't agree with Clune's implicit assumption. See McCarty and Brazer (1990) for a more detailed discussion of implications of equalization.

33. https://www.forbes.com/sites/frederickhess/2020/05/20/the-case-against-school-choice-is-unraveling

34. See the last chapter of Rose (2016).

Chapter 10

Diversity Issues

Choice opponents frequently assert that public school systems increase the interaction of children from different backgrounds, and that TPSs are the best way to establish and maintain the appropriate collectively chosen common set of values. Neither assertion has much theoretical or empirical support, and the desirability of a politically chosen common body of beliefs is anything but obvious (Raywid, 1992, pp. 112–113).[1]

Choice advocates do not adequately refute those claims. Therefore, choice opponents still claim that choice expansion will produce various forms of segregation and that choice will cause our society and political system to crumble for lack of an appropriate common set of core values (Goldhaber, 1996, p. 143). *The much greater threat to liberty is the current education system's failure to teach what we have learned about different political and economic structures, and thus the increasing inability to discern good policies from bad.*

Some choice opponents even claim that choice will cause the proliferation of extremist schools. In contrast, it is actually the status quo and its achievement deficit, lack of choice, and absence of competition that threatens the integrity of the political process and our national unity (Arons, 1997; McCluskey, 2007); witness the discovery of widespread teaching of critical race theory. Indeed, much extremism occurs on public school campuses.[2]

The current system forces the political process to address divisive issues that individuals could resolve for themselves (Arons, 1997; McCluskey, 2007; Rector, 1995). One reason for the system's inefficiency is that

> energized factions will waste resources trying to dominate that monopoly that could be much better spent on the education of their kids.[3]
>
> The majoritarian assumption transformed the public schools into a battleground for determining public orthodoxy. By requiring that the majority [of the politically active] decide how all children should be socialized we in effect

require that people contest the most intractable issues of individual conscience [through the political process]. (Arons, 1982, pp. 24–25, 30)

The dominant practice of defining choice expansion policies as tools to shuffle children among the schools in the current system sustains and exaggerates the segregation issue.

Choice advocates' mistakes are a major part of the problem. Their rebuttal of choice opponents' claim that choice will yield segregation is little more than a comparison of private and public school enrollments. The segregation issue persists largely because the rebuttals are inadequate, and almost entirely defensive. Much more than a stronger rebuttal is possible. Choice advocates must argue that an OEI will maximize the interaction of children from different backgrounds.

THE FOCUS ON LIMITED CHOICE AND CORRELATION VS. CAUSATION

"White flight" from the inner city is probably the phenomenon that lends credibility to assertions that whites will not voluntarily attend a school with a large minority population, though increasingly they do.[4] Prejudice certainly contributed to white flight, but income was probably the most important factor. Andrew Coulson (1999) reached the same conclusion:

> What is not so well known is the fact that the "white" in the "white flight" refers more accurately to the color of people's collars than to the color of their skin. That is to say, money, not race, is the best predictor of who fled. (p. 137)[5]

Though sorting by income was the dominant factor, prejudice certainly motivated some people. Prejudice still influences some families, but it is a much less important decision-making criterion now than when the "white flight" phenomenon became well known. The correlation between income and minority membership exaggerates the perception of past prejudice.

Since it's normal for neighborhoods to have people with similar incomes, the correlation between income and race often creates racially homogenous TPSs. That's an outcome of school choice exercised by changing where you live. Property taxes were once an even larger source of funding, so it was obvious that upscale neighborhoods had better-financed schools. When affluent families move, they leave behind a more homogenous lower-income neighborhood. The current system promotes devastating residential separation according to income.[6]

Though prejudice can increase such separation, it will occur even without prejudice. That is evident in comments by Angie Garcia, a former Texas director of the League of United Latin American Citizens (LULAC):

> Those who had enough money have left our inner-city neighborhoods to buy homes in better school districts. This has weakened our inner-city communities, both financially and culturally.[7]

With the likely propensity of an OEI to yield specialized schooling options,[8] choice expansion can foster racial and ethnic separation *only* when an academic specialty area is highly correlated with racial, ethnic, or socioeconomic characteristics. Modern stereotypes hint that a school specialized in science might attract a disproportionately Asian student body, and schools with an emphasis on athletics might attract a disproportionately African American student body, but *such correlations are still likely to be rare and harmless.*

The only other way choice expansion could create greater homogeneity is if student body composition mattered to parents more than any other difference between schools. That would take a sharp rise in prejudicial attitudes—the opposite of what seems to have occurred—or *tiny differences between TPS practices and policies*, for example, from so-called public school choice. We say so-called public school choice because even where it is legal to switch TPSs without relocating, it is typically rare, and it only yields a choice among different grades of an attempt at uniformity in comprehensiveness.

The best TPSs are typically full, and even when they're not—such as after post-pandemic enrollment losses[9]—school districts often refuse to take each other's students. We cannot pretend that an open enrollment declaration for TPSs will even yield much wider access to existing TPSs, much less the relentlessly improving menu of diverse schooling options we need.

The uniformity of TPS policies, especially within the same district, *exaggerates the importance of prejudice*. When parents compare school attendance zones, student body composition may be the only easily discernible difference between the zones. Student body composition influences choice to the extent that restrictions on parental choice keep the school system from changing and fostering specialization.[10]

THEORY AND REALITY

Kevin Smith and Kenneth Meier (1995) claimed that choice would lead to segregation and religious indoctrination and that "democratic institutions will seek to ensure such demands are not met." Smith and Meier offered no theoretical or empirical support for the alleged single-minded intolerance of individuals, their idealistic view of the political process, or the implied private-public decision-making schizophrenia implied by combining the two.

Since only evidence to the contrary comes to mind, the failure to support the bold Smith and Meier assertion is not surprising. Terms like "segregation" and "indoctrination" imply the use of force, and force is the essence of government.[11] A thorough refutation of the Smith and Meier claim is another book. The less ambitious rebuttal that follows includes some theoretical arguments, and one especially relevant example from the 51 U.S. school systems.

Segregation

Choice expansion can produce separation or stratification, but not segregation. The latter implies the use of force, that is, codified policy. Choice expansion can produce some geographic sorting of people, but the sorting factor is not necessarily race, ethnic origin, or even income. Sorting occurs by chance, or through illegal business decisions. Chance or decisions by organizations, or by independent people, may yield stratification. For example, the area near a sports arena might contain the city's most rabid sports fans. Sorting criteria amount to segregation only when the government enforces a doctrine like the longtime "separate but equal" policy, or when it ignores clearly discriminatory behavior.

In sharp contrast to Smith and Meier's (1995) claim about the political process, segregation by race was a longtime policy of many democratic[12] governments. U.S. history contains many examples of discrimination and institutional favoritism, including separate, and allegedly equal, TPSs. Segregated education facilities were an official policy until the *Brown v. Board of Education* (1954) U.S. Supreme Court ruling.[13]

The practice persisted as a popular unofficial policy in many places for decades thereafter. Indeed, its symptoms persist.[14] And despite expensive, controversial policies such as busing and court takeovers, the student body of many schools is much more homogenous than the population of its region; stratification is getting worse.[15]

"Black Americans in particular remain more residentially segregated than most other racial or ethnic groups. More than two-thirds of black and Hispanic children are still educated in segregated schools, and that proportion has increased sharply over the past decade."[16] Absent force, "stratified" is a more accurate characterization than "segregated." A key force underlying the persistent, growing stratification by income and race[17] is the phenomenon described by LULAC's Ms. Garcia described above and documented by Tim DeRoche (2020). *Limiting school choice to choosing a TPS attendance area drives up the price of homes in the better areas, which concentrates poverty in the attendance areas of the worst TPSs.*

States actively sought to disenfranchise a large share of the population. Political majorities use democratic institutions to dominate and oppress political minorities. Democratic institutions don't automatically do the right thing, even in the rare instances where the public interest is clearly defined, or even reflect the will of the people, for better or worse (Hayek, 1945, p. 42).

Term limits for legislators are good examples. Term limits are rare even though they enjoy overwhelming public support. The reality of the political process differs greatly from the idealized high school civics version of politics. Wishful thinking—hope triumphing over experience—seems to underlie advocacy of political-process-run public school systems and much of the opposition to parental choice.

The public school system reduces the interaction of children with widely differing backgrounds. For multi-school, multi-neighborhood towns, there is every reason to expect that result. As early as 1966, Christopher Jencks observed that neighborhood schools would keep children from different socioeconomic backgrounds from mixing. Daniel Akst's typical story of relocation to suburbs when the first child reaches school age shows how "lack of choice in schooling has helped segregate [stratify] our cities and keeps them segregated."[18] According to Angie Garcia, former Texas director of LULAC,

> Our schools are still segregated, not because the government dictates it, but because of flight from low-performing, often unsafe inner-city schools.[19]

In the 1970s, the federal government's predecessor to the cabinet-level Department of Education said that parental choice would help advance racial diversity because choice would diminish the importance of neighborhood homogeneity (Wyckoff, 1991).

Attendance zones reduce the mixing of children with different backgrounds by shrinking the area that schools draw students from. If the formal nonoverlapping official TPS attendance zones did not exist, the areas that contained each school's students would overlap, and neighbors would more frequently attend different schools. More children would interact with one set of children in their neighborhoods, and another set in their chosen school.

Indoctrination

Fear that democratic institutions would foster indoctrination was a key, well-founded reason for the First Amendment to the U.S. Constitution's Bill of Rights. Our highly political textbook selection and development processes invariably yield indoctrination (Sykes, 1995),[20] though it may be incoherent.

The founding fathers were superb political scientists. They knew that politics could foster intolerance of minorities, especially minorities defined by skin color, ethnic origin, or religious convictions. Such intolerance was a key source of immigration to the New World.

When a governing majority coalition is stable—when the majority coalition is about the same for every important decision—members of the majority can be especially tyrannical, often extracting tribute from the political minority to reward members of the majority constituencies for supporting those in power. As *Brown* demonstrated, the courts, the least democratic part of the government, are often the only way to eliminate discriminatory policies.

The Common School Myth

The claim that non-OEI, TPS-dominated school systems will establish and maintain the most appropriate common body of knowledge fails on several grounds. The most compelling reason to reject that claim is the global and persistent ineffectiveness of centrally planned schooling. Recall that the world's top-ranked systems outscore the "Nation at Risk," low-performing U.S. K–12 systems by about 10%. The dubious claim that democratic institutions will create and convey a curriculum that contains well-defined, uncontroversial critical elements is irrelevant if the favored TPSs struggle to convey the material.

Sykes (1995) and Finn and Ravitch (2004) described how politics infects curriculum development and the textbook production and selection process (Sykes, 1995).[21] Political correctness—the imperative to placate numerous special interests, each with its own view of what each course and book must include and omit—severely distorts and dilutes content. The curriculum development and textbook selection process is a glaring example[22] of the difference between the naive political theory of people working together to define common values and the reality of a nasty and contentious political process that yields "negotiated and compromised values" (Raywid, 1992, p. 113) and forces huge omissions to achieve agreement.

Especially devastating effects occur in subject areas such as history and social studies that matter most to unity and respect for democratic values. Consider the 1990s attempt to develop a national history standard. The National Governors Association's blue-ribbon panel had considerable difficulty reaching an agreement. Finally they "brought forth a politically correct screed [informal piece of writing] that was denounced by professional historians and rejected by a US Senate vote of ninety-nine to one."[23] Even subject areas such as math and physical sciences that don't seem to have any political content are not immune to political emasculation by the political correctness disease.

THE INADEQUATE REBUTTAL

A big part of the sorting/stratification issue is the narrow definition of choice expansion that pervades the debates. The typical choice expansion leaves many of the key elements of the status quo intact. That leaves little basis to argue that student body composition will become a less significant choice-making factor. It forces choice advocates into the misleading, difficult defensive position of having to assert that student composition would be a trivial choice-making factor. Then the rebuttal of claims that more parental choice will increase segregation rests on the reasonably diverse makeup of existing private schools and the current uses of restriction-laden versions of choice to pursue racial diversity goals.

Those facts are important, but they are just a starting point for a counterattack on the alleged segregation issue. Choice advocates can and should argue that parental choice in an OEI will make student body composition into a less significant choice-making factor.

Diversity Comparisons

James Coleman was among the first[24] to note the racial diversity of our systems' private schools (Coleman, 1987),[25] more so than a typical TPS, despite some public-private separation by income, and considerable grouping by religion. With parents having to pay private school tuition on top of their school taxes, income is a surprisingly small private school attendance barrier.

The high demand for privately funded, *partial* low-income vouchers has shown that many low-income families can find money for private school tuition. The religion factor exists because church-run schools dominate the tiny private school sector that results from the current systems' governance and funding policies, which causes many parents to send their children to a church-run school despite the religious orientation, not because of it.[26] Many parents tolerate religion courses because they prefer the academics, discipline, and safety of the church-run school over their assigned TPS.

Church-run schools will probably have a much smaller share of the larger private sector that an OEI would establish. Many parents who can afford the relatively low tuition still don't use church-run schools. In an OEI, those parents would keep their children in a likely improved TPS or choose a secular private school. Church-run schools would gain children currently kept away by tuition costs. However, church-run schools would lose students who attend because a secular private school was not available.

Evidence from Hypocrisy

Choice opponents say that parental choice will increase stratification even though we already use "parental choice as a strategy to racially integrate urban school systems" (Carl, 1994; Wells, 1993). Since the alternative was busing, limited choice expansion "was a politically advantageous response to school desegregation orders" (Raywid, 1992, p. 111). Magnet schools started as a way to recruit white, non-Hispanic children for schools in minority areas. That's still the primary purpose of many magnet schools.

Cambridge, Massachusetts, implemented controlled choice among TPSs (Fiske, 1991) to improve its schools' racial mix. District officials encouraged the schools to establish their own identities through unique programs, but to fulfill racial quotas the authorities had the final word on each child's school, which created many mismatches between unique programs and the interests and abilities of children. District officials denied some parents all of their top choices because the political process assigned a particular version of racial diversity a higher priority than the best possible match between a district's programs and student engagement factors. Perversely, the children forced into a mismatch are lucky that TPSs cannot pursue much specialization.[27]

FROM REBUTTAL TO COUNTERATTACK

Inside the intellectual prison bars of the status quo and misinterpreted past experience, uncontrolled choice that includes private schools can seem counterproductive (Wells, 1993). When choice is seen as something that just shifts a few students from TPSs to current private schools, prejudice-related criteria are going to be decisive more often for public school choice because public schools lack many possible, significant programmatic or pedagogical differences. State constitutions (e.g., Wisconsin) sometimes prohibit significant differences.

Desegregation through Specialization

The rationale underlying magnet schools and Cambridge's controlled choice policy is that most people care more about programmatic differences than integration (Wells, 1993), or the separation of certain groups. The increased diversity produced by the choice part of controlled choice will reflect the expected family priority of academics over racial or ethnic homogeneity.

By maximizing competitive pressures, and by minimizing the influence of politics, an OEI maximizes specialization by schools.[28] The resulting big programmatic and pedagogical differences would yield less homogenous student bodies than choice among TPSs. Those larger academic differences would further discourage prejudice-motivated behavior.

Borderless, Overlapping Attendance Areas

No policy can totally end neighborhood or student body sorting by socioeconomic background. But an OEI will minimize separation because with openness schools have informal, borderless, overlapping attendance areas determined by transportation costs. In comparison, 70%–80% of children attend an assigned TPS with a small, exclusive attendance area.[29] Efforts to completely eliminate student body income differences can easily do more harm than good.

Private-public tuition copayment, such as through voucher top-offs, could cause some separation by income. But flexible prices are much too important to consider banning copayment, especially since much of the separation effect is temporary until competition and experience drives down prices. Two factors will minimize that separation: (1) per-pupil public funding at a dollar level that a large number of schools will accept as nearly full payment—a practice strongly recommended throughout this book, and (2) philanthropists will expand means-tested scholarships to include top-off assistance. As noted previously, copayment will free up the donor funding paid directly to schools, especially CPSs.

Smaller Income Differences

Since market forces produce significant specialization and competitive behavior, at least in the private sector, schools would improve everywhere. Even without significant competitive behavior by TPSs, loss of poor-fit students improves TPS effectiveness.[30] The gains would be largest in the inner city where the worst schools and the least advantaged children live. Therefore, an OEI would likely gradually shrink the inverse correlation between family income and racial/ethnic minority membership. That would reduce the extent to which some natural sorting by income produces by-school or by-neighborhood racial or ethnic separation.

In the political arena, diversity of perspective produces bland compromises, acrimony, and deadlock. Eugene Smoley (1999) and the Twentieth Century Fund[31] cited electoral and special-interest diversity as a major reason why school boards performed so poorly. But in a market setting, diversity is an asset. Through the freedom that choice expansion entails, "the great cultural diversity of urban schools—so often cited as an excuse for failure—could be turned into a tremendous asset" (Lewis, 1996, pp. 5–7).

NOTES

1. According to Raywid (1992), libertarians and some conservatives believe that putting education practices in the domain of politics puts freedom in jeopardy, a belief famously expressed by John Stuart Mill in 1859.
2. For example, the recent spate of school shootings and the arguments for school uniforms.
3. Richard Sherlock, "Choice v. Conflict in Education," Sutherland Institute Public Policy Perspective, August 27, 1996.
4. https://www.theatlantic.com/education/archive/2019/07/kamala-harris-busing-politics/593797/
5. Coulson based his claim on Zafirau and Fleming (1982).
6. http://www.aei.org/publication/cpr-scholarships-using-private-school-choice-to-attack-concentrated-poverty-crime-and-unemployment/
7. Angie Garcia, "Vouchers Not Edgewood's Real Problem," *San Antonio Express-News*, December 6, 1998.
8. https://object.cato.org/sites/cato.org/files/serials/files/cato-journal/2005/5/cj25n2-9.pdf
9. https://reason.org/commentary/top-performing-public-schools-are-rejecting-students-even-though-they-have-open-seats/
10. https://object.cato.org/sites/cato.org/files/serials/files/cato-journal/2005/5/cj25n2-9.pdf
11. See Thomas Sowell, "Governments Have Fostered Discrimination," *Des Moines Register*, August 5, 1995, 7, for more discussion and examples. "Government Is Not Reason, It Is Not Eloquence—It Is Force," is true even if the phrase widely attributed to George Washington is apocryphal. http://volokh.com/2010/04/14/government-is-not-reason-it-is-not-eloquence-it-is-force/
12. In fact, we live in a republic. Few public policies are the result of democracy. As is common elsewhere, the term "democratic" is used to generally denote the participatory process of choosing and lobbying representatives, and less frequently choosing and deciding ballot propositions.
13. https://en.wikipedia.org/wiki/Brown_v._Board_of_Education
14. A *Newsweek* cover story (Joe Klein, "The Legacy of Summerton," *Newsweek*, May 16, 1994, 26–31) made that case largely through the example of a particular, supposedly typical, case. It included this statement: "Recent studies show that most school systems remain as profoundly segregated as those in Summerton, and those in the inner cities seem far more desperate" (p. 27). According to Robert L. Carter, an NAACP lawyer who helped argue *Brown v. Board of Education*: "More black children are in all or virtually all black schools today than in 1954." Quote from "Civil Rights Leaders Wear Scars of Controversy," *Washington Times*, May 17, 1994. According to Coleman (1987), "They [public schools] tend to be the most exclusive and segregated schools."
15. https://www.edweek.org/leadership/an-expansive-look-at-school-segregation-shows-its-getting-worse/2022/06

16. https://www.theatlantic.com/education/archive/2019/07/kamala-harris-busing-politics/593797/

17. https://www.edweek.org/leadership/an-expansive-look-at-school-segregation-shows-its-getting-worse/2022/06

18. Daniel Akst, "Why Liberals Should Love School Choice," *Wall Street Journal*, April 6, 1998.

19. Angie Garcia, "Vouchers Not Edgewood's Real Problem," *San Antonio Express-News*, December 6, 1998. Empirical evidence to support Ms. Garcia's assertion, and that the Akst story is not unique: Doyle and Munro (1997).

20. Also https://fordhaminstitute.org/national/research/mad-mad-world-textbook-adoption

21. Also https://fordhaminstitute.org/national/research/mad-mad-world-textbook-adoption

22. https://fordhaminstitute.org/national/research/mad-mad-world-textbook-adoption

23. Paul Gray, "Debating Standards," *Time*, April 8, 1996, 40.

24. More recently, a similar finding comes from Jay P. Greene and Nicole Mellow, "Integration Where It Counts: A Study of Racial Integration in Public and Private School Lunchrooms," Conference of the American Political Science Association Meeting, Boston, MA, September 1998.

25. The racial diversity of private schools was noted more recently by John Chubb and Terry Moe, "The Private vs Public School Debate," *Wall Street Journal*, July 26, 1991.

26. A poll of the New York City parents seeking privately funded scholarships to attend Catholic Schools indicated that the first concern of 85% of the parents was academic quality. Only 38% cited the religious instruction as their primary motivation. Ed Feulner, "Is School Choice a Bad Idea?," *Heritage Member News*, Autumn 1998.

27. According to Tony Wagner (1996), a prominent educator and a resident of Cambridge, "The majority of the 13 [Cambridge K–8 schools] seem virtually interchangeable and are mediocre."

28. https://object.cato.org/sites/cato.org/files/serials/files/cato-journal/2005/5/cj25n2-9.pdf

29. 80% in TPSs in 1993 to 73% in 2007 (https://nces.ed.gov/pubs2010/2010004.pdf); staying in that range, hard to pin down (https://nces.ed.gov/fastfacts/display.asp?id=55; https://nces.ed.gov/fastfacts/display.asp?id=6).

30. http://faculty.business.utsa.edu/jmerrifi/evp.pdf

31. The Twentieth Century Fund, *Facing the Challenge: The Report of the Twentieth Century Fund Task Force on School Governance* (New York: The Twentieth Century Fund Press, 1992).

Chapter 11

Important Policy Choices

With the world's current school systems as a starting point, the key outcome of policy imperatives, and various policy choices, is to have entrepreneur-created schooling options on an approximately level playing field with the schooling options staffed by the government (mostly TPSs). That would yield the urgently needed OEI. Chapter 3 adequately addressed the CPS policy options, so this chapter focuses on policy choices that would energize entrepreneurial initiative to develop relentlessly improving private schooling options.

There are several major policy options for achieving that approximately level playing field for the "consumers"—the parents—of an OEI. Nondiscrimination is a moral, economic efficiency, and equity ideal, which means the same amount of public money should follow a particular child no matter who owns the lawful school chosen by the child's parents. Since the public school system will have significant legacy costs such as bond debt and pension liabilities, exact nondiscrimination is probably not achievable. Approximate nondiscrimination is good enough.

A PAYMENT SCHEDULE—PROBABLY WEIGHTED STUDENT FORMULA

The first choice is the nature of the payment-through-parents schedule. That is, how much public money will follow a child to the chosen school, public or private? Because there are some obvious degrees of difference between the cost ranges for many delineatable categories of schoolchildren, a "weighted student formula" (WSF) is an appropriate basis for the public funding for a particular child's schooling. With copayment allowed, the WSF does not become a price control.

Since the constantly changing exact cost range differences between different observable student categories, which also vary geographically, are not knowable to the central planners who must devise the WSF schedule, deciding whether to allow or not allow top-off (synonyms: copayment, shared financing) of the public funding is *not* an OEI policy option. To achieve an OEI, shared financing *must* be allowed, though market forces may yield many schooling options that charge only the government-provided funding amount.

The potential for shared financing is the basis of (1) some family skin in the game; (2) the essential full price (tuition) formation and price adjustment process that will orchestrate (strongly influence what's taught, where, how, and to whom) the parental selection of, and entrepreneurial development of, the alternatives to the public schools; and (3) flexible funding for schooling without tax rate adjustment. *It is also well worth repeating from the equity chapter (Chapter 10) that the entire copayment need not, and indeed often cannot or should not, come from the child's family.*

Charities will provide means-tested copayment funding, hopefully always requiring some family skin in the game. Remember, for the families unable to fund a copayment from their own money or from a charity, there is still a zero-tuition public school—traditional (TPSs) and perhaps chartered (CPSs)—which will typically be better than the average current TPSs, at least because: (1) departure of outliers will reduce the need for differentiated instruction, and (2) perhaps competitive pressures. Then there is the matter of actually getting public funds to the alternatives to the TPSs.

DIRECT PAYMENT?

The United States has 51 school systems. State primacy means that the payment policy and funding are state government matters. In some countries, the government can simply send out checks based on verified enrollment reports. That likely maximizes the potential for, and intensity of, regulation of the alternatives to TPSs, especially the potential for the worst possible regulation—a copayment ban. Because of the way the U.S. Supreme Court interprets the First Amendment, direct payment is likely not an option in the United States. Because education tax credits and education savings accounts (both described below) can be designed to be superior means of achieving near nondiscrimination, unavailability of the direct payment option is very likely a positive factor.

TUITION VOUCHERS

This is the best-known vehicle for directing taxpayer dollars to eligible private schools. Voucher holders submit the document to an eligible private school, and the school cashes it. The cash value of the voucher may depend on a WSF and socioeconomic status (a proposed basis).

Except compared to direct payment, voucher use maximizes regulation, especially pressure for a copayment ban, which is a devastating constraint. And, compared to the options below, the voucher vehicle provides much less flexibility in how and when to buy education services. The full voucher amount must be offered to an eligible private school, which at least creates a price floor (bad) for each WSF-recognized category at the voucher amount. And if the policy bans or severely restricts shared financing of the tuition bill, it also creates devastating price ceiling effects such as shortages, quality erosion, scandal, and short-circuiting of the basis for decentralized planning.

For political reasons, it is probably good that tuition vouchers are obsolete relative to other ways of leveling the financial playing field between public and private schooling options. A nondiscrimination-targeted voucher policy, with copayment allowed, is an okay basis for an OEI, but unprincipled choice expansion opponents have exploited the fact that the actual experience with vouchers arises *only* from programs that lack key OEI elements.

As Thomas Sowell (2018) extensively documented, lack of one key element is enough to get totally different outcomes. Because of the limited nature of what have been widely deemed experiments (recall Chapter 2), choice expansion opponents can truthfully assert from the misleading and largely irrelevant "voucher evidence" that school choice hasn't made much difference in readily measured school system outcomes.

Choice expansion proponents often fail to add the caveat that the "treatment" has only been tested in very small doses. When this oversight is deliberate, it is a form of dishonesty—lying. People who painted with an overly broad brush have suffered no accountability for the devastating impact on lives severely diminished by an inability to escape a poor-fit TPS, or one of the many dysfunctional TPSs that fit no one.

When presented the facts, educated laypeople will understand the dosage dishonesty. Look at any medicine that you've taken and ask what effects would be seen if the consumed dosage was a small fraction of the MD-prescribed amount.

To achieve significant expansion of the menu of schooling options, Friedman (1955, 1962, and many others) prescribed the universal, nondiscrimination dosage for choice expansion, which has yet to be tried for a publicly funded U.S. program, or a non-restriction-laden foreign program.

The few privately funded voucher programs that applied a nontrivial dose of choice expansion yielded impressive results despite major shortcomings such as small scale, difficulty making comparisons because testing data do not match that from TPSs, low voucher funding levels, and investment discouraged by nonpermanence.[1] So, rather than trying to get public attention to detail-intensive issues that a lot of people may not grasp, we can ditch the use of vouchers in favor of the universal, nondiscrimination-dosage education tax credits or education savings accounts (ESAs).

EDUCATION TAX CREDITS

A refundable education tax credit can yield more private school tuition payment assistance than the tax liability against which the credit applies. So, for example, a $9,000 state income tax credit against a $5,000 state income tax liability yields zero income tax liability plus a $4,000 refund check. With 100% refundability, the only noteworthy difference between a tax credit and a tuition voucher policy with similar dollar value and eligibility rules is a Friedman-like objection to using the tax code to deliberately influence behavior.

A nonrefundable tax credit cannot yield more tuition funding than the tax liability against which the credit applies. *Critically*, with the nonrefundability aspect, courts rule[2] that tax credit seekers are spending their own money, not public funds, which greatly reduces the propensity to attach regulation to the use of the money. It also maximizes flexibility to bolster educational progress in ways other than just private school use.

But the nonrefundability aspect can create a major problem. Many families—probably the vast majority—do not have enough state tax liability, or even state plus local liability, especially if limited to a single direct tax—typically the state income tax—for even a nonrefundable 100% credit to significantly defray private school tuition costs of a single child.

Some states have partially addressed that problem by allowing businesses to claim a tax credit for contributing to private voucher funding for low-income families. Combining tax credits for families that opt a child out of the assigned TPS and tax credits for businesses that finance vouchers yields what are called tax credit scholarships (TCSs), which is a term used to avoid the politically incorrect term "voucher." Currently, sadly, TCSs are the most common private school expansion policy. It is sad because the tax credits and scholarship amounts are not close to near-nondiscrimination levels.

To understand why the tax credit for businesses can only partially address the nonrefundable credits' funding discrimination problem, we have to understand the source of public funding for K–12 schooling. Taxpayers directly and indirectly pay the taxes earmarked for K–12 schooling throughout their adult lives, not just when their children are in school.

To approach near-nondiscrimination levels, nonrefundable tax credits must be bankable. So, if a family spends, say, $250,000 on private schooling for two children, and the nonrefundable credit is an 80% credit (80% of

$250,000 is $200,000) against state taxes owed, that family must earn tax credits against actual taxes owed for as long as it takes for the credits to sum to $200,000. For most families, it will take years after their children have left high school to hit $200,000.

Even with that bankability feature to extend credit recovery beyond the schooling period, some families won't have enough tax liability in their entire lives to recapture a large amount of tuition spending, or they may simply suffer a cash-flow problem—the inability to make immediate large payments and then wait a long time to recover the X% allowed by a bankable credit. So, for a nonrefundable credit to achieve near-nondiscrimination levels, even with bankability, we'd need low-income family assistance through the business-targeted aspect of tax credit scholarship policies.

EDUCATION SAVINGS ACCOUNT (ESA)

In eight states, some families become eligible for an ESA[3] when they opt a child out of the assigned TPS. An ESA[4] provides public funding restricted to goods and services defined, formally, as educational. The account receives an annual deposit accessible through a special debit card. As some recent abuses have shown, the combination of debit card design and product coding is still improvable. We won't deal with that. We will describe the policy option of indirectly providing public funding for educational services, including but not limited to private school use.

That additional flexibility can be critical. It allows for spending on educational services such as tutoring and customization such as through course choice,[5] which can produce blended learning that can be far superior to what can be achieved within the constraints of a single school.[6] Course choice means having the flexibility to take different courses from different "schools"; some might be virtual.

ESAs allow frontloading of education spending through shared financing, or deferral of education spending, including for postsecondary schooling. The potential to carry year-end ESA balances forward into the next year has possibly great direct value to families, and the potential for shared financing and year-end balance rollover is critical to the decentralized planning process. A rollover possibility avoids a use-it-or-lose-it price floor at the annual public funding amount. Universal ESA access at near-nondiscrimination levels will foster efficient price formation and adjustment, providing the essential decentralized planning basis to determine what will be taught through the private sector, where, how, and to whom.

Example: Suppose eligible families get an annual ESA deposit of $9,000 for each child they opt out of the assigned TPS. They can spend $11,000 per year for three years (years 1–3) through a $2,000 copayment each year and then indirectly recover the $2,000 by spending only $7,000 per year for years 4–6. They can't directly shift money from the ESA to a personal bank account, but the $6,000 saved can offset future private spending on schooling, including college tuition costs. On the other hand, suppose a child attends a private school, K–12, through the ESA, but the private school tuition is only $8,000 per year ($1,000 less than the ESA amount). At the end of the 13 years, $13,000 plus interest is available to defray the teenager's college tuition.

With per-pupil TPS spending averaging over $13,000 per year,[7] an annual ESA deposit at near-nondiscrimination levels will cause the need for copayment (to which many people strongly object) to be rare and mostly negligible. Near-nondiscrimination would yield enough private choices in most places to force most private schooling purveyors to charge at or below the annual ESA deposit level. States with a large state government share of TPS funding (e.g., Hawaii at 100%) can provide near-nondiscrimination ESA funding levels without demanding that locally generated TPS funding follow the children opted out of the assigned TPS.

OKAY AND GOOD ELIGIBILITY TARGETING

Traditional eligibility targeting to children from low-income families, children assigned to TPSs formally designated failing, and children with diagnosed learning disabilities is to be avoided or assertively registered as a basis for low expectations for school system–wide improvement. *Such targeting wrongly implies that the assigned TPS is a good fit for all of the children outside the targeted categories.* For example, presence in an affluent neighborhood does not make TPS instruction adequately fit all. And the most prominent special need calling for choice is extraordinary ability—perhaps just in some subject fields—which typically is not included among the eligibility criteria for special needs–based school choice expansion.

Maintenance of appropriate expectations can make such targeting okay, which is better than no choice expansion. Only "okay" because very few families have genuine choice without out-of-pocket cost leveling between TPS and privately provided schooling options. Few are readily willing/able to pay for schooling twice (tuition on top of the taxes that fund TPSs).

In light of the political challenges of overcoming the inertia preventing implementation of near-nondiscrimination with universal eligibility, place-based targeting can be very good. Limiting universal choice to the poorest places avoids opposition from families near the best TPSs (typically still very inefficient), while it enlists the support of people eager to address the urban economic stratification that derives much of its basis from assigning children to TPSs.

Because the natural tendency of families to compete for the best possible TPS assignments causes higher housing costs in the attendance zones of the best TPSs, only the worst TPSs cost nothing other than taxes that must be paid. All of the other TPSs cost taxes plus a housing premium (Yinger & Nguyen-Hoang, 2011; DeRoche, 2020), which creates the economic segregation cited throughout this book. Shared financing of tuition is a far better way to finance schooling. It yields decentralized planning and a diverse menu of schooling options. Making families pay for better schooling through higher housing prices yields only better and worse versions of uniformly comprehensive.

Traditional attempts to direct economic development to high-poverty zones[8] have a very poor track record. School choice expansion targeted to poor places[9]—universal eligibility in the targeted zones—has an outstanding record of preventing flight of affluent families to areas with better TPSs, and even recruiting affluent families to lower-income areas.[10] Studies of Georgia,[11] Louisiana,[12] Tennessee,[13] and Texas[14] demonstrate the high degree of economic stratification present in every U.S. city mapped according to median family income or scrutinized through the "Opportunity Atlas."[15] Those studies provide the basis for the targeting of universal eligibility for private school choice to residents of lower-income areas.

Targeting choice eligibility to 100% of the children in large lower-income zip codes or census tracts creates real experiments in the high-dosage choice expansion that can be a transformational school system reform catalyst. We may need the evidence generated by such experiments to counteract the troublesome opposition narrative grounded in the existing, limited, low-dosage-only evidence. While experience accumulates from universal school choice eligibility in lower-income areas, especially the largest ones, private school choice expansion attacks the root causes of concentrated poverty and its devastating symptoms.

FACILITATING GOOD CHOICES

There are two key elements. First, to not leave children behind, entrepreneurs have to create a high-value menu of TPS alternatives as diverse as each area's schoolchildren, at minimum cost. Second, we need to inform wise selection from that menu. The price system is sufficient to inform and motivate entrepreneurship. That is, entrepreneurs will detect and act upon opportunities to at least temporarily charge a lot more for schooling than it costs them to deliver it. That will motivate innovation, as well as the copycat entrepreneurship that drives the cost and price of schooling options down to the costs of the most efficient producers of each instructional approach.

That same process would appropriately inform parents of differences in schooling option costs. Since the information needed to choose wisely from that diverse menu of schooling options is a public good, there is a case to be made for a government role in demanding information from schools and then making it public in a user-friendly format. Whether such a function can escape political bias, and whether it is worth its cost in light of private information sources driven by competitive pressures, is an empirical issue only experience and debate can resolve.

A critical information source will be private accreditations and certifications analogous to the Good Housekeeping Seal.[16] Schools will pursue such certifications to increase demand, and private certifiers seem to manage to retain the credibility needed to make the certifications valuable.

Regulatory restraint is a key part of facilitating the provision of good, diverse choices, along with the wisdom of families choosing. We have to keep in mind that school and district administrator accountability through the political process is a big part of how we got into our current "Nation at Risk" K–12 crisis.

Accountability to parents creates adequate attention to nearly all of the factors that legislators and regulators might be tempted to control. Very general rules such as the need to obey the law and minimum school sizes can adequately address factors such as discrimination and promoting hate. Competitive pressures will adequately address factors such as transportation and testing. Price system pressures will produce schools specialized in particular learning styles, including special needs, which is a much better approach to student diversity than directives requiring all schools receiving public funds, even indirectly, to accept all students.

In places with too little population density to support private schools addressing all special needs issues, the TPSs can continue their existing policies of providing appropriate services, which will be better informed as a result of practices by specialized private schools that exist in the larger urban areas. Course choice can address student diversity in low-population-density areas.

We have more than the sad long-term track record of political accountability as a basis to believe bottom-up accountability to schooling consumers will produce better results. Accountability to the political process occurs through objective measures such as specific subject test scores, for example, math, reading, and science. That has caused narrowing of the curriculum to the tested items and diversion of academic time to test-taking practice. Parents and society expect more from the schooling experience than high scores on specific standard tests.

Parents will certainly take test scores into account, which will prompt schools to adopt testing and publish scores. That parents will subjectively consider everything they know about a school will force schools to attend to quality across the spectrum of what schools can accomplish.

Expecting too much from the political process, and too little from subjective, bottom-up accountability to schooling customers, underlies many of the significant strategic and tactical mistakes discussed in the next chapter. The chapter also discusses the policy choices underlying a transition to an OEI.

NOTES

1. See Chapter 13 of *The School Choice Wars* (Merrifield, 2001).
2. https://ij.org/report/school-choice-and-state-constitutions/
3. https://www.edchoice.org/school-choice-in-america-dashboard-scia/ indicates that in 42 states, "no Education Savings Account programs are available."
4. https://www.edchoice.org/school-choice/types-of-school-choice/education-savings-account/
5. https://fordhaminstitute.org/national/resources/expanding-education-universe-explanation-course-choice-michael-brickman
6. https://fordhaminstitute.org/ohio/commentary/blended-learning-innovating-teaching-process-0
7. $13,118 in 2018: https://www.census.gov/newsroom/press-releases/2018/school-spending.html—estimates vary depending upon what is counted, and what sorts of adjustments are made. *Education Week* posted $12,526 as the national average.
8. https://www.heritage.org/taxes/report/opportunity-zones-understanding-them-the-context-past-place-based-incentives
9. https://www.aei.org/research-products/report/cpr-scholarships-using-private-school-choice-to-attack-concentrated-poverty-crime-and-unemployment/
10. http://faculty.business.utsa.edu/jmerrifi/evp.pdf and https://www.effective-ed.org/school-district-facts
11. https://static1.squarespace.com/static/59ca9008e45a7c444013ea43/t/5e1cb38d59e9f01e93c141ce/1578939283890/GA+Neighborhood+Hope+Scholarships.pdf
12. Not yet published when this was written; Google to find it.
13. https://static1.squarespace.com/static/59ca9008e45a7c444013ea43/t/5c5dd3299b747a2c78d52d76/1549652800870/TennesseeReport_Digital.pdf
14. https://drive.google.com/file/d/1mg5JJfVouKLt9L7_3Uj4BsuYPsW4Z90V/view
15. www.opportunityatlas.org/
16. https://www.goodhousekeeping.com/institute/about-the-institute/a31680/good-housekeeping-seal-faqs/

Chapter 12

Strategic and Tactical Mistakes

> It's time for major transformation of schools.
>
> —Jeanne Allen, director, Center for Education Reform[1]

Choice advocates talk about major reform, but nearly all of their proposals assume the key elements of the status quo. They celebrate every new option for anyone, even when the proposals could delay or derail more meaningful reforms. For example, the Center for Education Reform newsletter that contained Jeanne Allen's call for "major transformation of schools" also celebrated[2] a Florida voucher bill incapable of achieving any transformation. In the 1990s, the voucher plans in Cleveland and Milwaukee evoked the same unrealistic hype. Lately, it has been places with high concentrations of CPSs.

The story is equally depressing in Alabama. A 2014 report on the performance of Alabama's TPSs shows that nearly half of the students scored below basic on the Nation's Report Card (the NAEP test) (Merrifield & Ortiz, 2014). Despite such broad-based failure, Alabama's voucher program only allows for usage by failed school assignees who qualify for federally sponsored school lunches. Again, we can expect very little transformation from such a program. Alabama is especially far behind because it took until 2020 just to allow CPSs to operate in the state.

The education malpractice that children endure to become voucher eligible can mean that they've fallen so far behind that they may have to return to the TPS responsible for that. Because Alabama's participating private schools must accept the voucher as full payment, the voucher creates price control and lowers the private schools' money per student. Only the small share of TPSs near the failure standard have any additional incentive to change, far less than the share of children below the National Assessment of Educational Progress (NAEP) definition of basic reading and mathematics skills.

INCREMENTALISM?

In the decade preceding the 2001 publication of *The School Choice Wars*, choice advocates expected any additional choice for anyone to incrementally morph into their vision of adequate choice expansion, which was not always an OEI. Any extra choice supposedly moves us closer to "full school choice."[3] Low expectations and ideological confusion led to conclusions that progress can and must occur in "baby steps"[4] or with "piecemeal reforms."[5] Unfortunately, the piecemeal reforms became long-lasting stopping points, or even final destinations, rather than mileposts on an expressway to an OEI.

That hope for sufficient incremental change arose without any consistent evidence that major changes in the role of government can occur politically in stages, which means repeatedly revising and reenacting a policy. According to the incremental change hypothesis, there is no danger of stalling or lengthy detours.[6] A phase-in is better in that it only requires surviving the electoral and legislative gauntlet once, and it establishes a certain outcome at the outset. Create a plan to implement a determinate outcome in stages if necessary, but do not seek it in stages.

Though the private sector needs transformation, choice advocates act like the new private school users are rescued if they end up in schools like those in the current private sector. Choice advocates compare TPSs to the private schools present in the current system, when they should compare the average schooling outcomes of different governance, funding, and incentive *systems*.

Empirical support for the hypothesis that choosers will outperform their left-behind TPS peers means that choice expansion created effective escape mechanisms. After all, the implied hypothesis is mostly about giving students the option to attend better-fit-for-them schools that already exist, not about the effects, if any, of changes to the school system overall. The heavy focus on transferees ignores potential systemic benefits, which likely causes major underestimation of potential total OEI benefits.

The academic community's failure to recognize the obvious difference in research questions is a key reason for the persistent failure to address student diversity by properly building upon educator diversity. School researchers have been asking which type of school (CPS, TPS, or private) performs better than the other types of school. That approach set up the nearly irrelevant TPS vs. CPS and TPS vs. private political debates.

But we need to know whether a low-restriction system that fosters diverse schooling options performs better than systems that mostly support only TPSs. Few academic studies (Woessman, 2016), and zero non–peer reviewed reports, address the latter question. And low explanatory power in the key comparison (Woessman, 2016, note 8) of students in different systems suggests overlooked key variables.

Misleading information at least yields delay, which is the key downside of the hope that narrowly targeted programs can yield valuable insights and incremental change. The children stuck in a TPS that is not working for them may develop enough skills to earn a living, but not enough to differentiate objectively terrible policies from those with a legitimate basis for informed disagreement.

School system reform was urgent when *The School Choice Wars* was published in 2001, and from the intervening 20 years, we can see why delay yields an ever more dire "Nation at Risk" situation.[7] We are increasingly prone to existential-threat[8] policy errors that a better-educated public would not seriously consider.

Right after Chester Finn (a Reagan administration assistant secretary of education and prominent choice advocate) said he was "becoming more pragmatic [about choice advocacy]," he correctly noted that "piecemeal reform often slows the course of revolution,"[9] an understatement since it can abort it entirely. Low expectations led to conclusions that we cannot restructure the education system because "we do not live in an ideal world" (Chubb & Moe, 1990b, p. 21) or to conclusions that the public is just not ready for sweeping reforms.

The resulting "less sweeping reforms than vouchers" (Chubb & Moe, 1990b, p. 21) cannot produce, lead to, or reveal many effects of OEI conditions. Chester Finn and Rebecca Gau were correct: choice strategies are "mutating" (Finn & Gau, 1998, p. 79), but not for the better, as implied by the upbeat tone of their article. The first drastic mutations[10] eliminated the critical features of Milton Friedman's original proposal.[11]

Recall from Chapter 2 that choice opponents often attacked voucher proposals for their limited scope. The limited scope has become a common objection inadequately addressed by pro-choice campaign literature.[12] It means that incrementalism—stops on the "expressway"—may fortify, rather than reduce, resistance to choice expansion by creating new objections.

The typical choice advocate response to that common objection is that "lifeboat" programs for low-income families or children enrolled in low-performing schools are appropriate, or better than nothing. The correct response is that choice expansion is the best way to allocate all public funding of schooling.

Lowered expectations also lead to half measures, such as CPSs and choice limited to TPSs. But improvements over the status quo are not necessarily steps in the best direction. Both are probably one-way detours off the road to universal, nondiscriminatory choice expansion. Our country can't afford to neglect another generation of children, or the repeated misinvestment of tax dollars in the current system.

Progress toward an OEI will require a sustained assault on misconceptions. The shortcomings of the current system are a major reason why those misconceptions are getting harder to correct. Most voters, and their elected leaders, attended TPSs. Undereducation and miseducation, especially in economics,[13] make it harder to make the case for an OEI. It's another major source of urgency.

Bad Metaphor

John Hood (1991) said airline deregulation was a metaphor for gradual education reform. Hood said the controlled choice plan used in Cambridge, Massachusetts, to improve racial balance is an example of a good gradual reform starting point. Though airline deregulation was not done in one step, it had a much bigger first step than the Cambridge controlled choice plan. The Cambridge program limits parents' new choices to TPSs, and school administrators have the final say. With rare exceptions, choice-facilitated departures don't close schools or force ownership changes.[14] Many airlines dissolved or changed owners.

The poorly chosen metaphor illustrates several points. Unwittingly, Hood cast doubt on the assumed possibility of gradual reform. He admits that the airline industry has "*lingering* [emphasis added] impediments to competition." He claims that airline deregulation is an example of gradualism, even though most of the regulatory changes were not gradual. The original airline reforms were quite extensive. The original reform package was in place by 1982. The changes since have been much less extensive. Entrenchment of the original changes created the "lingering impediments." Likewise, the initial stages of restriction-laden reforms linger.[15] The end points of supposed gradual reform strongly resemble the starting point.

Stalled on a Detour

If choice supporters aren't told their destination, a hard-won victory will seem like a reasonable final destination to many. For example, though the key conditions of an OEI aren't present anywhere, the Center for Education Reform said "full school choice" already existed in Cleveland, Milwaukee, Vermont, and Maine.[16] Arguably, it only barely newly exists in Arizona and West Virginia, in the latter only if an appeals court reverses a lower court determination that it is illegal.

A similar example came from George Clowes (1998), then editor of *School Reform News*.[17] His version of "full school choice" is a voucher system that includes church-run schools without financial penalty. Clowes said, "The Milwaukee Parental Choice Program now offers a full working model for the broadest form of school choice." Limiting participation to 15% of children, as the Milwaukee plan does, and unequal financial support of TPS and private school students with price controls (copayment was forbidden in Milwaukee then—still true with a minor exception), must fall within his definition of "full school choice." The alleged linkages between the voucher program and Milwaukee public school behavior were unproductive, defensive reactions to embarrassment rather than competitive responses.

Clowes did not mention competition either, and he implied that each step follows naturally from the previous step. In contrast, many programs, including Milwaukee, skipped steps, and most stalled well short of Clowes's definition of "full school choice," often on their initial step. The five-step process outlined by Clowes—(1) intra-district, (2) inter-district, (3) CPS, (4) private-secular, and (5) all private—was, at best, wishful thinking, with a very modest wish. There is no reason you have to start with step 1 (intra-district choice among TPSs), and there is no reason to believe that each step is inevitably a temporary state of affairs that necessarily leads to the next step in a meaningfully short amount of time.

DOES UNILATERAL COMPROMISE REDUCE RESISTANCE?

Will restriction-laden choice proposals face less determined organized opposition? Already in the 1990s, evidence strongly suggested that the answer was no (McGroarty, 1998), and this has been recently reaffirmed.[18] Indeed, the key opponents of choice expansion never promised to oppose weaker versions with less vigor. Nevertheless, such appeasement is still common practice among parental choice advocates, in some cases right after acknowledging its futility. Consider this example. On page 5 of "Voucher Wars," Daniel McGroarty (1998) correctly observed that "the full force of the education establishment will always be brought to bear to beat back any voucher experiment, no matter how limited in scope or small in size," and then ignored his insight.

Universal, nondiscriminatory choice may not win right way, but the efforts will clearly establish what choice expansion advocates stand for and focus the public debate on stronger proposals. That will pay off as the public increasingly recognizes that other types of reforms produce only disappointment.[19]

Futility understates the negative effects of appeasement. If the countries of Eastern Europe had tried such an incremental march from dictatorship to democracy, the Iron Curtain and many dictators would still be there. The former socialist dictatorship countries that are trying to eliminate central planning in stages are far behind those that made the transition to full-fledged capitalism more abruptly. The incremental approach created many basket-case countries mired in "no-man's-land" between socialism and capitalism.

Many debilitating elements of the status quo are only rarely challenged. For example, choice advocates usually assume the dominance of school cartels called districts.[20] They champion competition in market settings with their rhetoric and publications, but then undermine competition with analytical and political mistakes. Sometimes compromise, appeasement, or the incremental progress hypothesis are key reasons that choice advocates enthusiastically support proposals that lack essential features of an OEI. However, carelessness and inertia are probably the most common reasons.

A fight for an OEI will differ from a fight for weaker versions of choice only in that the weaker versions contain debilitating restrictions that create additional grounds for criticism. In addition, weaker versions of choice leave more proponents of the status quo in positions of power from which they can cripple choice-based reforms or undermine their political support by misrepresenting their effects.

Choice advocates abandon some of their strongest arguments by letting their relentless, no-holds-barred opposition define the terms of the debate. It's like hoping the enemy will be nicer if you let them pick the site of the battlefield. Choice expansion advocates often seek validation through "the most challenging test case" (McGroarty, 1998). Many choice advocates apparently believe that choice expansion will occur only if they demonstrate that it works under the most adverse conditions, including the absence of any genuine competition.

Every major ballot proposition to expand choice has contained provisions designed to appeal to proponents of the status quo. Choice opponents still opposed them vehemently. Each proposition lost by a wide margin; in some cases they lost by more than 2 to 1. It is hard to imagine how reforms aimed at establishing an OEI could do worse.

Hype and Unrealistic Expectations

Already, 20 years ago, exaggerations, distorted perceptions of parental choice uses, and unrealistic expectations of restriction-laden programs were commonplace.[21] As *The School Choice Wars* warned then, the heated discussion of voucher vs. TPS student comparisons may have reduced OEI political feasibility. Monopoly proponents portray the same results their opponents brag about into a generalization that choice expansion is a failed reform (Drury, 2000).

Both sides ignore disclaimers like John Witte's that "this program should not be used as evidence for evaluating more inclusive choice programs" (Witte, Bailey, & Thorn, 1993, p. 29; see also Testa and Sen, 1999). Witte eventually ignored it himself. In 2000, Witte published a book about the Milwaukee program inappropriately entitled *The Market Approach to Education.*

The media spread and amplified the exaggerations. Milwaukee's voucher student outcomes were portrayed as general evidence of choice expansion effects. "School Vouchers on Trial in Milwaukee and Cleveland" was a typical headline.[22] Similar headlines appeared in major publications like the *Wall Street Journal* (October 11, 1996) and *Education Week* (August 5, 1998).

Bob Davis said, "Education scholars were hoping the Milwaukee experiment would finally settle whether vouchers help poor kids academically,"[23] a recurring plea that speaks volumes about persistent, deeply ingrained misperceptions of choice expansion rationales and school system deficiencies.[24] Milton Friedman said choice expansion through a universal voucher system should *replace* the TPS monopoly on taxpayer funding. But as Davis's comment illustrates, choice expansions have been widely portrayed as additions to the current funding system, a way to allow some disadvantaged children to escape their assigned TPS.

The small scale of the restriction-laden Milwaukee Parental Choice Program (MPCP) did not dampen the enthusiasm of the *Wall Street Journal*'s editors. They opined that even the tiny original Milwaukee program was a "pathbreaking voucher program"[25] and that the Wisconsin Supreme Court decision to allow the modest expansion of the Milwaukee program was a "thunderclap," "a huge boost to the school choice movement," and that the "Choice Debate Is Over."[26] In the continuing triumph of hope over reason and experience, choice advocates, including Wisconsin's governor Tommy Thompson (1998), "contend that [this time] competition for students will force [significant] improvements in Milwaukee's TPS."[27] That did not happen (Ford and Andersson, 2019).

Because the MPCP cannot generate valid generalizations about choice expansion, the attention given to its impact on voucher students should have been a cause for considerable concern by advocates of market-based reforms. But prominent choice expansion advocates rarely if ever raise such concerns. Many pro-choice-expansion newsletters described the alleged evidence of the benefits of choice without any caveats.[28] The debilitating impact of the restrictions, the absence of noteworthy rivalry behaviors, and the mistaken focus on helping a few children rather than improving the entire school system are rarely if ever mentioned.

The authors of the studies that found some small positive effects (Greene, Peterson, & Du, 1997)[29] said those findings demonstrated the benefits of competition. Daniel McGroarty (1994, pp. 95–96) noted the "small size and short duration" of Milwaukee's program and the huge political stakes but didn't explain that there was no basis for a high-stakes research battle or explain what a valid test would require. Instead, McGroarty complained that choice advocates were at a disadvantage because, at the time, only John Witte had access to the achievement data. After Witte published the data, McGroarty (1996) mistakenly asserted that choice advocates (disciples of "theoretical models that borrow from free market economics") could "test their theories against the reality of the one city [Milwaukee] where it [competition] exists" (p. xx).

Jeanne Allen,[30] longtime president of the Center for School Reform, said, "If these things [charges that the MPCP, with its minimal choice and limited rivalry, hadn't helped students academically or created more equity for racial minorities] were true, two of the key arguments of choice advocates would be refuted." The MPCP cannot demonstrate what Allen said it must. Moving a relatively few students among the choices available within the current system won't noticeably impact equity or achievement. Such an impact requires the genuine industry openness that would significantly change school systems. To make matters worse, statements such as Allen's include specific ways to discredit the choice expansion cause.

SUPPORT ANYTHING CALLED SCHOOL CHOICE?

Choice expansion advocacy organizations celebrated every favorable public mention of anything labeled "choice." They proclaim victory, even when little is accomplished. The event may only be a vague statement of support by a public official, or a weak proposal with little chance of enactment. A 1997 Heritage Foundation report[31] began with: "Nearly 32 states considered a school choice program *of some kind* [emphasis added] [in 1997]. At least 45 governors stated their support for different degrees of school choice or charter schools."[32] How many is "nearly" 32? Does "at least" 45 mean that there were unconfirmed rumors of support among the remaining governors?

Closer examination of what was actually said (very little) and done (even less) reveals that most of the governors are just astute politicians trying to ride a popular issue (choice devoid of specifics) without doing or saying anything that would anger powerful special interests. Contrary to the Heritage report, none of the proposed reforms, much less enacted legislation, offered any significant steps toward "principles of free-market competition." By the 1998 election campaign, only 15 of the 36 states with gubernatorial contests had a major party candidate who supported any kind of parental choice. Only five supported voucher programs, mostly restriction-laden versions. Even the *Wall*

Street Journal celebrated scraps; for example, it proclaimed 2011 the "year of school choice."

Another example is on page 12 of the March 1998 issue of *School Reform News*. The headline said, "1997 was a breakthrough year for market-oriented education reform." Again, the events of 1997 did not back the glowing headline. Changes that would establish an OEI were not even proposed, much less implemented, in any state legislature or by any ballot initiative. Relatively few children left their assigned TPS, and the system's critical elements remained intact everywhere.

What "school choice," "parental choice," "voucher programs," and, more recently, new policy tools such as education savings accounts (ESAs) mean even to the tiny minority that have heard of those terms depends mainly on what choice advocates support. Choice advocates' strong support for programs limited to special needs children, a relatively few low-income families, and "failed" TPS assignees fosters perceptions that choice expansion is just a way to allow disadvantaged children to escape especially poor-fit situations, including TPSs that are so bad that they fit no one. That implicitly contradicts calls for transformational school system reform.

Mainstream parental choice advocates provide their opponents significant opportunities to deceive the public about the aims of choice expansion advocates. Restriction-laden programs generate distortable evidence. A perception of choice expansion failure can have catastrophic political consequences. Even undeniable relative success with partial measures is not necessarily good. Widespread imitation might preclude more productive reforms.

Choice advocates chose their battles poorly and frequently ignored or abandoned high-caliber ammunition. Choice expansion advocates often transfer ammunition to the enemy. Language like the strong words of the 1983 *Nation at Risk* report seem to apply to a great many prominent advocates of real reform through choice expansion. If a foreign power was doing it to them, we and they would see it as an act of war, but they are doing it to themselves and placing the nation's future in greater jeopardy.

PRIVATE SCHOOL–PUBLIC SCHOOL COMPARISONS?

Most differences in current public and private schools are noteworthy only if we intend to leave the key elements of the status quo intact. Many analysts fall into the intellectual trap of assuming that current private school practices and outcomes will remain the main alternatives to public schools. Economists Masato Aoki and Susan Feiner used the existing private sector to assess pro-competition arguments. Especially revealing was their conclusion that the chiefly religious character of the private sector "profoundly colors the argument for market choice" (Aoki & Feiner, 1996).

Many choice advocates rest their case on the alleged superiority of current private schools. Jay Greene said choice expansion would promote integration because in Cleveland, "private schools, on average, are better integrated than are public schools."[33] Joseph Viteritti (1999) thought it very important that "inner city parochial schools are more effective in meeting the educational needs of poor children than are typical public schools in the same neighborhood" (p. 15).

Prominent choice expansion advocates John Chubb and Terry Moe said that "if there are no differences between public and private schools, there is little reason to support educational choice of any kind, public or private."[34] They reached that conclusion even though they noted that "private schools generally have smaller [per-pupil] budgets than public schools." They ignored the debilitating effect of having to charge tuition for a much less expensive service.

Unfortunately, the editors of the *Wall Street Journal* published the faulty Chubb and Moe analysis. The stakes are too high—our nation is at risk (Bennett et al., 1998; Clowes, 1998)—to keep making such blunders. We can't afford to assign immense relevance to irrelevant comparisons, pretend to assess competition when it does not exist, and confuse potential reforms—agents of school system transformation—with programs that only shuffle a few students among existing schools.

Dan Goldhaber's (1996) article is a later more extensive example of the same mistake. All of those scholars assumed that parental choice would not fundamentally change the public or private sector, that it could only change the public and private market shares.

Failure to recognize and celebrate the possibility of major private sector change, and the need for it, is a big political mistake. The private schools of an OEI would not look much like the low-budget, predominantly sectarian, nonprofit private schools that dominate the private sector now. Since some people mistakenly equate the private sector with elite prep academies, claims that choice expansion is a good idea because private schools are doing a better job create dangerously unrealistic expectations, even for the private schools of an OEI.

Public funding discrimination against users of TPS alternatives, and major regulatory barriers for private schools participating in choice programs, hinder the generation of large achievement gains for TPS leavers. For example, an evaluation of the DC voucher program found no statistically significant test score effects, but the vouchers were only worth about a third of what was spent in the nearby TPS (funding discrimination).[35]

Unqualified comparisons of public and private schools can make parental choice look like an expensive, disruptive waste of time. Defenders of the status quo exploit that mistake by citing data which indicate that private school academic outcomes are similar to public school outcomes, at least in terms of readily measurable criteria like standardized test scores. The small test score effects of the small programs convinced some prominent analysts that "school choice" is an inadequate reform catalyst.[36]

The unwarranted media hype and overblown rhetoric from school choice advocates[37] helped public school system monopoly proponents generalize the effects of small-scale, restriction-laden choice way beyond the conditions responsible for the small effects. The proper interpretation of similar private school and TPS test scores is that the whole education system is broken.[38] The current system significantly handicaps most private schools. We need an OEI not to move some children to different existing schools but to improve the entire school system by changing its composition, especially the private school sector.

Comparisons of public and private schools have other bad consequences. By asserting that private schools produce better results, choice advocates probably give many teachers (more on this in Chapter 13), and much of the general public, the impression that choice expansion is just an expensive new program that would operate within the current system.

The low teacher pay of existing private schools helps union leaders arouse rank-and-file support for the teacher unions' vehement opposition to choice expansion. In contrast, as an example in Chapter 13 will show, much-reduced public funding discrimination can simultaneously raise TPS teacher and private school teacher salaries.

Much-improved private schools, including many new profit-seeking firms, would be the alternative to TPSs unless choice expansion is severely restricted, for example, by capped programs such as Milwaukee and Cleveland. Those restricted versions generate little or no competition, while sometimes simultaneously increasing taxpayer burdens (Levin & Driver, 1997).

TRANSITION ISSUES

Among the most critical tactical issues is the management of a transition to an OEI. Specification of transition issues such as teacher retraining, school closures and transfers, and pension portability can influence enactment probability and potential for abandonment before full implementation is achieved or a new equilibrium can arise. Those issues are a chapter by themselves, and since they are discussed in Myron Lieberman's "The School Choice Fiasco"[39] and in *School System Reform: How and Why Is a Price-less Tale* (Merrifield, 2019), we won't include that discussion in this book.

NOTES

1. Jeanne Allen, *Center for Education Reform Newsletter* 53 (May 1999): 1.

2. Among others, so did *School Reform News* (June 1999—large "Victory in Florida" headline) and the Heritage Foundation (email announcement of Florida governor Jeb Bush appearance).

3. George A. Clowes, "Five Steps to Full School Choice," *School Reform News*, September 1998, 10–11.

4. Quentin L. Quade, "Strap on the Armor and Go: Never Give In!," *School Reform News*, June 1998, 16.

5. Chester Finn quoted in John Hood, "Educational Challenges: The Role of Choice," *Current*, December 1991, 11.

6. The rhetoric of competition is commonplace, but many—perhaps the vast majority—choice advocates are not aware of the requirements explained in Chapter 2. Many are quite willing to accept a noncompetitive system of parental choice. Most parental choice advocates' definition of "full school choice" falls far short of an OEI.

7. https://www.schoolsystemreformstudies.net/nation-at-risk-vi/

8. Thomas Jefferson: "If a nation expects to be ignorant & free, in a state of civilization, it expects what never was & never will be." http://tjrs.monticello.org/letter/327

9. Chester Finn quoted in John Hood, "Educational Challenges: The Role of Choice," *Current*, December 1991, 11.

10. See the discussion of the Christopher Jencks and Theodore Sizer 1960s voucher proposals in Viteritti (1999, p. 55).

11. Friedman, (1955).

12. For example, see https://www.edchoice.org/research-library/?report=whos-afraid-of-school-choice#report; Daniel McGroarty, "Voucher Wars," Milton and Rose Friedman Foundation, Indianapolis, *Issues in School Choice*, no. 2 (April 1998); Dorman E. Cordell, "Answering Objections to School Vouchers in D.C.," *National Center for Policy Analysis Brief Analysis* 266 (May 22, 1998): 2.

13. Economic illiteracy is rampant. Dave Kansas, "Illiteracy About Economics Abounds Among Americans, Survey Concludes," *Wall Street Journal*, September 11, 1992; Thomas Sowell, "Economic Literacy Escapes Most," *San Antonio Express-News*, January 4, 1995.

14. Exceptions: Some Giffen Elementary (Albany, New York) employees were fired after many parents responded to a privately funded rescue, and Harlem, District 4, where unpopular schools are closed.

15. The definition of "entrenched" is debatable. Most choice-based changes have changed very little. The least entrenched program is Milwaukee's low-income vouchers. Even so, it still took most of a decade to expand the program to 15% of the student population, and to give the majority of private schools a chance to be eligible. The

remaining significant restrictions preclude the development of a competitive education industry, and Milwaukee's "public" schools are under threat of a state takeover.

16. From CER's website, EdReform.com.

17. https://www.heartland.org/news-opinion/news/five-steps-to-full-school-choice

18. https://www.edchoice.org/research-library/?report=whos-afraid-of-school-choice#report

19. Omdahl and Ducote (1999) describe how Louisiana reached that point: "Louisiana has tried almost every one of them [reforms other than school choice], from enhanced pre-schooling to finance reforms, during the period from 1975 to 1995."

20. School districts satisfy the definition of a cartel: an association of producers that eliminates or significantly reduces competition. A school district is a much more stable anti-competitive institution than any cartel of private firms, or even a cartel of nations, like the OPEC oil cartel. See, for example, Dougherty and Becker (1995).

21. Fuller (1997); Rouse (1996); Wenman (1996); McGroarty (1996); Fuller and White (1995); Greene, Peterson, and Du (1997); Drury (2000).

22. February, 1998, *Mobilization for Equity* newsletter.

23. Bob Davis, "Dueling Professors Have Milwaukee Dazed over School Vouchers," *Wall Street Journal*, October 11, 1996, A1.

24. Chapter 5 discusses the fallacy that school system problems are limited to the inner-city schools of low-income families.

25. *Wall Street Journal* Editorial Board, "Choice Thunderclap," *Wall Street Journal*, June 11, 1998, A22.

26. *Wall Street Journal* Editorial Board, "Choice Debate Is Over," *Wall Street Journal*, April 6, 2000.

27. June Kronholz, "School Voucher Drive Bolstered by Court Action," *Wall Street Journal*, June 11, 1998, A24.

28. Not naming them is deliberate. The point here is the nature of the mistakes. Accountability should occur in a different venue, actually planned for the nascent Institute for Objective Policy Assessment.

29. It's controversial because it contradicted some of the findings of John Witte described by Bob Davis, "Dueling Professors Have Milwaukee Dazed over School Vouchers," *Wall Street Journal*, October 11, 1996, A1. Likewise, there are competing research results for the Cleveland low-income voucher program: A Kim Metcalf study summarized by Mark Walsh, "Vouchers Yield Mixed Results, Report Says," *Education Week*, December 2, 1998, 3, versus Greene, Peterson, and Howell (1997).

30. Jeanne Allen, "Serving Up a Skewed Look at Parents and School Choice," *Washington Times*, November 10, 1993.

31. The Heritage Foundation report, January 30, 1998, *F.Y.I.*

32. The April 21, 1997, *F.Y.I.* makes almost identical claims about the previous years.

33. Jay P. Greene, "Why School Choice Can Promote Integration," *Education Week*, April 12, 2000, 72, 52.

34. John E. Chubb and Terry M. Moe, "The Private vs Public School Debate," *Wall Street Journal*, July 26, 1991.

35. https://www.washingtonexaminer.com/opinion/school-choice-works-for-a-third-of-the-cost

36. https://www.city-journal.org/html/school-choice-isn't-enough-13064.html; https://thebulwark.com/school-choice-is-not-enough/; https://fordhaminstitute.org/national/commentary/tale-two-movements-why-standards-and-choice-need-each-other

37. Frederick Hess, "Solve School Problems, but Do Not Oversell," *Washington Examiner*, November 30, 2010: "Proponents oversell ideas as miracle cures . . . without attention to context."

38. The lack of significant differences between private school and government school test scores is repeated in national publications like the *Wall Street Journal* and *Newsweek*; Barbara Kantrowitz, Stryker McGuire, and Pat Wingert, "Take the Money and Run," *Newsweek*, October 11, 1999, 65: "In national tests, there's not much difference between public and private school students from the same socioeconomic backgrounds."

39. https://nationalaffairs.com/public_interest/detail/the-school-choice-fiasco

Chapter 13

Teachers

We treat them [teachers] badly, so they leave in droves.

—John Merrow[1]

Teachers Are [Still] Not Okay.

—Madeline Will[2]

An OEI will significantly change teachers' lives, likely mostly for the better. The current system treats teachers badly, so there is much room for improvement. Because OEI conditions will reduce teacher union membership and revenue, teacher unions will strongly oppose OEI conditions, at least initially. But strong, monolithic teacher opposition to OEI conditions is not inevitable. That's the primary point of this chapter. There are many signs of significant teacher dissatisfaction with the status quo, and abundant virtues of an OEI well worth bringing to the attention of teachers.

Reduced teacher opposition to, and even eventual teacher support for, an OEI is a realistic goal. As the teacher unions of some other countries illustrate, unions sometimes grudgingly accept parental choice after it operates for a while. Teacher union opposition is a significant political barrier, so well-crafted appeals to teachers could significantly improve OEI political feasibility.

TEACHERS VS. TEACHER UNIONS

Presidential nominee Bob Dole's speech at the 1996 Republican National Convention contained an attack on teacher unions that explicitly differentiated between union leaders and the rank and file.[3] Though support for teachers, but not their unions, is a recurrent theme,[4] choice expansion advocates rarely give that distinction the considerable attention it deserves.

Choice expansion advocates' statements usually reflect a belief that teacher opposition to openness is inevitable and that union leader opposition just reflects that. For example, Bast and Harmer (1997) said, "It's the system, not the people in it, that is evil. For those reasons, we find it possible to forgive TPS teachers for opposing the voucher movement."

But strong teacher opposition to an OEI is not inevitable. In 2001, *The School Choice Wars* noted that 79% of U.S. public school teachers joined a union or employee association,[5] and not all of the union members support the union's political stance.[6] Many more are just passive supporters, including many who have little issue awareness.[7] Even before the Janus (2018) effect on union membership, union representation of teachers had fallen nine percentage points.[8]

The OEI version of parental choice has much more to offer teachers, and fewer reasons to be feared, than the versions of parental choice that most often appear in the public debate. For example, a 2017 Texas education savings account proposal—approximately fiscally neutral at $6,500 per pupil per year—would have yielded $1,000 per public school teacher in savings to school districts and provided a basis for $27,000 per year average raises to private school teachers,[9] largely due to greater school funding through tuition copayment. That is, the $6,500 ESA would have significantly increased private spending on K–12 education (Merrifield & Ginn, 2016).

David Kirkpatrick was a longtime educator and former teacher union leader, and a leading supporter of school choice. His experience includes solid evidence of major differences between teachers and union leadership on school choice, including vouchers:

> I spoke to this effect [school choice issue] at a number of [union] meetings, and at no time was I criticized by a member of the [National Education] Association. Teachers are willing to consider new ideas and follow positive leadership. Unfortunately, such leadership is not forthcoming as officers or staff play to the weakest and most fearful of their members or adopt positions perceived to be in the interests of the organization, its officers and staff, rather than those of the rank-and-file membership.
>
> The first thing we [teachers] must do is stop defending a system we did not create, and which is not in the interest of our students or ourselves [teachers] to maintain. We have been victimized along with our students. (Kirkpatrick, 1997, p. 12)

Denis Doyle said, "The most ardent opponents of private school vouchers are public school teachers,"[10] when in fact "union officials constantly complain about the lack of grassroots participation"[11] in anti-choice campaigns.

Herbert Gintis made an even stronger misstatement: "It is well-known that teachers and their unions are virtually unanimous in opposing school choice" (Gintis, 1995, p. 508). But many teachers already support some forms of choice expansion, many are eager to learn more, and the key point already made above, but well worth repeating, is that an OEI is arguably more likely to appeal to teachers than the kinds of choice expansions that receive the most publicity.

There is even a teacher organization that overwhelmingly supports choice expansion. The Association of American Educators' 1997 membership survey[12] revealed that 62% thought vouchers were a good idea. Only 32% disagreed. AAE is the largest national, nonunion, professional educators' organization. AAE still openly supports expansion of parental choice.[13]

There are many teachers in choice (however limited) schools. They "seem ripe for the picking as allies in the struggle for choice expansion, and as human rebuttals to the teacher unions' incessant anti-choice rhetoric" (Murdock, 1998, p. 20). The same thing is probably true of private school teachers in general.

An OEI would end the need to choose between better-paying TPSs and more teacher-friendly private schools. Contrary to an Allen/Toma inference, public school teachers are not the "suppliers of a monopoly product" (Allen & Toma, 1996). They work for the public school system public finance monopoly. Monopolists don't appreciate competition, but their employees appreciate more competitive labor markets.

Despite choice advocates' failure to properly depict the reform pathways, some teachers already speak out against the status quo and advocate major reform,[14] often including parental choice. But for the fear of reprisals from their colleagues and employers, more probably would. Prominent teachers are among the vocal dissidents. They include John Gatto (1992a), a New York City and state teacher of the year; Tracey Bailey,[15] the 1993 national teacher of the year; and Kevin Irvine,[16] a Colorado state teacher of the year. Teacher Daniel Buck provides a modern (2019) description of the persistent tensions and unrealized opportunities.[17]

CHOICE ADVOCACY OPPORTUNITY

No one has come close to exploiting the differences between teachers and the teacher union leadership. The National Education Association (NEA) and the American Federation of Teachers (AFT) lead the name brand opposition[18] to every choice expansion proposal, so there is much to be gained from at least weakening teacher union opposition. Choice expansion advocates should at least be able to count on the one of five,[19] or "two out of five teachers that routinely vote Republican,"[20] depending upon when and how the poll is taken.

Instead of soliciting teacher support, choice expansion advocates unwittingly harden teacher opposition. The typical restriction-laden proposal makes choice expansion look like a limited transfer of students and teachers to the private schools of the current system. That helps the unions convince teachers that choice expansion will cause more teachers to earn the lower salaries of existing private schools. That's a distasteful outcome for many teachers despite the often better working conditions of private schools.[21] An OEI version of parental choice would not spread the conditions of existing private schools. The negative image of restriction-laden proposals inappropriately tarnishes proposals that would establish an OEI.

There is empirical evidence that many more teachers could become choice expansion supporters. "A survey of 2,372 teachers by the National Center for Education Information shows 53% say schools would be better if students could attend the school of their choice."[22]

Recently, Ashley Berner (2019) argued that

> many educators will find [this] pluralistic system professionally attractive. Funding an increasingly diverse spectrum of schools will likely generate innovative working environments and strong school cultures that mirror teachers' individual commitments and pedagogical styles.

Abroad, some teacher unions support school choice programs. Among 48 teacher unions in a dozen developed countries, 35% "are strongly in favor of choice or voucher programs."[23] Only 22% strongly oppose them.

MAKING THE CASE TO TEACHERS

Sources of teacher dissatisfaction with the status quo are a good starting point. The benefits teachers will realize from an OEI are the proper endpoint. The certain benefits include a more competitive teacher labor market,[24] opportunities to concentrate on what they are best at, increased mobility, linkage between productivity and compensation, and opportunities to become school entrepreneurs.[25] Better relations with parents are a likely effect of parents choosing schools, rather than having their children assigned to one. Public-private shared financing of tuition yields increased classroom spending without higher taxes.

Teacher Dissatisfaction with the Status Quo

Like Merrow at the beginning of the chapter, Murphy notes that "conditions of employment for teachers are unprofessional and stifling" (Murphy, 1996, p. 151). Many people still seek teaching careers, but teaching experience prompts a growing number to ask, "Who would want to become a technician [teacher] in such a field [teaching]?"[26] High teacher turnover is one of the two devastating effects of those conditions.

As the 2021 Madeline Will quote at the beginning of the chapter demonstrates, things haven't changed much since the 1990s[27] when the San Antonio news media displayed some of the concerns and deep dissatisfaction teachers were experiencing. A teacher said, "I'm doing a tough job with two hands tied behind my back."[28] A June 1, 1997, *San Antonio Express-News* Sunday Insight section titled "Schoolhouse Blues" described some of the underlying causes of discontent. The titles of the articles speak volumes: "I Need to Be in My Classroom"; "Treat Teachers as Professionals"; "Good Teachers Tired of Battling the System." The alleged teacher shortage problems are price control (single salary schedule) and retention problems, not recruiting problems. There'd be more and larger shortages but for the many teachers teaching outside of their fields of expertise.[29]

The "Schoolhouse Blues" articles noted that constantly changing programs create panic, low morale, and burnout; the latter is a second devastating result of the unprofessional, stifling conditions TPS teachers suffer. The current systems' tendency to inflate differentiated teaching pressures is a major irritant and a source of frustration.[30] "Teachers are in a virtual state of panic, caught between crushing district mandates and the need to raise standardized test scores."[31]

Scholar Gary Dworkin said that burnout is a widely researched topic. Burned out teachers often stay in their jobs because they lack comparable career opportunities (Dworkin, 1997). A longtime Milwaukee teacher said, "Very common are teachers who at one time were good, but after years of bureaucratic nonsense and dwindling morale, do not much like their job anymore" (Fischer, 1994, p. 35). Such strong signals of dissatisfaction with the system represent opportunities to weaken union opposition to the OEI version of choice expansion.

Union-sponsored publications and advertisements contain signs of dissatisfaction. A 1998 Today's Unions commercial said that unions gain teachers their employers' respect. But school district fear of union power differs from respect for teachers as competent professionals, and fear of union power has harmful side effects, including reduced accountability.[32] Both are major sources of the widespread "teacher bashing" that teachers resent.

By forcing nearly equal treatment of diverse teachers,[33] unions discourage superior performance. They also make it more difficult to purge bad teachers, which unsurprisingly yields statements like this: "Teacher unions seem to be driving good teachers out, coddling bad ones, and putting bureaucracy in the way of quality education."[34]

The unions claim they enhance teachers' professional image, but there is no broad-based movement toward greater teacher autonomy. Anecdotal evidence such as teacher complaints points toward greater micromanagement. Difficulty defining and consistently measuring professionalization and autonomy hinders systematic study.

Choice advocates must exploit TPS teachers' frustrations with the system. Analysis of teacher bashing could greatly increase teacher support all by itself. Seymour Sarason nailed it: If a large number of people "conclude that almost all people in a particular role are inadequate, should one not ask what there is about the system that makes or sustains such failures?" (Sarason, 1990, p. 15).

The reasons why teachers underachieve demonstrate why the current system causes teacher bashing. Political and administrative processes distort textbook content,[35] and they micromanage teaching methods and the curriculum, often through insulting "teacher-proof"[36] materials. Teachers are the "victim of job reduction and job simplification, prescriptive laws, the growing specter of legal liability and malpractice suits, and seniority rules" (Dworkin, 1987, p. 15).

"Policies that determine textbooks, course content, and even the style by which information is delivered are also removed from teacher's control" (Dworkin, 1987, p. 69).[37] Longtime AFT president Albert Shanker agreed that teachers had little say in policies, books, standards, or curriculum.[38]

The inability of parents to choose, and the resulting inability of schools or teachers to specialize much, creates unnecessary tension between overextended teachers and unhappy, trapped parents (Arons, 1997; McCluskey, 2007).[39] As a result of forced rather than chosen teacher-parent connections, many teachers dread speaking to parents so much that they'd forgo substantial raises if it would mean they'd never have to speak to a parent again (Sarason, 1990, pp. 25–26). Among the flood of people leaving teaching, many cite lack of support from parents as a major cause for their decision (Gallup, 1985, p. 10; Elam, 1987, p. 294–296).

The post-1983 reforms accelerated the erosion of teachers' working conditions. After *Nation at Risk* appeared in 1983, schools responded by "evolving . . . into institutions that prescribe top down management control of every aspect of the teaching process."[40] Professors Aldo Bernardo and Marianne Jennings said "big government is moving in on education," and "what is happening is not a dumbing down process, but [much worse] the emasculation of the American educational system."[41] "While reformers lip-sync homilies about creativity, empowerment, and involvement, they institute reforms that empower bureaucracies, reduce teachers to paraprofessionals, and marginalize parents" (King, 1996, p. 180).

More than ever, K–12 education suffers from "academically trained bureaucrats who believe that once they find the proper regulatory formula, they can make the world work properly."[42] If we see that for what it is—attempts at "central plan optimization"[43] (a virtual oxymoron)—we can see why it typically has a very high cost-to-benefit ratio.

Gary Dworkin and Merric Townsend (1994) said, "Texas is implementing site-based management, but the mandate involves micro-management of this implementation at higher levels. The effect has been a greater sense of powerlessness among teachers" (p. 77). Policy makers "want teachers to become technicians who will be able to follow directions very well."[44]

Nearly nationwide, "education reform has removed management of the classroom to the highest state levels. In most instances, the legislatures have micro-managed the school districts, campuses and classrooms."[45] Each so-called reform—a central plan revision—increased teachers' paperwork and frustration, including through contradictions among reforms.

Teachers often break the rules to educate children. They must endure fear of exposure and punishment and expend time and energy to hide their efforts and misrepresent their work. "A majority of public school teachers responding to a series of surveys conducted in Houston between 1977 and 1991 agreed or strongly agreed that school rules are so rigid and absurd that good teachers have to break them or ignore them" (Dworkin, 1997, p. 463). New York State teacher of the year John Gatto said he became "an active saboteur" (Gatto, 1992b, p. 9). David Kearns and Denis Doyle (1991) found that

> superb teachers share a trait not widely talked about: they are canny outlaws, system beaters, and creative and responsible rule benders. They have to be "outlaws" to succeed in most districts—especially the large ones—the deck is stacked against the creative, imaginative, and entrepreneurial teacher. (p. 64)

Former Milwaukee Public Schools superintendent Howard Fuller agrees that teachers have to break the rules to succeed (Fuller, 1997). Principals are often in the same situation. Tom Luce, an education reform activist and former candidate for Texas Governor, said a "principal must be an academic leader that knows how to get around the system."[46] A Heritage Foundation study described by Samuel Carter said that effective principals are "mavericks who buck the system" (Carter, 2000). The same study found that the effective principals found a way to free themselves from many of the personnel regulations, line-by-line budget requirements, and curricular mandates that hamstring most TPS principals. (Carter, 2000)

The system traps teachers to at least the same extent as parents. Most teaching credentials have little value outside teaching. Except when trained in math or science, teachers forfeit most of the investment in their skills if they leave teaching. TPS teachers have very little choice of where they work. District administrators choose each teacher's campus.

A principal's inability to hire or fire creates additional friction with teachers. Principals typically must accept district-approved candidates. Principals often receive just one candidate. Since they can't fire them, principals often conspire to make them miserable so they'll leave. A much better match would result if teachers and principals chose each other directly.

Ambitious, fairness-conscious teachers resent that their earnings reflect only credentials and time served. There is "no other profession where compensation and contract renewal are so largely divorced from evaluations of performance as they are in public school teaching" (Ballou & Podgursky, 1997, p. 81). G. Carl Ball and Steven Goldman found that "an excellent teacher who rocks the boat can receive poorer evaluations than less competent but 'safe' teachers" (Ball & Goldman, 1997, p. 230). The typical compensation policy—the single salary schedule—bases pay on just experience and training.

In the current system, teacher salary incentives are a mixed blessing. They can motivate innovation and spur creativity, but they can also create tension between teachers (Dworkin & Townsend, 1994). Increased productivity doesn't raise a public school's merit pay funding, or even its total budget. More money for one teacher may mean less for others. When someone else's good evaluation is bad for them, teachers can become more reluctant to share ideas and materials or to work in teams.

Public-private comparisons yield more empirical evidence of teacher dissatisfaction with TPS working conditions.[47] Ballou and Podgursky (1997) found that private schools had no difficulty filling openings, even though the average private school starting pay was 73.5%[48] of TPS pay. We agree that "the extra amount that public school teachers get is combat pay."[49] Salary differences for similar teachers are a good measure of a large number[50] of teachers' willingness to forgo income for better working conditions: "I'd rather teach here [private turned CPS] than in the TPS because I have a lot more latitude in what I teach, and how I teach it."[51]

A survey of Indianapolis non-public school teachers (Styring, 1998) found considerable dissatisfaction with TPS work environments.[52] Only about 20%, mostly younger teachers, said they would accept one of the higher-paying jobs in a suburban public school. About two thirds of them took their current teaching job because a better-paying suburban position wasn't available.

Only 10% of the veteran teachers would take the higher-paying job in a good suburban public school. Only 2% of the "non-public" veteran schoolteachers in the sample would leave their current job for a much-higher-paying job in [an inner city] Indianapolis Public School. Typical comments were: "No amount of money," "You've got to be kidding," and "Maybe for a million dollars." Half the non-public schools in the sample were urban. Many teachers make a large financial sacrifice to leave public schools.

Fewer private school teachers have teaching certificates, but more have a degree in the subject they teach, and more come from selective, prestigious universities; these factors are much more highly correlated with student achievement than certification (Ballou & Podgursky, 1997). Most teachers prefer the higher salaries of public schools to the better working conditions of private schools (Forster & D'Andrea, 2009), but many teachers are competing for the lower-salary, largely union-free private school openings. The much-better-paying public school openings fill slowly.

The preferred conditions (except pay) of many private schools exist even though most of them have much less money per student. Since the OEI described throughout this book would eliminate the funding gap, the already superior working conditions of many private schools would get better. Therefore, the current salary gap understates the value to teachers of the improvement in working conditions they can expect from an OEI.

Collective Bargaining Is Expendable

A few teachers may regret the decline in union power that an OEI will cause, but it's hard to miss something that produces many headaches and few benefits. The spread of collective bargaining did not produce noteworthy, general increases in teacher salaries (Lieberman, 1997).

"The American Legislative Exchange Council's 1994 Report Card on American Education found that since 1972, teacher salaries had gone up 3.5% in real dollars. Everything else in education other than teachers' salaries has gone up 90%" (Fischer, 1994, p. 33). The slightly different methodology of Ben Scafidi's "Back to the Staffing Surge"[53] indicated that teacher salaries, adjusted for inflation, fell 2% from 1992 to 2014.

Another headache is the time and money cost of union membership. Previous studies omitted those costs, yet some of them still found that collective bargaining left teachers worse off. The omitted membership costs might exceed the estimated net benefits that some studies found. Teachers like Michael Fischer describe their belief that collective bargaining harms teachers in articles with strong titles like "A Betrayal of Teachers by Their Union"

(Fischer, 1994). An article with a similar title (Glass, 1995) includes another example—pension fund mismanagement—of divergence in union leadership and teacher interests, and of the fact that the former usually takes precedence.

Teachers in an Open Education Industry

The private schools of an OEI will not have externally imposed budget caps. Of course, entrepreneurs can cause the public school merit pay problems described earlier by allocating a fixed sum for merit raises, but the market pressures of an OEI will discourage that practice. Classroom achievements that please parents raise enrollments, budgets, and profits, and therefore raise teachers' market value. Likewise, a reputation as a team player—someone who makes colleagues more productive with good ideas and useful materials—will raise a teacher's market value. That will further motivate teachers to develop such reputations.

Employers recognize merit or lose top teachers to competing school entrepreneurs. Since the flexible tuition price and teacher salary requirements of an OEI, varying by subject matter, means that parents can reward better teaching by supplementing public funding with private funds (tuition add-ons), there isn't even a system-wide budget constraint. Teachers can increase the system's total funding and their earnings by improving the quality of instruction.

When choice, rather than assignment, matches parents and schools, and teachers and children, they will all get along better, and children will learn more. Assignment of teachers to a neighborhood public school often creates mismatches, sometimes to the extent of culture shock (Dworkin & Townsend, 1994, p. 77). It is not unusual to have teachers from middle-class, suburban backgrounds start their teaching career in a school in an urban, largely minority, working-class neighborhood. It is one of the major reasons why there are so many extremely short teaching careers.[54]

Parents' freedom to choose among diverse offerings will free and pressure schools and teachers to specialize in what they do best. Schools will differ according to teaching styles, use of technology, governance structure, and subject emphasis, and some will focus on specific special needs. Teachers will enjoy higher productivity because they will work in the schools best suited to their particular skills and interests, and because they'll teach children matched to their interests and instructional style. "It [openness] is the one change that will permit teachers to emerge from the shadow of the bureaucracy and become professionals" (Doyle, 1992, p. 518).

Because the school cartels, called districts,[55] hire most schoolteachers, local teacher labor markets are often not competitive (Merrifield, 1999). There is often very little competition for teachers. No current teacher labor market is as competitive as the teacher labor market of an OEI. The existing analyses of data generated by public school district rivalry,[56] rather than competing profit-seeking entrepreneurs, understate the effects of competition, yet they still confirm the theoretically sound proposition that teacher salaries are higher in more competitive teacher labor markets.[57] An OEI's larger private sector would greatly increase the number of self-managed campuses that would compete for teachers.

In an OEI, more teachers would apply directly to the campuses where they want to work. That would increase teacher mobility and location choice, and it would reduce teacher vulnerability to arbitrary or personal administrative decisions. Teachers in regions with few school districts (including some single-district, large urban areas or entire states, like Hawaii) need such changes the most. Currently, teachers who run afoul of key administrators often have only unattractive alternatives. Termination is usually unlikely, but administrators can make teachers miserable.

It may take a change of residence, or a long commute, to work in another school district. The only other choices are (1) leave the labor force; (2) take a much lower-paying, non-teaching job; (3) return to college for retraining; or (4) seek a nearby lower-paying private school position. An OEI would have more independent employers, and private schools would receive nearly as much public money per student as TPSs. In a mature OEI, a teacher seeking a new position has a much better chance of finding a good one without a big jump in commuting time.

PARTICULAR GAINERS AND LOSERS

Some effects of market forces are fairly certain. Other long-term effects are not as easily foreseen, but some likely key factors are identifiable. Some teachers would regret weaker union political clout. Lacking the captive audience of a TPS, irretrievably burned out or incompetent teachers may find it difficult to get a job offer. They will suffer unless they take advantage of the adjustment aid and transition incentives proposed below.

Since supply and demand will probably both grow, the size and direction of teacher salary change is uncertain. Because of improved working conditions, the resulting entry of new teachers, the return of former teachers, and long-term turnover reductions could be large. But the major changes will also drive some teachers into early retirement or other careers.

Demand is likely to rise because opportunities to supplement vouchers with private add-ons, and the improved quality that would result from the stronger incentives and opportunities to specialize, will expand K–12 resources. However, that outcome is not certain. Technology applications may eliminate more teaching positions than they create, and the new positions may differ greatly from traditional teaching positions.

Certainly, the possible changes point to significant differences in the salary changes of different kinds of teachers. An OEI would replace the surpluses, shortages, and disguised exceptions of salary schedules based on general credentials and experience with market-based salaries based on subject area, technology skills, effectiveness working in teams, and popularity. Among the skilled and motivated, teachers in high-demand fields like math and science would enjoy larger raises than teachers in traditional lower-demand fields such as history and English.

Supply Changes

We believe that the improvements in the teaching profession that an OEI would bring about would greatly increase the supply of teachers. The professionalization of teaching would raise interest in teaching careers among college students and among the large number of former teachers. The increased size of the private sector, where certification matters less, would attract the people interested in teaching as a second career who aren't willing to get the education degree and teaching certificate that TPSs typically require.

Such supply increases would reduce the salary increase caused by transformational change-induced attrition, reduced spending on administration, and parents' ability to supplement public spending on K–12 with privately funded tuition add-ons only to the extent that teaching jobs become more desirable.

An OEI will not accommodate every existing teacher, and some will decline to adjust. Irreconcilable mismatches between the skills school operators will want and the skills that existing teachers have or are willing to learn would reduce the effective supply of teachers. Some teachers would want to change careers or retire early.

Use of Technology

Public schools see technology as something to teach much more than they see it as a potentially superior way to teach some things to some children. Chalk and talk remains the dominant education process. The relentless pressure to improve quality and cut costs inherent in open industries may change that much faster than the current system would. That could significantly change what a teacher does and the skill mix teachers need, as well as the total number of teachers that school operators will want at the market price.

CRITICAL TRANSITION ISSUES

Choice advocates have an arsenal of powerful arguments, but uncertainty is a powerful enemy, and a key to the status quo's defenses. A carefully crafted incentive package will significantly fortify the case that teachers should not fear an OEI and will increase the likelihood that teachers will accept the transition to a new system.

Assurances of pension portability are a must. Adjustment assistance measures also deserve serious consideration. Adjustment assistance is compassionate, and it is politically astute.[58] Adjustment assistance should at least include retraining assistance aimed at helping teachers adapt to labor market changes within the newly evolving OEI, or to begin new careers outside K–12 education. Other incentives, including severance payments for teachers in schools where ownership changes occur, are also worth considering.

A key political strategy and transition issue is choice advocates' ability to appeal to teachers without compromising the key elements of an OEI. Choice expansion advocates must make the case, often and loudly, that teachers can prosper in an OEI. The teaching profession has almost as much to gain from an OEI as children do. How to get there is the subject of the final chapter.

NOTES

1. John Merrow, "The Teacher Shortage: Wrong Diagnosis, Phony Cures," *Education Week*, October 6, 1999, 64, 48

2. Madeline Will, "Teachers Are Not Okay, Even Though We Need Them to Be," *Education Week*, September 5, 2021, 14, https://www.edweek.org/teaching-learning/teachers-are-not-ok-even-though-we-need-them-to-be/2021/09

3. Elizabeth Gleick, "Mad and Mobilized," *Time*, September 9, 1996, 52.

4. https://fee.org/articles/7-reasons-to-say-goodbye-to-teachers-unions/#0

5. https://blogs.edweek.org/edweek/teacherbeat/2017/10/participation_teachers_unions_down_likely_to_tumble_further.html

6. For example, in Milwaukee, a teacher opposed to the NEA position on school choice ran for school board against heavy NEA opposition (Kirkpatrick, 1997, p. 110). The AFT and NEA endorsed Al Gore, but a nationwide survey of teachers by the Alexis de Tocqueville Institution revealed that teachers' top three choices were "undecided," Bush, and McCain. Bush received more support than Gore and Bradley combined.

7. Education Intelligence Agency Communiqué, May 24, 1999. Nonparticipation follows from the low level of awareness of union representation. A survey of Alabama's NEA affiliate "revealed that only 2 percent of its members described the AEA as a labor union, and only 5 percent described the NEA as a labor union."

8. https://blogs.edweek.org/edweek/teacherbeat/2017/10/participation_teachers_unions_down_likely_to_tumble_further.html

9. http://taxpayersavingsgrants.org/sites/taxpayersavingsgrants.org/files/TSG_Teacher_Study.pdf

10. Denis Doyle, "Lessons in Hypocrisy," *Wall Street Journal*, June 13, 1995.

11. Education Intelligence Agency, *NEA Confidential: A Practical Guide to the Operations of the Nation's Largest Teachers' Union* (an EIA Annual Report from 1998).

12. The 1997 membership survey of the Association of American Educators posted on the internet at www.aaeteachers.org/survey97.html#7

13. https://www.aaeteachers.org/index.php/press-release-pages/012119-aaecelebratesnscw2019

14. "A Letter to the American People: From the Participants of the National Summit of Teachers for Education Reform"; published on the Mackinac Center for Public Policy website (mackinac.org) and described in *School Reform News*, December 1998, 3.

15. Drew Lindsay, "Turncoat, Part I," *Education Week*, May 7, 1997.

16. Drew Lindsay, "Turncoat, Part I," *Education Week*, May 7, 1997.

17. https://fee.org/articles/school-choice-also-gives-teachers-like-me-more-choice/

18. Teacher unions are actual organizations, name brand opposition. Suburban Republicans and rural Republicans are often significant—sometimes the most significant—choice expansion opponents. They are identifiable people, but not actual organizations.

19. http://verdantlabs.com/politics_of_professions/

20. *Wall Street Journal* Editorial Board, July 7, 1998, A16.

21. "Teacher unions oppose vouchers in part because the private schools they foster generally pay lower salaries than the public systems." Richard Lacayo, "They'll Vouch for That," *Time*, October 27, 1997, 74.

22. From *USA Today*, August 28, 1990, via David Kirkpatrick, "School Choice Choir Has Broad Range of Voices," *School Reform News*, July 1999, 9.

23. Alexis de Tocqueville Institute.

24. https://www.washingtonexaminer.com/opinion/school-choice-benefits-teachers-too

25. Robert Maranto and Scott Milliman, "In Arizona, Charter Schools Work," *Washington Post*, October 11, 1999, A25, found that Arizona's "best charter schools are started by entrepreneurial teachers who felt stymied by school administrators and school boards," not a competitive situation, but a demonstration of entrepreneurial spirit.

26. Paula M. Evans, "When I Grow Up, I Don't Think I Want to Be a Teacher," *Education Week*, June 2, 1999, 31.

27. Michelle Hackman and Eric Morath, "Teachers Quit Jobs at Highest Rate on Record," *Wall Street Journal*, December 28, 2018, https://www.wsj.com/articles/teachers-quit-jobs-at-highest-rate-on-record-11545993052; https://www.educationnext.org/why-are-teachers-leaving-their-jobs-turnover/; https://theconversation.com/teacher-turnover-is-a-problem-heres-how-to-fix-it-101584

28. More recent counterpart: a TED Talk about persistent teacher autonomy frustrations, https://www.youtube.com/watch?time_continue=21&v=GBRwcNL5LDg&feature=emb_title

29. National Academy of Sciences, National Academy of Engineering, and Institute of Medicine, *Is America Falling Off the Flat Earth?* (Washington, DC: The National Academies Press, 2007), https://doi.org/10.17226/12021. See also National Commission Report, 2001, p. 39, https://fas.org/irp/threat/nssg.pdf

30. SSRS blog post citing *Education Week* articles.

31. Denis Udall, letter to the editor, *Education Week*, July 8, 1998, 41, 43.

32. https://www.educationnext.org/why-are-teachers-leaving-their-jobs-turnover/

33. Thomas Jefferson: "Nothing is more unequal than to treat unequals equally."

34. Thomas Toch, "Why Teachers Don't Teach," *U.S. News & World Report*, February 26, 1996, 62.

35. https://fordhaminstitute.org/national/research/mad-mad-world-textbook-adoption

36. Dworkin (1997); Ravitch (1983, p. 233); Robert Chase, "Changing the Way Schools Do Business," *Vital Speeches*, May 1, 1998, 444. According to Ravitch, the rather demeaning "teacher-proof" term has its origin in the 1960s, and it has survived the power of teacher unions and was even recognized by Robert Chase, a president of the National Education Association.

37. A nearly identical statement is in Ball and Goldman (1997, p. 230).

38. Albert Shanker on *Jim Lehrer NewsHour*, August 22, 1996.

39. https://www.cato.org/publications/policy-analysis/why-we-fight-how-public-schools-cause-social-conflict

40. Letter to the editor, *Teacher Magazine*, November/December 1995.

41. "Professor: US Education Being Emasculated," *School Reform News*, December 1998, 3.

42. George Melloan, "Global Finance: Some Day We'll Get Organized," *Wall Street Journal*, May 4, 1999. Melloan was referring to international finance bureaucrats, but it applies equally well to most bureaucrats.

43. Chapter 7 in Merrifield (2019).

44. Paula M. Evans, "When I Grow Up, I Don't Think I Want to Be a Teacher," *Education Week*, June 2, 1999, 31.

45. Ibid, Evans.

46. Tom Luce, speaker, School Choice Conference, sponsored by the Federal Reserve Bank of Dallas, October 17, 1997.

47. See also https://www.edweek.org/ew/articles/2019/02/27/i-was-tired-of-how-politicians-treated.html

48. Based on full-time teachers in the 1987–1988 Schools and Staffing Survey.

49. Peters quoted by Murdock (1998, p. 20).

50. Teachers' willingness to pay (by accepting a lower salary than TPSs offer) for better working conditions will diminish as the total number of teachers sought by the private school sector increases. To greatly increase their market share (now about 10% nationally), private schools would have to reduce the private school–TPS salary gap.

51. Hugh Pearson, "An Urban Push for Self-Reliance," *Wall Street Journal*, February, 7, 1996.

52. Note that the survey takers are those who remain public school teachers despite the problems they described. Can you imagine how much worse the survey results would be if they included teachers who had quit in frustration, including many during the school year?

53. https://www.edchoice.org/wp-content/uploads/2017/05/Back-to-the-Staffing-Surge-by-Ben-Scafidi.pdf

54. https://theconversation.com/teacher-turnover-is-a-problem-heres-how-to-fix-it-101584

55. A cartel is an association that reduces competition. The organization of schools into districts with centralized personnel policies eliminates competition among schools for students (customers) and for personnel. That lack of competition between schools within districts is especially significant for teachers because, except in areas like math and science, the significant investment in teaching skills has little value outside of teaching.

56. See the findings and literature review in Merrifield (1999).

57. More competition will probably also produce better working conditions. Employees with options have to be treated better to retain them. Empirical support is harder to generate for this theoretically sound proposition because working conditions are not as easily measured and quantified in a consistent manner over time or among jurisdictions.

58. https://www.nationalaffairs.com/publications/detail/the-wall-and-the-bridge

Chapter 14

Outlook and Political Strategy

I sense that we are on the verge of a breakthrough in one state or another, which will then sweep like wildfire through the rest of the country.[1]

—Milton Friedman

The outlook—what spreads and how fast and to a big state, please—depends on strategy.[2] Sadly, the vast majority of recent choice expansion proposals are still losers, if not politically then as a reform catalyst. It will take wise strategy for Arizona's just-enacted universal $7,000 education savings account (ESA) to ignite the Friedman "wildfire," which would include further reductions in Arizona in the discrimination against children for whom the assigned TPS is a poor fit. Total TPS funding is much above $7,000 per pupil everywhere.

All eyes should be on schooling-related entrepreneurial initiative in the Phoenix and Tucson metro areas. Because of West Virginia's lower population density and smaller maximum ESA amount, its universal ESA is less likely to be a reform catalyst within the state, or a driver of the Friedman wildfire.

The Arizona and West Virginia expansions notwithstanding, persistent academic failure and exasperation with typical reform strategies continue to yield occasional small-scale parental choice expansion. The determination to protect the system—to, as Senator Joe Lieberman said, sacrifice children to sustain a process—seems to still dominate the determination to leave no children behind. Substantial evidence to the contrary, we still cling to the delusion that every student can succeed if we relentlessly pursue what amounts to central plan optimization and sporadically single out children from low-income families, disabled children,[3] and/or students from government-designated low-performing TPSs for escape on the cheap.

The persistence of school system failure alongside seemingly numerous school choice programs has already somewhat poisoned the well. For example, at a recent Texas Republican convention, there was much talk that school choice is an old idea whose time has passed; we need new ideas, please. What is old is trying to get "it" to work as a reform catalyst at a way below reform catalyst (OEI) dosage.

Another example arose, coincidentally, the day coauthor JM wrote the first draft of this chapter. Tennessee's narrowly targeted choice expansion was declared unconstitutional.[4] Tennessee Republicans imposed the program on two heavily Democratic, deep poverty areas, but they left out areas that might have disrupted the better TPSs in Republican-represented areas. It was declared unconstitutional for not being a statewide program, singling out just two parts of the state. Both parties preferred the status quo to avoid the disruption of a departure from TPSs.

It is too early to tell if universal choice for residents of poor places will be widely adopted. It seems to be gaining traction in several places, but the Tennessee experience is not promising. There are places throughout Tennessee in urgent need of the economic development known to follow school choice expansion. If some places large enough to fully exploit entrepreneurial initiative (Phoenix, Tucson) adopt it, at least the largest of those will constitute a real experiment in potentially transformational parental choice. Those experiences may then help yield the Milton Friedman wildfire.

Continued discrimination against taxpayers who use private schools will retard the transformation of the private sector. It will take 20–30 years to realize that helping some of an area's disadvantaged children will not produce widespread academic improvements. Another decade *may* be enough to convince the public that limited parental choice was an ineffective reform catalyst because of the limitations. Widespread economic illiteracy already makes that a hard sell, and alongside an increasingly overextended electorate, it won't get any easier.

To replace that dominant scenario with a more promising one, choice advocates must begin openly supporting choice expansion programs that contain every key element of an OEI. They must visibly subordinate movement within the system to system transformation. A key part of that is an end to one-dimensional perceptions of student ability, teacher talent, and school quality. For example, when people mistakenly see student ability as excellent, average, or poor rather than diverse in terms of strengths and weaknesses, they can worry about "cream skimming" (capturing the best), which can cause even meticulous economists (Sahlgren, 2013) to recommend devastating price control (banning shared financing of private tuition).

Small changes in the status quo should be left to legislatures, where caution and compromise approaches are inevitable during the time that political pressure builds for the necessary K–12 transformation. However, cautious compromise policies must not be allowed to diminish that pressure. Programs that help thousands of children are great as long as they don't jeopardize reforms that would help millions.

Choice advocates must articulate strong reservations when they support restriction-laden programs that lack key elements of an OEI. Unless they do, small choice expansions may continue to yield lengthy detours, perhaps even indefinitely poisoning the well for transformational choice expansion.

Choice advocates must use opposition to deficient proposals to educate the public and define choice advocacy as the pursuit of universal opportunity and empowerment. Something like this is appropriate:

> Today, Governor X proposed a low-income voucher program wherein the state share of public school funding follows the children of successful applicants—up to Y% (far below 100%) of district enrollment—to the school they prefer. It's only a small positive step when a much larger step is desperately needed. The state can do much more within the existing K–12 budget. Competition and improved fit through universal parental choice would help all children by improving the entire system. When public support follows every child without regard to school ownership, schools will join the vast majority of service providers and become directly accountable to the people they serve. Market forces would produce the relentless improvement that characterizes most of the economy.
>
> Governor X's restrictions on choice continue the long-standing practice of assigning the comfort of public school employees—public servants—and residents near the better TPSs a higher priority than a great education for the children the current system leaves behind. School taxes exist to support children, so their welfare should be our top priority. While we continue our pursuit of universal choice and empowerment, we'll support X's proposal so that the school system's worst victims can attend schools that their parents believe are better for them.

It will take smart political work to enact universal parental choice anywhere. It may then spread like wildfire. The smart political work must address the following:

1. Most suburbanites believe that their TPSs are fine.
2. Rural legislators struggle to oppose the interests of school districts, which can be their district's major employer.
3. Most states don't publish detailed, school-level academic data or academic standards for each grade.
4. Leaders of low-income groups often take choice expansion positions at odds with most of their constituents.
5. Teachers, the cornerstone of organized choice opposition, have much to gain from an OEI. Many teachers are conservative, and much of the support for the union position is only passive. The vast majority are apolitical and don't understand the choice expansion policy options.

6. Except for changes in the governance and finance system that would foster creation of TPS alternatives, every potential reform strategy has been tried many times and yielded only big expenditures and disappointment. "More of the same—harder" hasn't worked (Hess, 2010).
7. The public knows very little about the choice expansion options, and much of the available information is wrong, misleading, or irrelevant.
8. Greater access to the best choices currently available can hinder the supplementation and transformation of the choices.
9. Hardly anyone cares about openness to TPS alternatives, but most of the potential benefits of parental choice depend on it.
10. Winning will be easier in some places.
11. And, finally, the policy essentials and key options.

WINNING IN THE SUBURBS

Blissful ignorance is a formidable opponent. Its victims won't seek the truth. Their ability to deny the truth is evident in the persistence of the myth that suburban schools are good in the face of frequently published evidence to the contrary. The propensity to deny is even apparent in the title—"Reality Check 2000"[5]—of a prominent early piece of evidence. Lance Izumi's "Not as Good as You Think" series provided dozens of shocking examples.

The chorus of a popular song—"Tell me lies, tell me sweet little lies"—is quite relevant. The truth could hurt property values. Some families prefer living downtown but move to the suburbs because the schools are usually better.[6] They will not readily accept a contention that the better school that helped attract them is still pretty bad.

Apparently, deeply ingrained myths can survive even multiple doses of overwhelming general evidence. I often hear: "The system is struggling, but my children are in a good school." Asserting otherwise for specific schools is an implicit accusation of child neglect. Resentment of the messengers will outlast the eventual, grudging acceptance of the message.

However, the distastefulness and difficulty of the task doesn't alter the fact that school system transformation will not begin until choice advocates destroy the myth that major academic deficiencies exist only in the low-income inner city. Suburban bliss is a major roadblock on the road to an OEI, maybe more so than opposition from the establishment groups such as teacher unions.

Publication of detailed school-level data is the first step. The next step is to compare it to what children in each grade should know. Regional groupings of schools are appropriate. Since the top schools may still be pretty bad, school rankings should be avoided. For large urban areas, it might be helpful to compare subgroups of schools to what children should know. Subgroupings such as public school districts or inner-city vs. suburb might be useful.

Choice advocates should not attack the myth one school at a time. That approach would maximize the property value effects. The outcry could undermine the process and divert attention away from the critical message that the whole system is broken, that relocating to another neighborhood or switching to a private school may not help some students at all. Truly outstanding schools should be singled out so that the users of the other schools cannot cling to the widespread myth that problems exist in every school but their own.

WEAKENING THE OPPOSITION

Discord between labor and the poor, and between the poor (especially African Americans) and their leaders, could significantly weaken choice expansion opponents. Labor and the poor are core constituent groups of politicians, mostly Democrats, who currently oppose all but the weakest forms of choice expansion, and would feel the same about an OEI. Choice advocates must exploit such rifts in the opposition.

The teacher unions are widely seen as the biggest opponents of choice expansion; but they cannot stop it on their own, and they confront several problems that choice expansion advocates must exploit politically. Teacher union leaders struggle to maintain the backing of teachers, and they fight to preserve an anti-choice-expansion liberal coalition that supports public funding for many other kinds of choice. Liberals' discomfort with the contradiction between the teacher union position and other liberal causes was clearly evident in a Gore-Bradley debate. Both were eager to change the subject, to flee from what the *Wall Street Journal* correctly dubbed a "piece of Democratic Kryptonite."[7] Choice advocates must use those contradictions to reform or defeat the "liberal superhero" position on choice expansion.

The passionate opposition of teacher union leaders is not seen among teachers. Even though very few choice advocates vigorously solicit teacher support, few teachers show a strong interest in working to defeat choice expansion. Most teachers fear the union definition of choice expansion enough to support the union position, but they're unhappy with the status quo.

Teachers resent teacher bashing, which they see as condemnation for following orders and for the mistakes of others. They don't like mandates, micromanagement, teaching tests, or excessive differentiation of instruction. Teachers don't like coping with parents who want out but can't leave. They don't like mainstreaming everything, including revolving-door discipline problems and special needs children who require specialized services. Many want linkage between genuine merit and compensation.

Teachers want a transformation of the system, but not enough agree that genuine openness is the best way to do it. As teachers see more evidence that efforts to make the current system work are painful acts of futility that often further degrade their lives, more of them will realize that an OEI is the only viable alternative. Choice advocates must accelerate that process. Teachers may indeed be the best catalyst for change.

Teacher union leaders can maintain rank-and-file support only if they can make systems with much more choice look even worse than the current system. That's really tough. Since administrators and legislators will continue their frenzied efforts to make teachers succeed despite the system, maintaining teacher support for the union position will get tougher.

Choice advocates can accelerate the erosion of teacher opposition to choice expansion. It would help a lot if choice expansion advocates would just stop enthusiastically supporting the restriction-laden choice expansion proposals and stop making the analytical errors that help union leaders frighten teachers. Because teachers see little else discussed, and because choice advocates so enthusiastically embrace restriction-laden programs, teachers probably think of choice expansion as something that will extend to more teachers the existing opportunity to give up one third of their income to escape the problems described in the previous paragraph.

Choice advocates must point out that an OEI would do more than eliminate that trade-off. Other current disadvantages of the private sector, such as the scarcity of secular schools, would disappear, and the government-owned schools would either get better and more teacher friendly or become increasingly scarce.

The poor, especially minorities, represent another political opportunity. According to a recent *Time* magazine article, "inner city blacks are beginning to join the Republican cry for vouchers to pay private school tuition."[8] "The Joint Center for Political and Economic Studies, a left-leaning think tank that focuses on African-American issues, found in its [1999] annual survey that 60 percent of blacks support school choice" (Rees, 2000, p. 3). "School choice and charter schools are becoming the civil rights movement of the 1990s" (Shokraii, 1996), and "over 70 percent of blacks under 35"[9] support parental choice. In a "1997 Delta Kappa/Gallup Poll between 62 and 72 percent of African-Americans expressed their support for vouchers."[10] The figure has held steady, with 70% of African Americans supporting choice expansion in 2022.[11]

Such polling data continue to signal still unrealized, potentially "serious trouble for Democratic legislators and school choice opponents, given blacks' status as the most loyal of all Democratic constituencies" (Loomis, 1998, p.

80). The survey respondents probably understood choice expansion to mean restriction-laden vouchers worth less than the per-pupil funding of TPSs.

We believe that the parental choice system advocated throughout this book—properly explained in the survey instrument—would produce even better polling data. Unlike every existing voucher and tax credit program, the system advocated in this book would put all but the elite prep academies within reach of every family.

The current situation presents enormous dangers and opportunities. The opportunities will come from the growing pressure on leaders of low-income groups to profess support for choice expansion with public funding through vouchers, tax credits, or education savings accounts. The danger is that their proposals won't include the key elements of an OEI.

Reluctant, born-again choice advocates—leaders of low-income groups—will try to pile on the restrictions. They will do so to appear consistent with previous commitments and to appease their longtime allies in the liberal coalition. They are more likely to get away with it if restriction-laden proposals continue to dominate the public debate,[12] a situation that choice expansion advocates can avoid by demanding large first expansions. Light must accompany heat. Choice advocates must explain how each type of restriction hurts low-income groups.

DOCUMENTING FUTILITY

The authorities are under enormous pressure to improve K–12 education. Repeated failures to make the current system produce satisfactory results produce growing frustration and anger. The authorities have had enough time to try every elixir for the current system, and some policies, nearly everywhere (Barry & Hedeman, 2000). Some reform strategies resurface often in a never-ending triumph of hope over experience. Already in 2000, Kearns and Harvey said, "Education reforms recycle"; they appear, "disappear, and then reappear again" (p. 56).

The MOTS-H (more of the same—harder) approach (Jennings, 1998, p. 1) wastes time, money, and young minds. Indeed, MOTS-H sounds like a longtime definition of insanity. "Insanity is repeating something that doesn't work and expecting different results."[13] Better documentation can reduce the repetition of costly acts of futility.

Some parental choice advocacy organizations must produce a report that catalogs those disappointments by major plan ingredient; they should highlight things such as teacher raises, alleged merit pay, ending social promotion, and reduced class sizes. The report should also report what each government tried. Such a report is an indispensable advocacy tool. It will comprise a cornerstone of the urgently needed campaign to convince reformers that a reform package will produce satisfactory results only if it fosters OEI conditions.

Proper interpretation of findings is vital. For example, merit pay isn't a bad idea because it hasn't produced significant gains. It's a big advantage of an OEI. Competition forces managers to reward true merit. Without genuine competition, managers are under much less pressure to recognize merit, and measurement is much more difficult. We must recognize that the political process rarely enacts genuine merit pay and that the rare exceptions are predictably ineffective, even counterproductive. Parent/consumers voting with their feet and money will reward and raise genuine merit much more than an administrator trying to allocate an externally fixed budget according to scheduled performances ("observations" of teachers) or test scores.

Similar points should be made about most of the other efforts to make the system work better, including especially teacher raises, increased K–12 spending, and reduced class size (Kirkpatrick, 1997, p. 9). For example, consider the political approach to class size. If enough vocal supporters believe class size reductions warrant the political price of higher taxes or cuts in other areas, class size is capped for certain grades.

In contrast, profit-seeking entrepreneurs would find out exactly where class size reductions matter the most, advertise general class reductions, and minimize cost and maximize benefits by implementing the largest class size reductions where it would matter most, and smaller reductions, perhaps even some increases, where it mattered least. The political process cannot produce such an outcome because it would be seen as unfair.

Again, it's not that teacher pay, class size, and K–12 spending don't matter. It's that the political process hasn't used them in a way that would bring about improvements, and that for theoretical as well as empirical reasons we should not expect it to do so in the future. Choice advocates can summarize with a key generalization. Markets cause resources to flee failure, but in the government's share of K–12, failure often attracts additional resources.

CHANGING BLISSFUL IGNORANCE

A Public Agenda opinion poll said that "a vast majority of the American public has little knowledge about CPS, education vouchers, or for-profit schools"—something that is still true—but that "debate at the top levels of national leadership was crisp, and well-defined."[14] With so many wrong, misleading, or irrelevant statements, the assertion that the top levels are on track is alarming, and the high degree of ignorance within the general public remains, sadly, for the time being, a blessing. It is much easier to inform people than to dispel their misconceptions.

The survey results also repudiate a key premise of the incrementalism strategy. That approach to some version of "full school choice" began with the premise that the public is not ready for radical changes in the status quo. Since a substantial segment of the public doesn't even know what expansion advocates proposed, they are not necessarily against it. They are "not ready for radical change" because ignorance makes people more resistant to change, and more gullible. Choice opponents skillfully exploit both. Since they usually have more money to get their message out, they can get away with more emotion-evoking distortions.

A reality check, followed by relentless truth in labeling, is the only way out of the encumbrance of public ignorance and the more devastating mistaken beliefs of the longtime participants in the school choice wars. The reality check should begin with what is, by now, evident in places such as Milwaukee and Cleveland. Narrowly targeted, restriction-laden choice expansions are not tentative reform procedures.

Choice expansion advocates should celebrate the extra freedom and academic progress each student transfer produces and remind everyone that each escape attempt is at least a rejection of discrimination in favor of uniformly comprehensive schooling, and that tweaking the status quo is not good enough. Particular school managers, including the government, can best serve only a fraction of our diverse population.

OEI advocates must use words like "freedom" and "escape" loudly and frequently, especially when they condemn choice program restrictions, including the large number left behind[15] and the minimal effect on the system.[16] That's more important than celebrating the exhilaration of the escapees. The emotional reaction of many escapees causes the word "rescue" to come to mind, but that term should be used sparingly. That term can imply that current private schools are in good shape, when in fact there is much room for improvement there.

RECONCILING PRAGMATISM AND PRINCIPLES

In many places, an OEI may not be politically feasible yet. In the meantime, the inevitable pursuit of lesser objectives must not conflict with that ultimate objective. In other words, choice advocates must push for an OEI to effect systemic reform while efforts to provide some additional choices, and limited chances to use alternatives to TPSs, continue in a manner that does not undermine the reform effort.

The key is truth in labeling. With truth in labeling, the limited-choice escape valves that John Hood (1991, p. 11) mistakenly called "gradual reform" can continue without "the limitations and risks that entails" or the risk of being intellectually "right but outmaneuvered" politically with an OEI-or-nothing policy. Interim, limited victories are often necessary to maintain the morale of the key choice advocates and broaden support by publicly demonstrating political strength.

Truth in Labeling in Practice

Here's how advocates of an OEI should have described the passage of the 1990 choice expansion enacted for Milwaukee, Wisconsin:

> Today, the State of Wisconsin decided to help 1% of the students trapped in the reform-resistant Milwaukee Public Schools (MPS) attend certain private schools—nonsectarian schools willing to enroll a child for about half as much as MPS spends. Only the children of low-income families will have the freedom to attend a private school with some of the tax money earmarked for their education. The families that pay most of the school taxes can't use their taxes to find a better fit.
>
> Escape attempts represent rejection of the uniformly comprehensive schooling forced on TPSs by attendance areas and its low quality. The modest rise in MPS's per-pupil funds will have no immediate impact on the remaining MPS students, including unsuccessful voucher applicants and many more low-income children stuck in the worst MPS schools. Because of the restrictions on private schools, the extremely low cap on participation, and the unequal funding of MPS captives and escapees, the escapes will produce no discernible competitive pressures. We can only hope that embarrassment[17] alone is enough to motivate some constructive reactions by MPS officials.

OEI advocates should have said this after the voucher applications were in:

> The private schools have much less money per child than MPS does, yet many more parents want in than the existing private schools can enroll. That occurred despite MPS harassment and the legal cloud of uncertainty that hangs over a new program. But for crippling restrictions, the private sector could eventually serve everyone who's not finding a good fit in their assigned TPS.
>
> The cap on participation and the ban on adding private money to the voucher are especially troublesome. In addition, the large voucher waiting list only contains low-income applicants. Some of the families that supposedly have enough money to pay for education services twice are so desperate for escape assistance that they risk the punishment for filing false income statements.[18] The high demand for vouchers directly contradicts the claims of some choice critics that parents, especially low-income families, can't compare schools.

The voucher applicants were so unhappy with their much better funded MPS school that they greatly preferred a much leaner private school that they have no personal experience with, and which probably means some inconvenience and discomfort, such as separating their children from their friends and transportation requirements. Right now, many children want a better fit, and each departure saves taxpayers' money or increases the funding per MPS user. If private school and MPS users had equal public funding and a wider array of private schools could cash vouchers, the number of applications would be far greater.

Citizens tax themselves to educate children by the best possible means, not to support school systems. Therefore, the authorities should make the program universal and eliminate the TPS funding advantage. That would allow us to reap the benefits of competition.

COMPETITION: THE CRITICAL PROCESS

A key misleading finding is that "competition does not matter to anyone."[19] But nearly all of the things that do matter depend on the openness that fosters genuine competition. That's the correct message to choice advocates. Since citizens care about academic outcomes and fairness, not underlying processes, choice expansion advocates must connect the outcomes to openness and the critical process of competition. The truly alarming, but not surprising, implication of that finding is that people do not make the connection on their own. Poor economic education is one of the most glaring defects of the current system. Myron Lieberman (1993) pointed out that economic illiteracy makes choice advocacy much more difficult:

> Public education has flourished because it fails to educate effectively. Its failure to foster an understanding of market systems has led citizens to accept a larger public education sector than a more informed citizenry would permit.[20]

The parents of TPS leavers and unsuccessful applicants are a natural, politically active OEI constituency. They already believe that the political process hasn't fixed the public school system. Regular reminders of the difference between system transformation and a move within the system are especially important. They must be convinced that an OEI will make private school choices much better.

WHERE TO START THE WILDFIRE

For the sake of our children and our country, it would be great if OEIs could be started up everywhere at the same time. But the economic realities of limited resources and the geographically uneven barriers to change require that we carefully choose wildfire ignition points. The first modern OEI will not be an experiment. Competitive forces already have an impressive track record, even in education.

ESSENTIALS AND OPTIONS

The critical elements of an OEI described in Chapter 2, political pragmatism, and the recommendation of a high minimum level of support for every child come down to some policy essentials and some policy options. The policy essentials are as follows:

1. State and local public funding of K–12 instruction must be entirely child based so that parents' choices exclusively decide each school's share of state and local public funding.
2. Each child's share of state and local K–12 instruction spending is the same whether they attend government-owned, private nonprofit, or private for-profit schools. This policy essential can be phased in.
3. There must be no restrictions on private spending on K–12 instruction. Families must have the right to use private funds to help buy more instruction than the public funds will buy.
4. As required by existing federal law, federal K–12 funding must provide supplemental public support to "special needs" children on a case-by-case basis.
5. There must be a minimum enrollment to qualify an "operation" to receive public funding to educate children. This will deter fraud and extremist schools and stop families from earning income educating their own children.
6. There must be a way to verify the enrollment of each school.

There are several significant policy options:

1. The public funding mechanism: Bankable, nonrefundable education tax credits and education savings accounts are best. Vouchers are okay but not necessary, a plus given the "V-word" phenomenon discussed earlier. Another option is a fully refundable tax credit. Then schools would only bill parents, and the government would only have to issue checks to families with K–12 credits larger than their tax liabilities.
2. Providing the same level of public support to government and private school users does not preclude age-based or place-based differences in the government support per child. For example, private school tuition

levels are now typically higher for high school grades than for the elementary grades, an indication that it costs more to educate older children. Therefore, more government support for, say, 10th graders than 2nd graders may be deemed appropriate. Likewise, the authorities may decide that regional cost differences warrant regional differences in the government support per child.
3. The authorities will have to decide how much of current government spending to allocate to instruction and how much to allocate to administrative functions. As long as there are no restrictions on private K–12 copayment spending, the political tug-of-war over appropriate age- and region-based differences and instructional vs. administrative spending won't be too damaging.
4. Another important policy decision is the government's role as an information provider and data generator, including standardized testing. Test score comparisons will still matter to some parents, but with the specialized schools of an OEI, test scores won't matter as much as they matter with the uniformly comprehensive schooling that dominates public schools now.

States have to define "school" to determine eligibility for public K–12 instructional funding. The pressure to add regulations to the definition in compulsory attendance laws must be resisted. The market will resolve personnel qualifications, textbooks, curricula, food service, and transportation services. Those are specialization and competition areas.

Market forces deter and punish mistakes more effectively than costly, stifling, change-resistant government regulations can prevent them. Choice and tolerance, not regulation, is the answer to disagreement over what schools should teach. One of the reasons regulations would be counterproductive is the same as the demand for them: the ever-changing controversy over what the rules should require. The other reason is that they would hinder the relentless pursuit of improvement that characterizes open industries.

PROCESSES AND OUTCOMES

Most of the specific effects[21] of market forces are utterly unforeseeable. The example in the next paragraph illustrates the key elements of a child-based funding process and connects the process to likely general effects. The ones that might stand out during a transition are especially noteworthy. Unless choice advocates prepare the public for a bumpy transition period, market forces could be stifled before they completely take hold.

Let's say a county with 100,000 K–12 age children implements the policy essentials described above for the next school year. For simplicity, assume that K–12 enrollment in that area will stay at 100,000, and that in the previous year, state and local public funding for K–12 was $1 billion. The authorities must service debt, administer the child-based funding process, and monitor rule compliance. Suppose that debt service consumes $50 million per year and that it takes $1 million to administer the requirements of child-based funding. For a margin of safety, in case the federal funds are not enough of a supplement for special needs families, the county school authorities set aside another $24 million for that.

In the first years of child-based funding, the authorities should also allocate money for severance and retraining support, a function with significant economic and political benefits. It will help educators adjust to changing job opportunities or change careers. Assume the authorities allocate $25 million per year for that. With the same state and local funding level next year, that will leave $900 million ($1,000 − $50 − $1 − $24 − $25) to allocate to schools according to parental choices, an *average* of $9,000 per K–12 child ($900 million ÷ 100,000 children). However, the level of support per child will probably vary by grade level, with more than $9,000 for older children.

If the county is typical and 12% of the students attended private schools or were homeschooled when the public schools had their monopoly on public funding, child-based funding—ending the government's discrimination against private school users—will cause a 12% drop in the district-owned schools' per-pupil funding.

Even though schools will be free to charge more than the average $9,000 public funding level, and child-based funding will eliminate some costs (see below), some people will cite potential hardship for low-income families to justify increased public spending on K–12, and they'll find ready allies in private school operators eager for opportunities to raise their prices.

Charities can eliminate that justification for increased public funding by providing a low-income safety net and help for families that don't live near a school that will accept the $9,000 public funding as full payment and can't afford a required add-on. A true scholarship program that gives low-income families access to schools that demand large add-ons would also have a great deal of economic and political value.

Child-based funding will eliminate costly tasks, some directly, and it will undermine the rationale for others. School budgets will depend on the choices of parents, not decisions of the district central office. That will significantly weaken the rationale for an expensive district superintendent and their raft of associates, assistants, directors, and program coordinators. In addition, district administrators won't have to develop budgets or maintain, adjust, or enforce school attendance areas.

The government-owned schools can maintain their district identity, but schools will probably perform many former district-provided services themselves. Personnel is a good example. Schools want to hire their own staff. They don't want district administrators to do it for them.[22] Schools will increasingly resist funding district-provided support services. District schools will not benefit from those services equally. In addition, the changes that will come with the pressure to specialize will require a wider range of service providers.

Ending the government's discrimination against private school users will increase the demand for private schooling. Even if there is enough time to expand facilities and establish new schools, some schools will have more applicants than space. When oversubscribed schools discover the problem after it is too late to change advertised prices, they can use a lottery or exercise selectivity.

It is in schools' self-interest to select based on the school's unique mission. But given the politics of the possibility that socially harmful discrimination may occur, it is important to recognize that the shortages that empower bigotry will be very short-lived. Copycat entrepreneurs will quickly offer more of the most popular services. When explaining this facet of the transition to an OEI, parental choice advocates should also point out that selectivity—school choice, by public school officials, rather than parents—already exists in the current system. However, the current system contains no market mechanism to quickly eliminate space shortages in magnet schools, or in some states, charter schools.

Some people may fear that the large private school sector of an OEI will create a second strong lobby for higher school taxes. Certainly, extra public funding per child can produce price increases and higher short-term profits, but that produces unwanted additional competition that restores the rate of return to the level that is normal for businesses with comparable risks. Many school operators will conclude that such a cycle of change is not worth lobbying for.

Basic economics texts often discuss a phenomenon called "limit pricing," a practice whereby firms forgo short-term profit to avoid an intensification of competition and a possible drop in long-term profitability. In the current system, school operators see no downside to across-the-board funding growth. An OEI will create much weaker pressures for government funding increases, and school operators cannot stifle signals such as falling tuition copayment levels and excess capacity that justify public spending restraint.

MOUNTAINS AND TRENCHES AS METAPHORS

Reformers can achieve the OEI summit, but the summit is hard to see from the trenches, especially when the trenches are enshrouded in the fog of war. Small changes in the status quo, like low-income vouchers, education savings accounts for the disabled, public school choice, and even strong charter laws, can seem like the summit or on the road to it. But such changes are sub-peaks, tempting objectives that raise the distance to the OEI summit and that could become permanent detours. False summits can easily sap enough time and energy to put the summit out of reach or push a successful summit attempt into the distant future.

This book made some observations from behind the front lines. It aimed to define the significant differences between the OEI summit and the sub-peak detours and chart the route to the summit. The OEI outcomes of social justice and the relentless pursuit of improvement are worth the difficulties that must be endured to reach them. Our civilization hangs in the balance.

NOTES

1. Milton Friedman, "Public Schools: Make Them Private," *Washington Post*, Weekly Edition, February 27, 1995.
2. https://www.aei.org/op-eds/school-choice-is-on-a-roll-here-are-3-ways-to-keep-it-going/
3. I avoided the term "special needs" because I regard many gifted-and-talented children as special needs. School choice programs have not addressed those special needs. Conditions that cause children to be outside the mainstream, and thus seen as having a learning disability, are addressed by school choice policy changes in some states.
4. Anonymous, "Tennessee Voucher Law Ruled Unconstitutional," *Education Week*, May 13, 2020, 3.
5. Public Agenda and *Education Week*, "Reality Check 2000," *Education Week*, February 16, 2000, S1–S8.
6. Daniel Akst, "Why Liberals Should Love School Choice," *Wall Street Journal*, April 6, 1998, A14.
7. *Wall Street Journal* Editorial Board, "No Choice for Democrats," *Wall Street Journal*, February 23, 2000.
8. Sally B. Donnelly and Tamala M. Edwards, "They'll Vouch for That," *Time*, October 27, 1997, 72–74.
9. Nina Shokraii Rees, "School Choice 2000 Annual Report," *The Heritage Backgrounder*, no. 1354 (March 30, 2000).
10. Rochelle Stanfeld, "A Turning Tide on Vouchers," *National Journal*, September 27, 1997, 1911.

11. https://www.federationforchildren.org/new-poll-72-support-for-school-choice/

12. Stephen Talbot, "The Battle Over School Choice," *PBS Frontline*, May 23, 2000. The hour-long TV special did not discuss competition or how parental choice might bring about a system transformation. The possibility of universal choice was not considered. Instead, the program stated that there was "not much need for school choice in some places." Parental choice was presented strictly as a way for low-income families to escape bad "public" schools.

13. G. K. Chesterton, cited in Center for Education Reform, *Newsletter*, no. 60 (February–March 2000).

14. Education Policy Institute, "New Poll Finds Public in Dark About Charters and Vouchers," *EPI-Update*, November 19, 1999.

15. "Fifteen Percent of Eligible Cleveland Public School Children Apply for Vouchers," *The Buckeye Institute for Public Policy Solutions*, June 19996. There is huge excess demand for the latest CEO voucher offering.

16. Wisconsin governor Tommy Thompson gives MPS ultimatum: Improve significantly by June 2000, or be taken over by the state. Beth Reinhard, "Thompson Threatens a Takeover for Milwaukee," *Education Week*, January 28, 1998, 8.

17. Some MPS changes, such as increased school autonomy, have been attributed to embarrassment about the escapes. In Albany, New York, Virginia Gilder funded some low-income vouchers for students at woeful Giffen Elementary. The overwhelming response to the offer prompted some changes at Giffen. According to Albany superintendent Lonnie Palmer, "The real catalyst may not have been competition, but the subsequent media attention."

18. Mark Walsh, "Audit Criticizes Cleveland Voucher Program," *Education Week*, April 15, 1998.

19. Frank Luntz and Bob Castro, "Dollars to Classrooms and Parental Choice in Education," *Memorandum*, April 14, 1998.

20. Based on a general observation by Mancur Olson, in Lieberman (1993, p. 160).

21. Size, number, and specialization area(s) of each school; typical modes of instruction; salary levels of different types of educators; market shares of government-owned, private for-profit, private nonprofit, church-run schools, etc.

22. Describing a typical urban school principal, Rexford Brown noted that "his greatest frustration is his inability to hire and fire his own teachers. You're the boss, but you're not able to hire and fire your own employees." Brown (1993, p. 104).

References

Abdulkadiroğlu, A., Pathak, P. A., & Walters, C. R. (2018). Free to choose: Can school choice reduce student achievement?. *American Economic Journal: Applied Economics, 10*(1), 175–206.

Alger, V. E. (2016). *Failure: The federal misedukation [sic] of America's children.* Oakland, CA: The Independent Institute.

Allen, W., & Toma, E. (1996, November). *A new framework for public education.* Lansing, MI: Governors Office.

Aoki, M., & Feiner, S. F. (1996). The economics of market choice and at-risk students. In W. E. Becker & W. J. Baumol (Eds.), *Assessing educational practices.* Cambridge, MA: MIT Press.

Armor, D. (1997). *Competition in education: A case study of interdistrict choice.* Boston: Pioneer Institute for Public Policy.

Arons, S. (1982). Educational choice: Unanswered question in the American experience. In M. E. Manley-Casimir (Ed.), *Family Choice in Schooling* (pp. 22–31). Lexington, MA: Lexington Books.

Arons, S. (1997). *Short route to chaos.* Amherst: University of Massachusetts Press.

Ascher, C., Fruchter, N., & Berne, R. (1996). *Hard lessons: The promises of privatization.* New York: The Twentieth Century Press.

Ball, G. C. (1990, Fall). In search of educational excellence. *Policy Review.*

Ball, G. C., & Goldman, S. (1997). Improving Education's Productivity. *Phi Delta Kappan 79,* #3: 228–32.

Ballou, D., & Podgursky, M. (1997). *Teacher pay and teacher quality.* Kalamazoo, MI: W. E. Upjohn Institute for Employment and Training.

Barry, J. S., & Hedeman, R. S., Jr. (2000). *Report card on American education: A state-by-state analysis, 1976–99.* Washington, DC: American Legislative Exchange Council.

Bast, J. L., & Harmer, D. (1997). *Vouchers and educational freedom: A debate* (Policy Analysis Monograph No. 269). Washington, DC: The Cato Institute.

Bastian, A. (1986). *Choosing Equality: The Case for Democratic Schooling.* Philadelphia: Temple University Press.

Baumol, W. J., Schramm, C., & Litan, R. E. (2007). *Good Capitalism: Bad Capitalism* New Haven: Yale University Press.

Baumol, W. J., Panzar, J. C., & Willig, R. D. (1982). *Contestable markets and the theory of industry structure*. New York: Harcourt Brace Jovanovich.

Bedrick, J. (2016). The folly of overregulating school choice. *Education Next*. Retrieved from https://www.educationnext.org/the-folly-of-overregulating-school-choice/

Bedrick, J., & Burke, L. (2018). Surveying Florida scholarship families: Experiences and Satisfaction with Florida's Tax-Credit Scholarship Program. *EdChoice*.

Benbow, C., & Stanley, J. C. (1996). Inequity in equity: How equity can lead to inequity for high-potential students. *Psychology, Public Policy, and Law, 2*, 249–292.

Bennett, W. J., Fair, W., Finn, C. E., Jr., Flake, F., Hirsch, E. D., Marshall, W., Ravitch, D., et al. (1998, July/August). A nation still at risk. *Policy Review, 90*.

Berends, M., Waddlington, J., & Schoenig, J. (Eds.). (2019). *School choice at the crossroads: Research perspectives*. New York: Routledge.

Berliner, D., & Biddle, B. (1995). *The manufactured crisis*. Reading, MA: Addison-Wesley.

Berliner, D. C. (1993). "Mythology and the American System of Education." *Phi Delta Kappan 74*: 638.

Berner, A. R. (2017). *Pluralism and American Public Education: No One Way to School*. New York: Palgrave-MacMillan.

Blumenfeld, S. (1981). *Is Public Education Necessary?* Boise, ID: The Paradigm Company.

Bonsteel, A., & Bonilla, C. A. (1997). *A choice for our children*. San Francisco: ICS Press.

Borenstein, S. (1992). The evolution of U.S. airline competition. *Journal of Economic Perspectives, 6*.

Boyd, W. L. (1987). Balancing Public and Private Schools: The Australian Experience and American Implications. *Educational Evaluation and Policy Analysis 9*, #3: 183–97.

Bradford, D. F., & Shapiro, D. (1998, October). The politics of vouchers. In *Vouchers and Related Delivery Mechanisms: Consumer Choice in the Provision of Public Services*. Conference Papers (p. 52). Washington: Brookings Institution.

Brown, B. (1992). Why governments run schools. *Economics of Education Review, 11*(4).

Brown, R. G. (1993). *Schools of thought*. San Francisco: Jossey-Bass.

Buckley, J., & Schneider, M. (2003). Shopping for schools: How do marginal consumers gather information about schools. *Policy Studies Journal, 31*(2), 121–145.

Burke, L. M., & Bedrick, J. (2020). Myth: School choice needs regulation to ensure access and quality. In C. DeAngelis & N. McCluskey (Eds.), *School choice myths: Setting the record straight on education freedom*. Washington, DC: Cato Institute.

Carl, J. (1994). Parental choice as national policy in England and the United States. *Comparative Education Review, 38*(3).

Carnegie Foundation for the Advancement of Teaching. (1992). *School choice: A special report*. Princeton, NJ.

Carnoy, M., Chuggar, A., & Adamson, F. (2007). *Vouchers and Public School Performance* Washington, DC: Economic Policy Institute. https://www.epi.org/publication/book_vouchers/

Carpenter, P., & Hall, G. (1971). *Case Studies in Educational Performance Contracting: Conclusions and Implications*, Report #R-900/1-HEW. Santa Monica, CA: Rand Corporation.

Carter, S. C. (2000). *No excuses: Lessons from 21 high-performing, high poverty schools*. Washington, DC: Heritage Foundation.

Cavazos, L. F. (1991). Achieving our national education goals: Overarching strategies. *Harvard Journal of Law and Public Policy, 14*(2).

Chakrabarti, R. (2008). Can increasing private school participation and monetary loss in a voucher program affect public school performance? Evidence from Milwaukee. *Journal of Public Economics 92*, #5–6.

Chubb, J., & Moe, T. (1990a). *Educational choice*. San Antonio: Texas Public Policy Foundation.

Chubb, J., & Moe, T. (1990b). *Politics, markets, and America's schools*. Washington, DC: Brookings Institution.

Churchill, A. (2015). *The 2014 Education Choice and Competition Index*. Washington, DC: Fordham Institute. https://fordhaminstitute.org/national/commentary/2014-education-choice-and-competition-index-0

Clowes, G. (1998, September/October). After 15 years, nation is still at risk. *Intellectual Ammunition*.

Clowes, G. (2000, January). The Dark Side of Suburban School Achievement. *School Reform News*, 7.

Clune, W. (1994). The Shift from Equity to Adequacy in School Finance. *Educational Policy 8*, 376–94.

Cobb, C. W. (1992). *Responsive schools, renewed communities*. San Francisco: The ICS Press.

Cohn, E. (1974). *Economics of state aid to education*. Lexington, MA: D.C. Heath.

Coleman, J. (1987). *Public and private schools*. New York: Basic Books.

Collinge, R. A., & Ayers, R. M. (1997). *Economics by design*. Upper Saddle River, NJ: Prentice Hall.

Cookson, P. (1993a). Assessing private school effects: Implications for school choice. In E. Rasell & R. Rothstein (Eds.), *School choice: Examining the evidence*. Washington, DC: Economic Policy Institute.

Cookson, P. (1993b). Response to Bruce Cooper's review of the choice controversy. *Journal of Education Finance, 19*, 223–225.

Coons, J., & Sugarman, S. (1999). *Education by choice*. Troy, NY: Educator's International Press.

Cordell, D. E. (1998, May 22). Answering objections to school vouchers in D.C. *National Center for Policy Analysis Brief Analysis*, 266.

Coulson, A. (1999). *Market education*. New Brunswick, NJ: Transaction Publishers.

Cubberly, E. P. (1905). *School Funds and Their Apportionment, Contributions to Education No. 2*. New York: Columbia University Teachers College.

Cushman, K. (2000). Shrink big schools for better learning. *The Education Digest, 65*(6), 36–39.

Danzberger, J. P., Kirst, M. W., & Usdan., M. D. (1992). *Governing Public Schools*. Washington, DC: Institute for Educational Leadership.

DeAngelis, C. A. (2018). Is public schooling a public good? An analysis of schooling externalities (Cato Institute Policy Analysis No. 842).

DeAngelis, C. A. (2019a). Divergences between effects on test scores and effects on non-cognitive skills. *Educational Review*, DOI: 10.1080/00131911.2019.1646707

DeAngelis, C. A. (2019b). Regulatory Compliance Costs and Private School Participation in Voucher Programs. *Journal of School Choice*.

DeAngelis, C. A., & Burke, L. (2017). Does regulation induce homogenisation? An analysis of three voucher programmes in the United States. *Educational Research and Evaluation*, 23(7–8), 311–27.

DeAngelis, C. A., Burke, L. M., & Wolf, P. J. (2019). The effects of regulations on private school choice program participation: Experimental evidence from Florida. *Social Science Quarterly*, 100(6), 2316–36.

DeAngelis, C. A., & Dills, A. K. (2019). Is School Choice a "Trojan Horse?": The Effects of School Choice Laws on Homeschool Prevalence. *Peabody Journal of Education*.

DeAngelis, D., & McCluskey, N. (Eds.). (2020). *School choice myths: Setting the record straight on education freedom*. Washington, DC: Cato Institute.

DeRoche, T. (2020). *A fine line: How most American kids are kept out of the best public schools*. Los Angeles: Red Tail Press.

DiLorenzo, T. (2005). *How Capitalism Saved America*. Corbridge, UK: Forum Books.

Dougherty, J. C., & Becker, S. L. (1995). *An Analysis of Public-Private School Choice in Texas*. San Antonio: Texas Public Policy Foundation.

Doyle, D., & Munro, D. (1997). *Reforming the schools to save the city*. Baltimore, MD: The Calvert Institute.

Doyle, D. P. (1992, March). The challenge, the opportunity. *Phi Delta Kappan*, 518.

Drury, D. W. (2000, Summer). Vouchers and student achievement. *Policy Research* (Newsletter of the National School Boards Association).

Dworkin, A. G. (1987). *Teacher burnout in the public schools*. Albany: State University of New York Press.

Dworkin, A. G. (1997). Coping with reform: The intermix of teacher morale, teacher burnout, and teacher accountability. In B. J. Biddle, T. L. Good, & I. F. Goodson, *International Handbook of Teachers and Teaching* (Vol. 1). Dordrecht, Netherlands: Kluwer Academic Publishers.

Dworkin, A. G., & Townsend, M. L. (1994). Teacher burnout in the face of reform: Some caveats in breaking the mold. In Bruce A. Jones and Kathryn M. Borman (Eds.), *Investing in U.S. Schools: Directions for Educational Policy*. Norwood, NJ: Ablex Publishing Company.

EdChoice. (2019). *The ABCs of School Choice*. Indianapolis, IN: EdChoice. https://www.edchoice.org/wp-content/uploads/2019/01/The-ABCs-of-School-Choice-2019-Edition.pdf

Egalite, A. J. (2013). Measuring competitive effects from school voucher programs: A systematic review. *Journal of School Choice*, 7(4), 443–464.

Elam, S. M. (1987, December). Differences between Educators and the Public on Questions of Education Policy. *Phi Delta Kappan*, 294–96.

Epple, D., Calabrese, S., Romer, T., & Sieg, H. (2005). Local Public Good Provision: Voting, Peer Effects, and Mobility. NBER Paper 11720.

Epple, D., Romano, R. E., & Urquiola, M. (2017). School vouchers: A survey of the economics literature. *Journal of Economic Literature, 55*(2).

Ekelund, R. B., & Tollison, R. D. (1997). *Microeconomics: Private markets and public choice* (5th ed.). Reading, MA: Addison Wesley Longman.

Feng, C., & Harris, D. N. (2020). The effects of market-based school reforms on student outcomes: A national analysis of charter effects on district-level school systems [Mimeographed].

Finn, C., & Ravitch, D. (2004). *The Mad, Mad World of Textbook Adoption.* Washington, DC: Thomas Fordham Institute. https://fordhaminstitute.org/national/research/mad-mad-world-textbook-adoption

Finn, C. E., Jr. (1992, Summer). Up from mediocrity. *Policy Review*, 80–83.

Finn, C. E., Jr. (1995). The schools. In N. Kozodoy (Ed.), *What to Do About. . . .* New York: HarperCollins.

Finn, C. E., & Gau, R. L. (1998, Winter). New ways of education. *The Public Interest.*

Finn, C. E., Jr., Manno, B., & Vanourek, G. (2000). *Charter schools in action: Renewing public education.* Princeton, NJ: Princeton University Press.

Finn, C. E., & Rebarber, T. (1992). *Education reform in the '90s.* New York: Macmillan Press.

Fischer, M. (1994, Fall/Winter). A Betrayal of Teachers by Their Union. *Wisconsin Interest*, 35.

Fiske, E. B. (1991). *Smart schools, smart kids.* New York: Simon & Schuster.

Fiske, E. B., & Ladd, Helen F. (2000). *When schools compete: A cautionary tale.* Washington, DC: Brookings Institution Press.

Fondy, A. (1998). *School Vouchers in Pennsylvania: Bad Education Policy, Worse Public Policy.* Philadelphia: Pennsylvania Federation of Teachers.

Ford, M. R., & Andersson, F. O. (2019). Determinants of organizational failure in the Milwaukee school voucher program. *Policy Studies Journal, 47*(4), 1048–1068.

Forster, G., & D'Andrea, C. (2009). *Free to teach: What America's teachers say about teaching in public and private schools.* Indianapolis, IN: The Friedman Foundation for Educational Choice.

Forster, G., & Woodward, J. L. (2012). *The Greenfield school revolution and school choice.* Indianapolis, IN: The Friedman Foundation for Educational Choice.

Fox, M. (1997, February). Remarks of Ohio State Representative Michael Fox. *State Legislator Guide to Teacher Empowerment.* Washington, DC: American Legislative Exchange Council, 17.

Freiwald, L. (1996, October). Recognizing the horses. *Phi Delta Kappan 78*(2), 180.

Frey, D. E. (1992). Can privatizing education really improve achievement? An essay review. *Economics of Education Review, 11*(4), 427–438.

Friedman, M. (1955). The role of government in education. In R. A. Solo (Ed.), *Economics and the Public Interest.* New Brunswick, NJ: Rutgers University Press.

Friedman, M. (1962). *Capitalism and freedom.* Chicago: University of Chicago Press.

Friedman, M. (1997). Programs for the poor are poor programs. In A. Bonsteel & C. Bonilla, *A Choice for Our Children: Curing the Crisis in America's Schools*. San Francisco: ICS Press.

Fuller, H. (1997). A research update on school choice. *Marquette University Current Education Issues, 97*(3).

Fuller, H. L., & White, S. B. (1995). *Expanded School Choice in Milwaukee: A Profile of Eligible Students and Schools*. Thiensville, WI: Wisconsin Policy Research Institute.

Gallup, A. M. (1985). *Gallup Poll of Teachers' Attitudes toward the Public Schools*. Bloomington, IN: Phi Delta Kappa, 10.

Gatto, J. T. (1992a). *Dumbing us down*. Philadelphia, PA: New Society Publishers.

Gatto, J. T. (1992b). *Confederacy of dunces: The tyranny of compulsory schooling*. New York: John Taylor Gatto.

Gintis, H. (1995). The political economy of school choice. *Teachers College Record, 96*(3).

Glass, S. (1995, Winter). A pension deficit disorder: Teacher unions betray their members. *Policy Review*.

Glenn, C. L. (1998). Where public education went wrong. *Family Policy, 11*(5).

Goldhaber, D. D. (1996). Public and private high schools: Is school choice an answer to the productivity problem? *Economics of Education Review, 15*(2), 93–109.

Goldhaber, D. D. (1999, December). School choice: An examination of the empirical evidence on achievement, parental decisionmaking, and equity. *Educational Researcher*.

Greene, J. P. (2000). The effect of school choice: An evaluation of the charlotte children's scholarship fund program. *Civic Report, 12*, 1–15.

Greene, J. P., & Forster, G. (2002). Effects of Funding Incentives on Special Education Enrollment. *Civic Report, 32*, 1–13.

Greene, J. P., Peterson, P., & Du, J. (1997). *The effectiveness of school choice: The Milwaukee experiment*. Cambridge, MA: Program in Education Policy and Governance, Harvard University.

Greene, J. P., Peterson, P., & Howell, W. (1997). *Test scores from the Cleveland voucher experiment*. Cambridge, MA: Program in Education Policy and Governance, Harvard University.

Greene, J. P., Peterson, P. E., & Du, J. (1999). Effectiveness of school choice: The Milwaukee experiment. *Education and Urban Society, 31*(2), 190–213.

Greene, J. P., & Marsh, R. H. (2009). *The Effect of Milwaukee's Parental Choice Program on Student Achievement in Milwaukee Public Schools* (SCDP Comprehensive Longitudinal Evaluation of the Milwaukee Parental Choice Program, Report #11).

Hakim, S., Seidenstat, P., & Bowman, G. (Eds.). (1994). *Privatizing education and educational choice*. Westport, CT: Praeger.

Hall, J. C. (2006). Positive externalities and government involvement in education. *Journal of Private Enterprise, 21*(2).

Hanushek, E. A. (1996). School resources and student performance. In G. Burtless (Ed.), *Does Money Matter?* Washington, DC: Brookings Institution.

Hanushek, E. A. (1997, Winter). Why true reform of schools is so unlikely. *Jobs and Capital*, 23–27.

Hanushek, E. A. (Ed.). (2006). *Courting failure*. Stanford, CA: Hoover Institution Press.

Hanushek, E. A., & Woessmann, L. (2008). The role of cognitive skills in economic development. *Journal of Economic Literature, 46*(3), 607–668.

Harmer, D. (1994). *School choice*. Washington, DC: Cato Institute.

Hassel, B. (2003). "Friendly Competition." *Education Next* 3:1.

Hayek, F. (1945, September). The use of knowledge in society. *American Economic Review*.

Hayek, F. A. (1994). *The road to serfdom*. Chicago: The University of Chicago Press.

Hayes, K. J., & Taylor, L. L. (1996). Neighborhood Characteristics: What Signals Quality to Homebuyers? *Federal Reserve Bank of Dallas Economic Review* (4th Quarter).

Hegarty, S. (2003, October). *Disability heals but voucher remains*. Obtained online at http://www.sptimes.com/2003/10/04/news_pf/State/Disability_heals_but_.shtml]

Henig, J. R. (2008). *Spin cycle: How research is used in policy debates: The case of charter schools*. New York: Russell Sage Foundation.

Hess, F. M. (1998, Fall). Courting backlash: The risks of emphasizing input equity over school performance. *The Virginia Journal of Social Policy & the Law, 6*.

Hess, F. (1999). *Spinning wheels: The politics of urban school reform*. New York: Brookings Institution.

Hess, F. (2002). *Revolution at the margins: The impact of competition on urban school systems*. Washington, DC: Brookings Institution.

Hess, R. (2010). *The same thing over and over: How school reformers get stuck in yesterday's ideas*. Cambridge, MA: Harvard University Press.

Hill, P. (1995). *In* Responses to a Harvard study on school choice: Is it a study at all? The Pioneer Institute for Policy Research. *Dialogue*, 1–11.

Hirsch, J. (1943). *Price control in the war economy*. New York: Harper.

Hirschman, A. O. (1970). *Exit, voice, and loyalty*. Cambridge, MA: Harvard University Press.

Hitt, C., McShane, M. Q., & Wolf, P. J. (2018). Do impacts on test scores even matter? Lessons from long-run outcomes in school choice research. *American Enterprise Institute*. Retrieved from http://www.aei.org/publication/do-impacts-on-test-scores-evenmatterlessons-from-long-run-outcomes-in-school-choice-research

Hood, J. (1991, December). Educational Challenges: The Role of Choice. *Current*.

Hoxby, C. (1998, March). What do America's traditional forms of school choice teach us about school choice reforms? FRBNY. *Economic Policy Review*, 4.

Hoxby, C. (1996). The effects of private school vouchers on schools and students. In H. F. Ladd, *Holding schools accountable*. Washington, DC: Brookings Institution.

Hoxby, C. (2000). Does Competition among Public Schools Benefit Students and Taxpayers. *American Economic Review 90*:5, 1209–1238.

Hoxby, C. (2004). Productivity in education: The quintessential upstream industry. *Southern Economic Journal, 7*(2), 209–231.

Hoxby, C. (2006). *School Choice: The Three Essential Elements and Several Policy Options.* Auckland, NZ: NZAE Education Forum.

Hubbard, G., & Kane, T. (2013). *Balance: The economics of great powers from ancient Rome to modern America.* New York: Simon & Schuster.

Jabbar, H., Fong, C. J., Germain, E., Li, D., Sanchez, J., Sun, W. L., & Devall, M. (2019). The Competitive Effects of School Choice on Student Achievement: A Systematic Review. *Educational Policy.*

Jencks, C. (1966). Is the Public School Obsolete? *The Public Interest 2,* 18–27.

Jennings, W.. B. (1998, Spring). Lets ride the wave of change. *Enterprising Educators,* 6(2), 1.

Kearns, D. T., & Doyle, D. P. (1991). *Winning the brain race: A bold plan to make our schools competitive.* San Francisco: ICS Press.

Kearns, D. T., & Harvey, J. (2000). *A legacy of learning.* Washington, DC: Brookings Institution Press.

King, W. S. (1996). A simpler conclusion. *Phi Delta Kappan 78,* #2, 180.

Kirkpatrick, D. (1997). *School choice: The idea that will not die.* Mesa, AZ: Bluebird Publishing.

Kozol, J. (1992). *Savage inequalities: Children in America's schools.* New York: Harper Perennial.

Lamdin, D. J., & Mintrom, M. (1997). School choice in theory and practice: Taking stock and looking ahead. *Education Economics,* 5(3).

Lee, M., Mills, J. N., & Wolf, P. J. (2019). Heterogeneous impacts across schools in the first four years of the Louisiana Scholarship Program. EDRE Working Paper No. 2019-11.

Levin, H. (1991). The economics of educational choice. *Economics of Education Review,* 10.

Levin, H. M., & Driver, C. E. (1997). Costs of an education voucher system. *Education Economics,* 5(3).

Lewis, A. C. (1996). A Modest proposal for urban schools. *Phi Delta Kappan 78,* no. 1, 5.

Lieberman, M. (1993). *Public education: An autopsy.* Cambridge, MA: Harvard University Press.

Lieberman, M. (1994, Winter). The school choice fiasco. *The Public Interest.*

Lieberman, M. (1997). *The teacher unions.* New York: The Free Press.

Lieberman, M. (2007). *The Educational Morass: Overcoming the Stalemate in American Education.* Lanham, MD: Rowman & Littlefield Education.

Lieberman, M., & Haar, C. K. (2003). *Public education as a business: Real costs and accountability.* Lanham, MD: Scarecrow Press.

Loomis, B. (1998, October). The Politics of vouchers. In *Vouchers and Related Delivery Mechanisms: Consumer Choice in the Provision of Public Services.* Conference Papers (p. 80). Washington: Brookings Institution.

Lott, J. R., Jr. (1987, Fall). Why is education publicly provided? A critical survey. *Cato Journal,* 475–501.

Lowe, R., & Miner, B. (Ed.). (1996). *Selling out our schools.* Milwaukee, WI: Rethinking Schools.

Lund, J. (1999). How much bureaucracy is carried by classroom teachers? *Policy Highlighter,* 9(5).

Mader, N. (2010). School Choice, Competition, and Academic Quality: Essays on the Milwaukee Parental Choice Program. https://eric.ed.gov/?id=ED520755

Manna, P., & McGuinn, P. (2013). *Education governance for the twenty-first century: Overcoming the structural barriers to school reform.* Washington, DC: Brookings Institution Press.

McCarty, T. A., & Brazer, H. E. (1990). On equalizing school expenditures. *Economics of Education Review,* 9(3), 251–264.

McCluskey, N. (2007). Why we fight: How public schools cause social conflict. *Cato Institute Policy Analysis #587.* https://www.cato.org/policy-analysis/why-we-fight-how-public-schools-cause-social-conflict

McGhan, B. (1998). Choice and compulsion. *Phi Delta Kappan 79,* no. 8, 610–615.

McGroarty, D. (1994, Fall). School choice slandered. *The Public Interest.*

McGroarty, D. (1996). *Break these chains.* Rocklin, CA: ICS Press, Prima Publishing.

McGroarty, D. (1998, April). Voucher wars: Strategy and tactics as school choice advocates battle the labor leviathan. Milton and Rose Friedman Institution. *Issues in School Choice,* No. 2.

Merrifield, J. (1999). Monopsony power in the market for teachers. *Journal of Labor Research,* 20(3).

Merrifield, J. (2001). *The school choice wars.* Lanham, MD: Scarecrow Press.

Merrifield, J. (2005, Spring/Summer). Specialization in a competitive education industry: Areas and impacts. *Cato Journal 25, #2.*

Merrifield, J. (2008a). The twelve policy approaches to increased school choice. *Journal of School Choice,* 2(1), 4–19.

Merrifield, J. (2008b). The school choice evidence and its significance. *Journal of School Choice,* 2(3), 223–259.

Merrifield, J. (2019). *School system reform: How and why is a price-less tale.* New York: Covenant Press.

Merrifield, J. (2020). Myth: Any school choice is welcome school choice. In C. DeAngelis & N. McCluskey (Eds.), *School choice myths: Setting the record straight on education freedom.* Washington, DC: Cato Institute.

Merrifield, J., & Ginn, V. (2017). The effects of education savings accounts (ESAs) on teacher pay in Texas. *Texas Public Policy Foundation Center for Education Freedom.* https://www.texaspolicy.com/wp-content/uploads/2018/08/2017-03-PP07-ESAsTeacherPay-CEdF-GinnMerrifield.pdf

Merrifield, J., & Gray, N. (2009). An evaluation of the CEO Horizon, 1998-2008, Edgewood tuition voucher program. http://faculty.business.utsa.edu/jmerrifi/evp.pdf

Merrifield, J., & Ortiz, J. (2014). Reinventing the Alabama K–12 school system to engage more children in productive learning. In D. Sutter (Ed.), *Freeing the invisible hand: A vision for economic freedom and prosperity in Alabama.* Troy University: Johnson Center. https://www.troy.edu/academics/colleges-schools/business/johnson-center/policy-papers/improving-lives-in-alabama.html

Miller, J. (1992, November 30). Opting out. *The New Republic,* 12–13.

Mills, J. N., & Wolf, P. J. (2017). Vouchers in the bayou: The effects of the Louisiana Scholarship Program on student achievement after 2 years. *Educational Evaluation and Policy Analysis, 39*(3), 464–484.

Moe, T. (1995). *In* Responses to a Harvard study on school choice: Is it a study at all? Pioneer Institute for Public Policy Research. *Dialogue.*

Molnar, A. (1996). School reform: Will markets or democracy prevail? In R. Lowe & B. Miner (Eds.), *Selling out our schools* (pp. 16–17). Milwaukee, WI: Rethinking Schools.

Morrison, L. (1998). *The tax credits program for school choice* (Policy Report No. 213). Mackinaw, MI: National Center for Policy Analysis.

Morrison, S. A., & Winston, C. (1987). Empirical implications and tests of the contestability hypothesis. *Journal of Law and Economics*, 30.

Munk, L. R. G. (1998). *Collective bargaining: Bringing education to the table.* Midland, MI: Mackinac Center for Public Policy.

Murdock, D. (1998, April). Teachers warm to school choice. *Headway*, 20.

Murphy, J. (1996). *The privatization of schooling.* Thousand Oaks, CA: Corwin Press.

Nathan, J. (Ed.). (1989). *Public schools by choice.* St. Paul, MN: The Institute for Learning and Teaching.

National Commission on Excellence in Education. (1983). *A nation at risk: The imperative for educational reform.* Washington, DC: U.S. Department of Education.

Neal, D. (2018). *Information, incentives, and education policy.* Cambridge, MA: Harvard University Press.

Omdahl, R., & Ducote, J. (1999). Education accountability and the role of school choice. *Public Affairs Research Council of Louisiana, Inc.*, Analysis No. 299.

Osborne, D. (2017). *Reinventing America's schools: Creating a 21st century education system.* New York: Bloomsbury.

Peters, T. (1990, Fall). In search of educational excellence. *Policy Review.*

Peterson, P. E., Greene, J. P., & Noyes, C. (1996, Fall). School choice in Milwaukee. *The Public Interest.*

Pierce, R. K. (1993). *What are we trying to teach them anyway?* San Francisco: Institute for Contemporary Studies.

Pogrow, S. (1996). Reforming the wannabe reformers. *Phi Delta Kappan 77*, #10, 656–667.

Pondiscio, R. (2019). *How the other half learns.* New York: Penguin Random House.

Powell, A. G., Farrar, E., & Cohen, D. K. (1985). *The shopping mall high school: Winners and losers in the educational marketplace.* Boston: Houghton Mifflin.

Quade, Q. (1996). *Financing education.* New Brunswick, NJ: Transaction Publishers.

Quade, Q. L. (1997). *The National Education Association vs America's parents* [Mimeographed]. Marquette University, Wisconsin.

Ravitch, D. (1983). *The troubled crusade.* New York: Basic Books.

Ravitch, D. (1994, Fall). Somebody's children. *Brookings Review.*

Ravitch, D. (2003). *The language police.* New York: Knopf.

Ravitch, D. (2010). *The death and life of the great American school system.* New York: Basic Books.

Raywid, M. A. (1992). Choice orientations, discussions, and prospects. *Educational Policy*, 6(2).
Rector, R. (1995). The importance of vouchers for social health. In Independence Institute, *Colorado in the Balance*. Denver, CO: Independence Institute.
Rees, N. S. (2000). *School choice 2000 annual report*. Washington, DC: Heritage Foundation.
Reisman, G. (1998). *Capitalism*. Ottawa, IL: Jameson Books.
Richman, S. (1994). *Separating school and state*. Fairfax, VA: The Future of Freedom Foundation.
Rickover, H. G. (1959). *Education and freedom*. New York: E. P. Dutton & Co.
Roberts, D. J. (1990, Fall). *Policy Review*, 58.
Rockoff, H. (1984). *Drastic measures: A history of wage and price controls in the U.S.* New York: Cambridge University Press.
Rockwell, L. (1993, August 28). Costly initiative will hurt private schools. *Human Events*, 10.
Rockwell, L. (1998, September). School vouchers: An enemy of religion. *The Wanderer*.
Rose, T. (2016). *The end of average*. New York: HarperCollins.
Rothbard, M. (1994, January). *Free market*.
Rouse, C. E. (1998). *Private school vouchers and student achievement: An evaluation of the Milwaukee Parental Choice Program*. National Bureau of Economic Research.
Sahlgren, G. H. (2013). *Incentivizing excellence: School choice and educational quality*. London: The Center for Market Reform of Education.
Sarason, S. B. (1990). *The predictable failure of educational reform*. San Francisco: Jossey-Bass Publishers.
Savas, E. S. (1982). *Privatizing the Public Sector*. Chatham, NJ: Chatham House.
Savas, E. S. (1987). *Privatization: The key to better government*. Chatham, NJ: Chatham House.
Sawhill, I. V., & Smith, S. L. (1998, October 2–3). Vouchers for elementary and secondary education. In *Vouchers and related delivery mechanisms: Consumer choice in the provision of public services* (Conference proceedings). Washington, DC: Brookings Institution.
Schneider, M., Teske, P., Marschall, M., & Roch, C. (1997, Fall). School choice builds community. *The Public Interest*, 86–90.
Schuettinger, R. L., & Butler, E. F. (1979). *Forty centuries of [disastrous] price controls*. Washington, DC: Heritage Foundation.
Schundler, B. (1998, Fall). Public money for the public. *Michigan Education Report*, 12.
Segal, L. G. (2004). *Battling corruption in America's public schools*. Cambridge, MA: Harvard University Press.
Shakeel, M. D., & Wolf, P. J. (2018). Does private Islamic schooling promote terrorism? An analysis of the educational background of successful American homegrown terrorists. *Hungarian Educational Research Journal*, 8(1).
Shlaes, A. (2019). *Great society*. NY: Harper.

Shleifer, A. (1998). State versus private ownership. *Journal of Economic Perspectives, 12*(4), 133–150.

Shokraii, N. (1996, November/December). Free at last: Black America signs up for school choice. *Policy Review*.

Singal, D. J. (1991, November). The Other Crisis in American Education. *The Atlantic Monthly*.

Smarick, A. (2012). *The urban school system of the future*. Lanham, MD: Rowman & Littlefield.

Smith, K. B., & Meier, K. J. (1995). *The case against school choice*. New York: M. E. Sharpe.

Smoley, Eugene R., Jr. (1999). *Effective school boards*. San Francisco: Jossey-Bass Publishers.

Solmon, L. C., Block, M. K., & Gifford, M. (2000). *A market-based education system in the making*. Phoenix, AZ: Goldwater Institute.

Sowell, T. (2004). *Basic economics: A citizen's guide to the economy*. New York: Basic Books.

Sowell, T. (2018). *Discrimination and disparities*. New York: Basic Books.

Sowell, T. (2020). *Charter schools and their enemies*. NY: Basic Books.

Stuit, D., & Doan, S. (2013). *School choice regulations: Red tape or red herring*. Washington, D.C.: Thomas B. Fordham Institute.

Styring, W, (1998, Spring). Teachers and school choice, *American Outlook*, 49–51.

Sude, Y., DeAngelis, C. A., & Wolf, P. J. (2018). Supplying choice: An analysis of school participation decisions in voucher programs in Washington, DC, Indiana, and Louisiana. *Journal of School Choice, 12*(1), 8–33.

Sykes, C. J. (1995). *Dumbing down our kids*. New York: St. Martin's Press.

Testa, W. A., & Sen, S. (1999). School choice and competition (A conference summary). *Chicago Fed Letter* #143a.

Thomke, S. H. (2020). *Experimentation works: The surprising power of business experiments*. Boston, MA: Harvard Business Review Press.

Tiebout, C. (1956). A pure theory of local expenditures. *Journal of Political Economy*, 64.

Tooley, J. (2003). *Government failure: E. G. West on education*. London: Institute of Economic Affairs.

Tooley, J., Bao, Y., Dixon, P., & Merrifield, J. (2011). School choice and academic performance: Some evidence from developing countries. *Journal of School Choice, 5*(1), 1–39.

Turtel, J. (2005). *Public schools, public menace*. Liberty Books.

Twentieth Century Fund. (1992). *Facing the challenge: The report of the Twentieth Century Fund Task Force on School Governance*. New York: The Twentieth Century Fund Press.

Vanourek, G. (1996, December). The choice crusade. *Network News and Views*.

Viteritti, J. (1999). *Choosing equality*. Washington, DC: Brookings Institution.

Wagenheim, W. (1998, Fall). Why public money shouldn't go to private schools. *Michigan Education Report*, 12.

Wagner, T. (1996). School choice: To what end? *Phi Delta Kappan, 78*(1), 71.

Walberg, H. J., & Bast, J. L. (2003). *Education and capitalism: How overcoming our fear of markets and economics can improve America's schools.* Stanford, CA: Hoover Institution Press.

Weinschrott, D. J., & Kilgore, S. B. (1998). *Educational choice charitable trust: An experiment in school* (Hudson Institute Briefing Paper No. 189).

Wells, A. S. (1993). *Time to choose.* New York: Hill & Wang.

Wenman, C. (1996, December). Choice cuts: The real impact of Milwaukee's vouchers. *Reason.*

West, E. G. (1992). Autonomy in school provision: Meanings and implications. *Economics of Education Review, 11*(4).

West, E. G. (1994). *Education and the state* (3rd ed.). Indianapolis: Liberty Fund.

West, E. G. (1996, February). *Education Vouchers in Practice and Principle: A World Survey.* Washington: Human Capital Development Working Paper #64.

Wirt, F., & Kirst, M. (1997). *The political dynamics of American education.* Berkeley, CA: McCutchan.

Witte, J. F. (2000). The *market approach to education: An analysis of America's first voucher program.* Princeton: Princeton University Press.

Witte, J. F., Bailey, A. B., & Thorn, C. A. (1993). *Third-year report, Milwaukee Parental Choice Program.* Madison, WI: Department of Political Science and The Robert La Follette Institute of Public Affairs, University of Wisconsin.

Witte, J. F., Carnoy, M., Adamson, F., Chudgar, A., & Luschei, T. (2007). *Vouchers and public school performance: A case study of the Milwaukee Parental Choice Program.* Washington, DC: Economic Policy Institute.

Witte, J. F., & Rigdon, M. E. (1993, Summer). Education choice reforms: Will they change American schools? *Publius: The Journal of Federalism.*

Woessman, L. (2016). The importance of school systems: Evidence from international differences in student achievement. *Journal of Economic Perspectives, 30*(3), 3–31.

Wolf, P. J., Witte, J. F., & Kisida, B. (2019). Do voucher students attain higher levels of education? Extended evidence from the Milwaukee Parental Choice Program (EdWorkingPaper, Brown University).

Wolfram, G., & Coulson, A. J. (2009). Commentary on Andrew Coulson's "Comparing public, private, and market schools: The international evidence." *Journal of School Choice, 3*(2), 197–199.

Wyckoff, P. (1991). A new case for vouchers. *Journal of Policy Analysis and Management, 10*(1), 112–116.

Yergin, D., & Stanislaw, J. (1998). *The commanding heights.* New York: Simon & Schuster.

Yinger, J., & Nguyen-Hoang, P. (2011). The capitalization of school quality into house values: A review. *Journal of Housing Economics, 20*(1), 30–48.

Zafirau, S. J., & Fleming, M. (1982). A Study of *discrepant reading achievement of minority and White students in a desegregating school district: Phase IV.* Cleveland, OH: Cleveland Public Schools, Department of Research and Analysis.

Index

AAA. *See* Alabama Accountability Act
AAE. *See* The Association of American Educators
Abbott School District. *See* New Jersey
accountability, xxvi–xxvii, 5–6, 39–42, 47, 68, 71, 79–80, 87, 93, 156, 160–61, 181–82
Adamson, Frank. *See* Witte, John
AFT. *See* American Federation of Teachers
Aguirre, Robert, 112
Akst, Daniel, 145
Alabama Accountability Act (AAA), 77
Alger, Vicki, 118
Allen, Jeanne, 41, 163, 170
American Federation of Teachers (AFT), 107, 182
American Legislative Exchange Council, 185
Andersson, Fredrik, 25, 29, 169
Aoki, Masato, 171–72
arena shopping, 121
Arizona, 28, 44, 48, 108, 112, 166, 193
Armor, David, 30
Arons, Stephen, xxii, 141–42, 182
Ascher, Carol, 67–71
Association of American Educators (AAE), 179
Australia, 80

Ayers, Ronald, 5

Bailey, Andrea, 169
Ball, Carl, 31, 74n15, 94, 184
Ballou, Dale, 4, 101n44, 184–85
Bao, Yong. *See* Tooley, James
Barry, John, 199
Bartoletti, JoAnn, 119
Bast, Joseph, xxvi, 3, 6, 80, 178
Baumol, William, 5
Bedrick, Jason, 22
Bell, Terrel, xiii
Benbow, Camilla, 133
Bennett, William, 172
Berends, Mark, 52n11
Berliner, David, 63, 72, 108–9
Berner, Ashley, 180
Biddle, Bruce, 63, 108–9
Blaine amendments, 120
Block, Michael, 33
Blumenfeld, Samuel, xx
Bonilla, Carlos, 36n56
Bonsteel, Alan, 33
Booker, Corey, 111
Borenstein, Severin, 5
Bowles, Erskine, xxiii
Bowman, Gary. *See* Hakim, Simon
Bracey, Gerald, 109
Brazer, Harvey, 138n8, 139n32

Brickman, Michael, 125
Broder, David, xxviiin2
Brown, Byron, 91–92, 96, 101n42
Brown, Rexford, 131–32, 209n22
Brown v. Board of Education, 144, 146
Buckley, Jack, 5–6
Burke, Lindsey, 22–25
Bush, Jeb, 106
Butler, Eamonn, 13, 42–43

Cambridge, 32, 88, 148, 166
Carl, Jim, 148
Carnegie Foundation for Advanced Teaching, 25
Carnoy, Martin, 25. *See* Witte, John
Carter, Samuel, 9, 183–84
caste system, 130
Cavazos, Lauro, 95
CEI. *See* competitive education industry
Center for Education Reform, 41, 46, 163, 166
Center for Research and Education Outcomes (CREDO), 49
charity voucher. *See* Friedman, Milton
chartered public schools (CPS), xix–xxvii, 33, 39–51, 122, 154, 163–65, 167, 184, 200; comparison of TPS with, 44, 48–49, 149; constraints of, 44, 49, 51, 94, 157; market based tuition within, 43–47, 50–51; shortages within, xxvii, 40–48; specialization, 40; uncertainty within, 40, 45
charter law, xix, 39–51, 106, 117, 122, 208; consequences of, 44; shortage induced qualities of, 42
Charter Schools and Their Enemies. *See* Sowell, Thomas
Chase, Bob. *See* National Education Association
Chase, Robert, 103, 107
Chubb, John, 32, 165, 172
Chudgar, Amita. *See* Witte, John
Cleveland, 22, 27, 32–33, 107, 163, 166, 169, 172–73, 201

Clowes, George, 166–67, 172
Clune, William, 136
Cobb, Clifford, 22
Cohen, David. *See* Powell, Arthur
Cohn, Elchanan, 136–37
Coleman, James, 147
Collinge, Robert, 5
Colorado, 27, 109, 125, 179
Competition in Education: Case Study of Interdistrict Choice. *See* Armor, David
competitive education industry (CEI), 1
comprehensive uniformity, xix, 9, 30, 60, 92, 96–97, 132, 143, 159, 201, 202, 205
Cookson, Peter, 63, 79
Coons, John, xxi, 134, 139n27
Cordell, Dorman, 174n12
correlation, 57–58, 142–43, 149
cost issues, xxviii, 81–82, 93–95
Coulson, Andrew, xx, 20, 47, 49, 70, 94, 109–10, 112–13, 142
COVID-19, xiii–xviii, 3, 89, 106, 123–24
Cowen, Joshua, 20
CPS. *See* chartered public schools
CREDO. *See* Center for Research and Education Outcomes
Cushman, Kathleen, 15n3

D'Andrea, Christina, 185
Davis, Bob, 169
Davis, Carl, 121
Davis, Gray. *See* Broder, David
DeAngelis, Corey, xxvi, 22–25, 119
Deroche, Tim, 144–45, 159
Discrimination and Disparities. *See* Sowell, Thomas
diversity, xiv–xv, xvii, xxiv, xxviii, 8–9, 20, 32, 40, 48–49, 123, 137, 141–49, 160, 164
Dixon, Pauline. *See* Tooley, James
Doyle, Denis, 64, 72n1, 178–79, 183–84, 186
Driver, Cyrus, 88–89, 173

Drury, Darrel, 168–69
Du, Jiangtao. *See* Greene, Jay
Duncan, Arne, xiii
Dworkin, Anthony, 181–86

ECCI. *See* Education Choice and Competition Index
economists, 5, 29–30, 91, 171–72, 194; attention to charter law, 43–45
Edgewood School District, 10, 28–30, 105, 108
The Educational Morass, xiv
Education Choice and Competition Index (ECCI), 30
Education Savings Account (ESA), xxii, xxviii, 13, 22, 28–29, 60–64, 108, 121, 124, 154, 156–57, 171, 178, 193, 199, 204, 208
education voucher. *See* Friedman, Milton
educator initiative, xvii
Egalite, Anna, 15, 25
Eisenstadter, Ingrid, 133
Ekelund, Robert, 5
Elias, Ken, xvii
entrepreneurial initiative, xvii–xxi, 8–10, 20, 124–25, 129, 134, 153, 193
Epple, Dennis, 44, 70
equity, xix–xxviii, 42, 45, 50, 61–63, 113, 123–26, 129–37, 153–54, 170
ESA. *See* Education Savings Account
Espinoza v. Montana Department of Revenue, 120–21
Every Student Succeeds Act (ESSA), xvii, 117
Experimentation Works. *See* Thomke, Stefan
extremism, 71, 141

Failure: The Federal Misedukation [sic] of America's Children, 118. *See* Alger, Vicki
Fair, Williard. *See* Bennett, William
Farrar, Eleanor. *See* Powell, Arthur
Feng, Chen, 43, 51

Feiner, Susan, 171–72
Finn, Chester, xxv, 33, 46, 58, 146, 165
Fiske, Edward, 30–33, 88, 148
Flake, Floyd. *See* Bennett, William
Florida, 28–29, 34n15, 58, 81, 106–8, 163
Ford, Michael, 25, 29, 169
Forster, Greg, xxi, 25, 185
Forstmann, Ted, 103
Frey, Donald, 86–87
Friedman, Milton, ix–xxi, 20, 29–31, 104–5, 155–56, 165, 169, 193–94
Friedman, Rose, 31
Frutcher, Norm. *See* Ascher, Carol
Fuller, Howard, 19, 27, 106, 183

Garcia, Angie, 143, 145
Gatto, John, 103, 179, 183
Gau, Rebecca. *See* Finn, Chester
Geiger, Keith. *See* National Education Association
Gifford, Mary, 33
gifted, 131–33, 208n3
Gintis, Herbert, 33, 179
Glass, Stephen, 185–86
Glenn, Charles, 104–5
Goldhaber, Dan, 86–87, 106, 141, 172
Goldman, Steven, 94–95, 184
government policy. *See* monopoly
Greene, Jay, 22, 24–26, 169–70, 172
growth impediments, 40

Haar, Charlene, 85
Hakim, Simon, 99n12, 99n15
Hall, Joshua, xxvi, 67
Hanushek, Eric, xxvi, 16n19, 86
Harmer, David, 80, 178
Harris, Douglas, 43, 51
Harvey, James, 199–200
Hassel, Bryan, 45
Hayek, Friedrich, 6, 43–44, 144–45
Hedeman Jr., Rea, 199–200
Henig, Jeffrey, 42–43
Hess, Frederick, xxiv, 23, 29–31, 57, 132–33, 196

Hill, Paul, 129
Hirsch, Julius, 42
Hirschman, Albert, 59
Howell, William. *See* Greene, Jay
Hoxby, Caroline, 3–4, 22–23, 29–30, 47–48, 86, 88–89
Hubbard, Glenn, xiv, 42–43

Idaho, xxviii
incrementalism, xxii, 164–65, 201
Indiana, 28–29, 48
Indianapolis, 184–85
indoctrination, 91, 143–46
Information, Incentives, Education Policy. *See* Neal, Derek
Institute for Objective Policy Assessment (IOPA), xiv
Izumi, Lance, xxv, 58, 196

Jefferson, Thomas, xiv, 37n59, 42, 132, 191n33
Jencks, Christopher, 145

Kane, Tim, xiv, 42–43
Kansas City, xiii
Kearns, David, 188, 199
Kemp, Jack, xxiii
Kirkpatrick, David, xxviii, 80–81, 178, 200
Kirst, Michael, xxiii, 96
Kisida, Brian. *See* Wolf, Patrick
Kozol, Jonathan, xiii, 130–31

Ladd, Helen, 30–31, 33
Lamdin, Douglas, 29–30
League of United Latin America Citizens (LULAC), 143–45
Levin, Henry, 71, 88–89, 173
Levine, Arthur, 110
Lieberman, Joe, 103, 106, 193
Lieberman, Myron, xiv–xxvi, 14–15, 85, 87, 91, 95, 107, 173–74, 185, 203
lottery, 41–42, 44, 135, 207
Lott Jr., John, 91–92
Louisiana, 20, 22, 159

Lowe, Robert, 63–64, 73, 108
LULAC. *See* League of United Latin American Citizens
Lund, Jami, 99n11
Luscher, Thomas. *See* Witte, John

Manna, Paul, xxv
Manno, Bruce. *See* Finn, Chester
The Market Approach to Education, 169
Market Education. *See* Coulson, Andrew
Marschall, Melissa. *See* Schneider, Mark
Marshall, Will. *See* Bennett, William
McCarty, Thomas, 138n8, 139n32
McCluskey, Neal, xxii, 119–20, 141–42, 182
McGroarty, Daniel, 23, 61, 65, 110–11, 167–68, 170
McGuinn, Patrick, xxv
Meier, Kenneth, 86–87, 143–44
Merrifield, John, xix, xxvi, 1, 4, 9, 15, 20–21, 42, 87, 162–63, 174, 178, 186
Merrow, John, 177, 181
Miller, John, xxii, 59
Milwaukee Public Schools, xxii, 22, 24–33, 43, 81, 106, 163, 166–73, 181–83, 201–2
Milwaukee voucher program. *See* Milwaukee Public Schools
Miner, Barbara, 63, 73, 108
Mintrom, Michael, 29–30
Mobilization for Equity, 62
Moe, Terry, 32, 123, 165, 172
Molnar, Alex, 109–10
monopoly, xxiii–xxviii, 1–4, 8, 10, 14, 29, 46, 67, 92, 105, 108, 111–12, 118, 129, 141, 168–69, 173, 179, 206; finance, xxv, 1, 3, 104, 107, 110, 179; public funding, 121
Morrison, Linda, 74n21
Morrison, Steven, 5
MPS. *See* Milwaukee Public Schools

NAEP. *See* National Assessment of Education Progress
Nathan, Joe, 31–32

National Assessment of Education
    Progress (NAEP), 50, 58, 87, 163
National Center for Education
    Information, 180
National Commission on Excellence in
    Education, xxvii
National Education Association (NEA),
    107, 109, 179–80
National Governors Association, 146
Nation at Risk, xiii, xvii–xx, xxv–xxvi,
    68, 70, 108, 146, 160, 165, 171, 182
NCLB. See No Child is Left Behind
NEA. See National Education
    Association
Neal, Derek, 44–45
New Jersey, xiii, 47–48, 86
New York, 20, 27, 70, 86, 103, 179, 183
Nguyen-Hoang, Phuong, 129, 159
No Child is Left Behind
    (NCLB), xvii, 117
nondiscrimination, 7–10, 62, 64, 82,
    105–6, 136, 153–58
North Dakota, xxviii
Novel Way to Assess School
    Competition. See Hoxby, Caroline
Noyes, Chad. See Peterson, Paul

Obama, Barack, xiii, 25, 111, 117
OECD, 3–4, 94
open enrollment, 32, 143; impediments
    of, 40; isomorphism, 46;
    requirements of, 41, 46
Ortiz, Jesse, 87–88, 163
Osborne, David, 47–49

Panzar, John, 5–6
Peters, Tom, 31
Peterson, Paul, 24, 26–27, 169–70
Pierce, Ronald, 100n32
Podgursky, Michael, 4, 184–85
Pondiscio, Robert, 49, 51
Powell, Arthur, 15n3
prejudice, 121, 142–43, 148–49
Price, Hugh, 103

price control, xix, 2, 9, 13–14, 21–22,
    32, 40–45, 60, 62, 79, 81, 122, 135,
    153, 163, 167, 194
privatization, 67–69, 120
Pudelski, Sasha, 119
Puerto Rico, 88

Quade, Quentin, 51, 60, 78–79, 104,
    107, 112–13

Rasell, Edith. See Cookson, Peter
Raspberry, William, 112
Ravitch, Diane, 4, 20, 33, 43, 46,
    95–96, 111, 146
Raymond, Margaret. See Center for
    Research and Education Outcomes
Raywid, Mary, 141, 146, 148
Rebarber, Theodore, 58
Rees, Nina, 27, 189
reform, xiv, xxvii–xxviii, xxi–xxii, xxvi,
    19–20, 23, 25–27, 33, 29, 41–42, 47,
    51, 59, 61–63, 67, 69, 72, 81–82, 85,
    93, 95, 106–10, 113, 117, 121, 123–
    25, 159, 163–74, 179, 183, 193–94,
    196–97, 199–202, 208
Reisman, George, 14, 42, 53n18
Republican-in-name-only, 123
restriction-laden choice expansion,
    xxviii, 15, 19–21, 24, 27–28, 39,
    64–66, 70, 72, 77, 81, 85, 88–89,
    117, 137, 147, 155, 166–73, 180,
    195, 198–99, 201
Richman, Sheldon, 47
Richter, Bob, 132
Rickover, Hyman, 131
Rigdon, Mark, 32
RINO. See Republican-in-name-only
The Road to Serfdom. See
    Hayek, Friedrich
Roberts, Donald, 94
Roberts, John. See Espinoza v. Montana
    Department of Revenue
Robin Hood effect, 131
Rockoff, Hugh, 42
Rockwell, Llewellyn, 77–78

Romano, Richard, 53n28
Rose, Todd, 129
Rosenberg, Bella, 86–87
Rothbard, Murray, 42
Rothstein, Richard. *See* Cookson, Peter
Roukema, Marge, 104
Rouse, Cecilia, 22, 24

Sahlgren, Gabriel, 61, 194
Sarason, Seymour, 95, 182
savage inequalities. *See* Kozol, Jonathan
Savas, Emanuel, 67, 87
Sawhill, Isabel, 36n46
Scafidi, Ben, 185
Schneider, Mark, 5, 71
Schoenig, John, 52n11
school choice demonstration, xxi
The School Choice Fiasco. *See* Lieberman, Myron
The School Choice Wars, xiii–xviii, 1, 15, 43–44, 57, 79, 108, 164–65, 168, 178, 201
the School House Blues, 181
School System Reform: How and Why Is a Price-less Tale, 173–74
Schuettinger, Robert, 13, 43–44
Seidenstat, Paul. *See* Hakim, Simon
Selling Out Our Schools. *See* Lowe, Robert; Miner, Barbara
Shakeel, Danish, 14–15
Shanker, Albert, 86–87, 107, 183
Shapiro, Walter, 104–5
Sherman Act, 3
Shleifer, Andrei, 114n34
Shokraii, Nina, 35n32, 198
Smarick, Andy, 54n49
Smith, Kevin, 86–87, 133–34, 143–44
Smith, Shannon, 36n46
Smoley, Eugene, Jr., 93–94, 149
Solmon, Lewis, 33
Sowell, Thomas, 6, 42–43, 117, 155
special education, 45, 87–88, 97, 119, 130–34, 158, 160, 171, 186, 197–98, 204, 206
Spin Cycle. *See* Henig, Jeffrey

Stanislaw, Joseph, 114n34
Stanley, Julian, 133, 138n13
Sude, Yujie, 22, 25, 77
Sugarman, Stephen, xxi, 134, 139n27
Sykes, Charles, 145–46

TEA. *See* Texas Education Agency
teacher union, xxviii, 93–95, 107, 117, 123–24, 173, 177–82, 196–98
Tennessee, 72, 159, 194
Teske, Paul. *See* Schneider, Mark
test scores, xxiv–xxv, 21, 23–24, 26, 44, 48, 50, 59, 67, 69, 71, 73n4, 85, 86, 160–61, 173, 181, 200, 205
Texas, xxvii, 3, 10, 28–29, 47, 58, 94–95, 112–13, 133, 143, 145, 159, 178, 183–84, 193–94
Texas Education Agency (TEA), 94–95
Texas Justice Foundation, 112
textbook, 91, 95, 182, 205
Thomke, Stefan, 21
Thorn, Christopher, 169
Tiebout, Charles, 8, 22–23
Tollison, Robert, 5
Tooley, James, xxvii
Townsend, Merric, 183–86
traditional public schools (TPS), xviii–xxv, 1–13, 22–31, 39–51, 58–72, 77–82, 85–92, 95–98, 103–13, 120–26, 129–34, 141–49, 153–60, 163–73, 178–84, 187–89, 193–96, 199–203; choice expansion, 62–63; contracting out within, 67–69; criticisms of, 66; deep education crisis of, 59; opposition to; 20, 77, 145, 158–59; specialization, 143, 148
Turtel, Joel, 138n14
Twentieth Century Fund. *See* Smoley, Eugene, Jr.

United States, xx–xxi, xxv, xxviii, 1,3, 48, 80, 94, 118, 120, 154
Urquiola, Miguel. *See* Epple, Dennis
U.S. Constitution, xxii, 121, 145

U.S. Department of Education, 91, 118, 145
Utah, xxviii, 32

Vanourek, Gregg, 57–58
Virginia's Arlington Public Schools, 123
Viteritti, Joseph, xxi, 31–33, 106–7, 109, 111, 172
voucher, xviii, xxi–xxviii, 8–14, 20–33; 58–60, 62–64, 77–80, 88, 104–8, 110–13, 119–21, 124–25, 131, 147, 154–56, 163, 165–74, 178–80, 187, 195, 198–204, 208; add-on, 13, 60–62, 67, 135–36, 186–88, 206; top-off, 47, 60–61, 64, 149, 154

Waddington, Joseph, 52n11
Wagner, Tony, 32, 109–10
Walberg, Herbert, xxvi, 3, 6, 32, 114n24
Warren, Elizabeth, 111
Washington D.C., xxi, 8, 43, 86, 121
weighted student formula (WSF), 8, 13, 46–47, 62, 89, 153–56

Weinschrott, David, 35n17
Wells, Amy, 148
West, Edwin, xx, 19–20
West Virginia, xxii, 28–29, 112, 166–67, 193
white flight, 142
Will, Madeline, 177, 181
Willig, Robert, 5
Winston, Clifford, 5
Wirt, Frederick, xxiii, 96
Witte, John, 21, 24–25, 32, 169, 170
Woessman, Ludger, xxvi, 164–65
Wolf, Patrick, 14–15, 20–22
Wolfram, Gary, 94
WSF. *See* weighted student formula
Wyckoff, Paul, 145
Wyoming, xxviii

Yergin, Daniel, 114n34
Yinger, John, 129, 159
Youngkin, Glenn, xviii

Zelman v. Simmons–Harris, xxix, 120

PRAISE FOR *UNPRODUCTIVE SCHOOL CHOICE DEBATES*

"*Unproductive School Choice Debates* is an important and well-timed analysis of how to create an educational system in the United States that leads to optimal education for all children. It's discussion of the confusion regarding educational choice terminology and interpretation of research findings provide a road map for those who engage in the debate over how to move from a largely failed educational system to one that is truly transformational in improving our children's education."

—**Gary Wolfram**, William Simon Professor of Economics and Public Policy, Hillsdale College

"Merrifield and Gray provide a real service to the school policy debates. They extensively document the way political forces shape the language of school choice—and by implication the way school decisions are made. In the post-COVID world, issues of parental options and richer arrays of schools assume a sudden relevance. This is an opportunity that should not be missed. This book helps to guide clearer thinking about options and potential improvements."

—**Eric Hanushek**, senior fellow, Hoover Institution, Stanford University

"John Merrifield's ability and willingness to identify and challenge what he calls weak, perhaps heroic assumptions; to go against the supposed conventional wisdom is incredible."

—**Kent Grusendorf**, former State Legislator and Education Committee Chair

"The world desperately needs a school system reform movement, and Merrifield's work leads the way on that. His unique perspectives provide a basis to escape unproductive reform strategies and generate evidence to support new approaches."

—**James Tooley**, The University of Buckingham

"Merrifield and Gray offer a disruptive solution to the failures of US K–12 education. Traditional Public Schools and School Choice options, alike, have proven to be ineffective in addressing educational ills—especially for underserved poor and minority students. They demonstrate how an 'Open Education Industry' transcends school choice options such as public charter, vouchers, and private schools by creating a niche for decentralized planning.

It is the authors' thesis that an 'Open Education Industry'—based on economic principles—has the greatest potential to positively impact education inequity, academic under achievement, and social acrimony. For those of us looking for real debate about school choice and true options for education reform, *Unproductive School Choice Debates*, is a must read!"

—**Alexandra Penn**, author, senior consultant, GoldenPair & Company

"John Merrifield knows more about school choice than anyone else."

—**Neal P. McCluskey**, Cato Institute

"This insightful book by Merrifield and Gray couldn't have come at a better time. It has arrived just as the once 'politically impossible has become politically inevitable' (Milton Friedman) in many states. It explains how to achieve further progress in those states, and how to productively spread school choice expansion to the rest of the country."

—**Corey A. DeAngelis**, senior fellow, American Federation for Children

www.ingramcontent.com/pod-product-compliance
Lightning Source LLC
Chambersburg PA
CBHW031708230426
43668CB00006B/155